A Photo Guide to
Flowers *of*
BHUTAN

Thinley Namgyel

Karma Tenzin

WWF - Bhutan

Front cover photos
Clockwise from top left - *Cosmos bipinnatus*, a naturalised exotic in front of Paro Rinpung Dzong (Thinley Namgyel), *Rosa sericea* (Thinley Namgyel), *Lloydia flavonutans* (Karma Tenzin), *Paphiopedilum fairrieanum* (Thinley Namgyel).

Back cover photo
Meconopsis horridula along trekking route in Gasa Dzongkhag (Thinley Namgyel).

Book layout and design
Sonam Payday Dorjee & Thinley Namgyel

A Photo Guide to Flowers of Bhutan
by Thinley Namgyel and Karma Tenzin
© 2009 WWF-Bhutan

Published November 2009
by WWF-Bhutan, Thimphu, Bhutan

ISBN: 978-99936-785-0-2

Contents

About the authors

Thinley Namgyel has a B.Sc. in Natural Resources (Forest Science and Botany) from the University of Wisconsin-Madison and a M.Sc. in Sustainable Development and Conservation Biology from the University of Maryland at College Park. He currently manages Bhutan's climate change program at the National Environment Commission. As an avid photographer and outdoor enthusiast, he has been capturing the natural beauty of Bhutan since 1999.

Karma Tenzin has a Bachelors Degree in Forestry from India and a Masters Degree from Cornell University in the US. He was initially appointed as Ethno-botanist in Nature Conservation Division under the Department of Forest and was involved in numerous botanical surveys in the Protected Areas of Bhutan. He is currently Park Manager of Bumdeling Wildlife Sanctuary.

Acknowledgements

Although the idea to produce an illustrated guide to the Flowers of Bhutan was proposed in 2004 with Dr. Bruce Bunting (then vice president at WWF-US, and now president of the Bhutan Foundation) the project was put on hold due to time constraints. It was with Bruce's encouragement and fund raising support that work on this project began in 2008.

We are also extremely grateful to Mrs. Tania Whitman Stepanian from the USA for making the production of this book possible.

We are deeply grateful to Rebecca Pradhan at the Royal Society for the Protection of Nature (RSPN) for reviewing our manuscript and help with the identifying some of the flowers in our photographs. Our thanks also to Tashi Choden of the Center for Bhutan Studies (CBS) for proof reading portions of the text.

Thinley also thanks his parents and family for the constant support and encouragement with his photographic and botanical interests.

Preface

A considerable portion of the Kingdom of Bhutan lies within the great Himalayan range, one that houses some of the world's highest mountain peaks. Besides, it is also the world's largest trove of untainted beauty. Across this greatly inaccessible and rugged landscape, lies an immense spectacular ecosystem which makes this region stand out as one of the most sought-after biodiversity destinations in the world. The Himalayas is estimated to be home to more than 10,000 plant species, many of which are flowering plants.

Bhutan has a unique eco-floristic appeal with its own share of infinite assortment of flowering plants. Lying in the heart of the eastern Himalayas, Bhutan is indeed a sight to behold at the peak of its flowering season, made possible by its altitudinal variations and pleasant monsoon showers.

"A Photo Guide to Flowers of Bhutan" showcases over 400 flowers commonly encountered in the country. This photographic guide book also contains useful descriptive text and where available vernacular names of the species. As one leafs through the pages of this floral extravaganza, one will not only identify those flowers that commonly adorn the Bhutanese roadside and trails but also marvel at their exquisite 'uncommon' beauty.

Tashi Delek.

Kinzang Namgay
Country Representative
WWF-Bhutan

I: Introduction

Bhutan and its environment

Although the Kingdom of Bhutan is one of the smallest countries in the world, it has one of the richest concentration of biodiversity. Around 6000 plant, 670 bird, and 180 mammal species have been recorded in Bhutan, all in an area of around 38,000 square kilometers. This is one of the highest species richness per unit area for any country.

The reason such high diversity is found in Bhutan is a result of its biogeography and conservation policies. Located in the Eastern Himalayas, Bhutan's landscape is extremely varied and influenced by the monsoons. Biogeographically, the country lies in a global ecotone, in between the warm Indo-Malayan ecozone in the south and the temperate Palearctic ecozone in the north. In a distance of less than 115 km running north to south, the altitude ranges from subtropical lowlands at 150m near the border with India to snow capped peaks over 7000m at its northern borders with Tibet in China. The country is also divided into major valleys and mountain systems by seven major rivers, Amo Chhu, Wang Chhu, Puna Tsang Chhu, Mangde Chhu, Bumthang Chhu, Kuri Chhu, Kulong Chhu, all running north to south. The forests and ecoregions of Bhutan can be broadly described in three eco-floristic zones; the *subtropical zone* found from 150m to 2000m, a *temperate zone* extending from 2000m to 4000m and an *alpine zone* above 4000m elevation.

Another important factor for the rich floristic diversity is the seasonal monsoon rains falling from June to September. The rainfall pattern also varies spatially, with very heavy rains in the southern foothills and the more exposed slopes of the interior mountains. The amount of rainfall received generally decreases towards the north as the monsoon clouds shed most of their rain near the foothills. Several valleys like, Paro, Thimphu and Punakha are also relatively drier due to the local topography.

Furthermore, led by the visionary conservation policy of His Majesty the Fourth Druk Gyalpo, Jigme Singye Wangchuck, Bhutan has about 70% of its land under forest cover, protecting the fragile mountainous landscape and its immense natural beauty and biological diversity.

Scope of this book

This guidebook covers 404 flower species from Bhutan. While around 6000 species of plants have been recorded in the country, we included some of the more common flowers that one might encounter along roadsides and trails. The elevation range covered by the flowers in this book is concentrated mainly from 1500-4000 meters. This elevation range is what one will experience traveling along much of the East-West highway in Bhutan. However, many of the species have ranges that extend beyond this elevation. In terms of the localities, the records are not complete but we have included the administrative districts where these flowers are found based on the *Flora of Bhutan* (F.O.B.) and our own records during the collection of the photographs for this book.

The taxonomy of plants is constantly changing, and more so in recent times with the use of molecular systematics. Consequently there have been revisions in the taxonomy of many of the species, genera and families of plants found in Bhutan since the F.O.B was published. However, we have used the nomenclature and description in the F.O.B. mainly for simplicity and consistency in the local context.

How to use this book

The method of presenting the flowers in this guidebook is quite common in North American guidebooks and elsewhere, but not yet seen in our region. The flowers are first grouped by the dominant colour of the flower and then by shape or cluster type. This arrangement allows the non-specialist to quickly narrow down the identity of the flower of interest. The descriptive text for each photograph is cross-referenced in the third part of the book.

Photographs

We have chosen to use photographs to illustrate this book rather than drawings or paintings, as they are more realistic and less dependent on artist's interpretation. Another factor is that with the advent of digital photography it is also much quicker and relatively cheaper to produce photographic illustrations.

The photographs of the flowers presented in this book were taken in the field by the authors and contributors. Each photograph is captioned with an index number, botanical name and the page number for the descriptive text. The photographs are grouped first by colour of the flowers, and then within each colour group further arranged by shape or structure of the flower and/or flower heads.

Colour

Colour is often the most striking feature of a flower that people notice, so the photographs are first arranged by colour of the flower (mainly the petals or other showy parts).

It should be noted that colour in the natural world exists in a continuum and delineating boundaries is not so clear-cut. So while many flowers are easy to put into discrete colour groups, others intergrade into different colours. In such cases we have used the dominant colour as described in the F.O.B. to assign a colour category to the flower. Another note of caution is that some species have several colour variants in flowers. Therefore, one should look in more than one colour group to narrow down the identity of the flower of interest.

The colour groupings used in this book are as follows:

White

White flowers can be pure white to pale cream, and includes white flowers with hues of very light yellow, blue, pink, purple or green.

Yellow

Yellow flowers and those ranging into orange and reds.

Red

Reds and deep orange. These colours can also intergrade into yellows, purple or brown.

Pink

Predominantly pink, but can intergrade to purple and reds.

Brown-Green

Flowers with predominantly green and brown shades.

Blue

Blues can turn towards purples, lavenders and pale pastel colours turning white.

Purple

Purple is an interesting colour as it does not exist naturally in the colour spectrum but is a result of our brain interpreting it from a mixture of colours. Purple flowers can intergrade into pinks, reds and blues, and also includes mauves.

Shape

Within each colour group, photographs are further divided by the general shape of the flower heads.

Radially symmetrical flowers

Flowers that are solitary on a stalk. They have a very symmetrical shape, like a wheel, when viewed from above.

Composite flowers

Flowers in this group look like sunflowers and dandelions. They may look like radially symmetrical flowers but are actually composed of many flowers. "Sunflower-like" flowers have a central disk with numerous non-showy "disk flowers" surrounded by a ring of "ray flowers" with showy petals. "Dandelion-like" flowers lack a central disk and are composed entirely of many petal-like flowers.

Bilaterally symmetrical flowers

These flowers are solitary and when viewed straight on will have only one possible line of symmetry. Examples are beans and orchids.

Long cluster of flowers

This group contains flowers clustered on an elongated stalk. The flowers can be clustered tightly together or in loose branches. The individual flowers can be radially symmetrical or bilaterally symmetrical

Rounded cluster of flowers

Rounded clusters are many flowers growing on a single stalk to form a rounded mass. The cluster can be tight or loosely formed but in both cases appear to grow from a single point.

Fruits

Some plants that have attractive fruit have been included in this group.

Description of Flowers

The descriptions of the flowers in this book are arranged alphabetically by family. The description is based on the F.O.B., which is the authoritative work on Bhutanese plants. The text has been simplified where possible and additional information such as vernacular names have been added, as well as new locations and ranges.

The first part of the descriptive text for each flower is the botanical name (*Genus* and *species* plus author). For many flowers, the Dzongkha (Dzo.), traditional Bhutanese medicinal (Med.) and common English (Eng.) names are also given.

The next part of the text describes the plant starting from its habit (herb, shrub, tree, etc.), to the vegetative parts (stems, leaves), and then flowering parts and fruits.

The last part is the ecological and geographical ranges where the species may be found. Locations provided are administrative districts. It should be noted that the range provided here or in the F.O.B. is not complete since the Flora was based on specimens collected from a limited geographic range during collecting expeditions. Further long term research is needed to establish the full geographic ranges of plants in Bhutan. Nevertheless, the elevation range, flowering time and ecological habitats included in the text can help to confirm suitable locations. Additional notes for some species such as uses and origins are also included.

The illustrations in Part I and the glossary in Part III of this book will help in deciphering some of the botanical terms used in the descriptions.

References

Grierson, A.J.C. and D.G. Long, (1983-1991) Flora of Bhutan, Vol. 1 Part 1-3; Vol.2 Part 1, Royal Botanic Garden Edinburgh, UK.

Grierson, A.J.C. and D.G. Long, (1999-2001) Flora of Bhutan, Vol.2 Part 2-3, Royal Botanic Garden Edinburgh & Royal Government of Bhutan.

Gurung, D.B., (2006) An Illustrated Guide to the Orchids of Bhutan, DSB Publication, Thimphu, Bhutan.

Harris, J.G. and M.W. Harris, (1994) Plant Identification Terminology: An Illustrated Glossary, Spring Lake Publishing, Utah, USA.

Noltie. H.J., (1994) Flora of Bhutan Vol 3 part 1, Royal Botanic Garden, Edinburgh, UK.

Noltie, H.J., (2000) Flora of Bhutan Vol 3 part 2, The Grasses of Bhutan, Royal Botanic Garden Edinburgh & Royal Government of Bhutan

Pearce, N.R. and P.J. Cribb, (2002) The Orchids of Bhutan, Royal Botanic Gardens Edinburgh, UK.

Polunin, O. and A. Stainton, (1997) Flowers of Himalaya, Oxford University Press, New Delhi, India.

Polunin, O. and A. Stainton, (1997) Flowers of Himalaya–A Supplement, Oxford University Press, New Delhi, India.

Pradhan, R. (1999) Wild Rhododendrons of Bhutan. Thimphu, Bhutan.

Nakao, S. & K. Nishioka, (1984) Flowers of Bhutan, Asahi Shimbun Publishing Company, Tokyo, Japan.

Thinley, U., (2004) Know the Plants of Bhutan, Vol. 1, 2nd Edition, Thimphu, Bhutan.

Flower parts & arrangements

Parts of a Flower

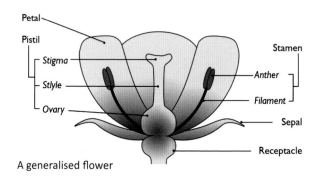

A generalised flower

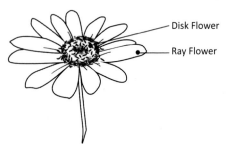

A generalised composite flower

Flower symmetry

Radially symmetric

Bilaterally symmetric

Types of flower clusters

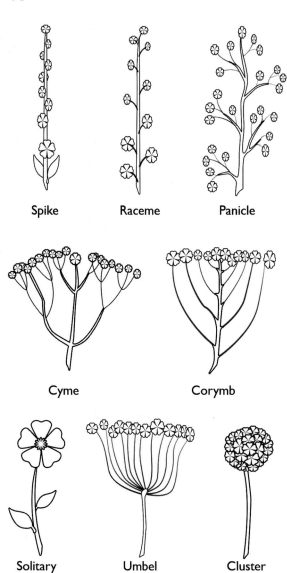

Spike   Raceme   Panicle

Cyme   Corymb

Solitary   Umbel   Cluster

Parts of a leaf

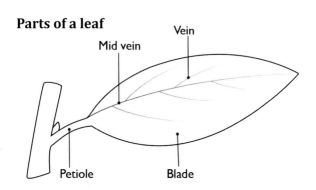

Types of leaf margins

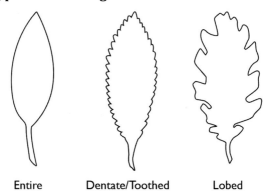

Entire   Dentate/Toothed   Lobed

Types of compound leaves

Tri-foliate   Pinnate   Palmate

Leaf shapes

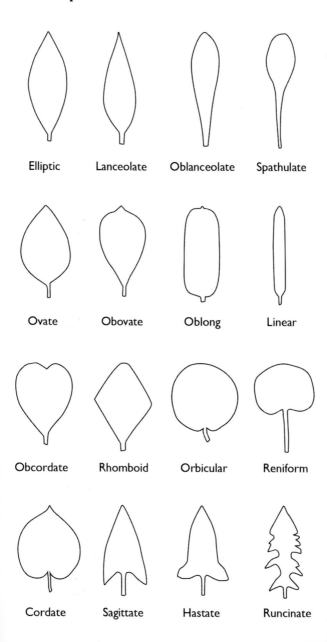

Elliptic   Lanceolate   Oblanceolate   Spathulate

Ovate   Obovate   Oblong   Linear

Obcordate   Rhomboid   Orbicular   Reniform

Cordate   Sagittate   Hastate   Runcinate

Bhutan: Land cover

Legend

Dryland Cultivation
Mixed Cultivation
Tseri/orchards
Wetland Cultivation
Landslips/erosion
Marshy Areas
Rock Outcrops
Snow/glaciers
Conifer Forest
Chir Pine
Mixed Conifer
Broadleaf Forest
Natural Pasture
Water spreads
Forest Plantation
Scrub Forest

Bhutan: Administrative boundaries

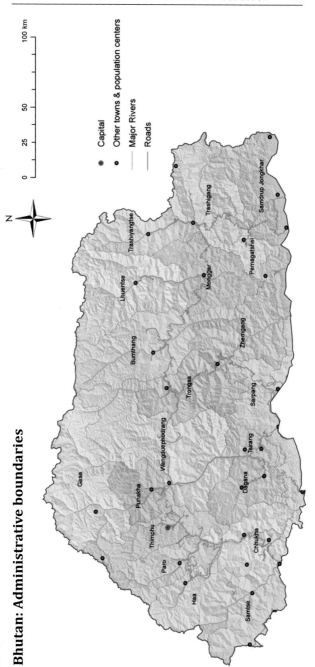

II: Colour Photographs

For an explanation about the arrangement of photographs in this section, please see "How to use this book" on page 11.

The name given under each photograph is the scientific name of the species. The number preceding the name is the plate number and the number after the name refers to the page that contains its description in section III.

1 Anemone rivularis   p. 353

2 Anemone rupicola   p.354

3 *Anemone vitifolia*   *p.354*

5 Clematis tongluensis   p.355

7 *Cotoneaster sherriffii*   *p.358*

9 Malus baccata   p.359

11 Prinsepia utilis   *p.363*

12 Rosa sericea   *p.364*

13 Rubus biflorus   p.365

14 Rubus ellipticus   p.365

15 Rubus indotibetanus   p.366

17 Magnolia globosa p.314

19 Brugmansia suaveolens   p.378

21 Solanum pseudocapsicum   p.379

23 *Lilium wallichianum var. wallichianum*   p. 311

24 *Lloydia longiscapa*   p.312

25 Streptopus simplex   p.313

26 Arenaria polytrichoides   p.243

27 *Stellaria vestita* p.243

29 *Swertia bimaculata*   p.292

31 Cassiope fastigata   *p.270*

32 Citrus limon   *p.370*

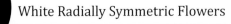

33 Disporum cantoniense   p.388

34 Elaeagnus parvifolia   p.269

35 Geranium nepalense   *p.293*

36 Holboellia latifolia   *p.302*

37 *Houttuynia cordata*   p.372

38 *Jasminum grandiflorum*   p.320

39 *Leontopodium jacotianum*   p.254

40 *Parnassia delavayi* p.340

41 *Philadelphus tomentosus* p.340

42 Podophyllum hexandrum   p.343

43 Schima wallichii   p.383

44 Aster ageratoides   p.246

46 *Bidens pilosa*   p.248

47 *Galinsoga ciliata*   p.252

49 *Myriactis wallichii*   p.255

50 *Tagetes minuta*   p.259

52 Bauhinia variegata   p.303

53 Pleione humilis   p.333

55 Cephalanthera damasonium   *p.323*

57 *Eria coronaria* p.331

59 *Aletris pauciflora*   p.315

61 *Gaultheria fragrantissima*   p.271

63 *Hedychium spicatum*   p.395

65 Capsela bursa-pastoris   p.265

69 Colebrookea oppositifolia   p.298

71 Stachys melissaefolia   p.301

73 Saussurea obvallata p.256

75 Lyonia ovalifolia   p.272

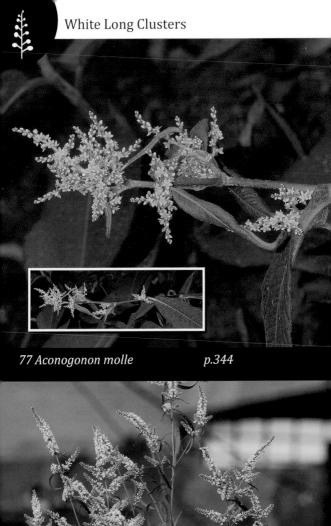

77 *Aconogonon molle* p.344

79 *Cuscuta reflexa*   p.268

81 Justicia adhatoda   p.221

83 Maesa chisa p.318

85 *Heracleum obtusifolium*   p.385

87 Selinum wallichianum

89 Torilis japonica   *p.387*

91 *Anaphalis contorta* p.245

92 *Anaphalis margaritacea* p.245

93 Anaphalis nepalensis var. nepalensis p.246

94 Chromolaena odorata p.249

95 *Saussurea gossipiphora* p.255

96 *Rhododendron anthopogon* p.273

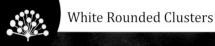

97 Rhododendron campylocarpum   p.275

98 Rhododendron dalhousiae var. rhabdotum   p.276

99 *Rhododendron falconeri*   p.276

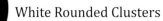

101 Rhododendron lanatum   *p.279*

103 *Fagopyrum dibotrys* p.345

104 *Persicaria chinense* p.346

105 *Viburnum cotinifolium*   *p.241*

106 *Viburnum erubescens*   *p.241*

107 *Viburnum grandiflorum*   p.242

109 Rosa brunonii   p.364

111 Dipsacus inermis   p.269

113 *Androsace geraniifolia*   p.349

115 Daphne bholua p.383

116 Deutzia corymbosa p.340

118 Murraya paniculata   *p.370*

120 Pavetta indica   p.369

121 Sambucus adnata   p.240

122 Solanum verbascifolium   p.381

123 Symplocus paniculata   p.382

124 Trifolium repens   p.309

125 Valeriana jatamansi   p.388

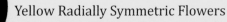

126 Oxygraphis endlicher   p.356

127 Ranunculus brotherusi   p.357

128 *Ranunculus chinensis*   p.357

130 *Potentilla arbuscula*   *p.360*

132 Potentilla griffithii   p.362

134 *Potentilla peduncularis*   p.362

136 *Cathcartia villosa*   *p.338*

138 *Lilium nepalense* p.310

140 Abelmoschus manihot   p.315

142 Opuntia vulgaris   *p.235*

144 *Rhododendron lepidotum* p.279

145 *Schisandra neglecta* p.374

147 Helianthus annus   p.252

149 *Senecio laetus*   *p.257*

156 *Coelogyne ovalis*   *p.325*

157 *Dendrobium jenkinsii*   *p.330*

159 Spathoglottis ixioides   p.335

160 Cassia occidentalis   p.304

161 *Piptanthus nepalensis*   p.308

162 *Impatiens cristata*   p.230

163 Lonicera quinquelocularis   p.240

165 Dendrobium chrysanthum   p.328

167 *Dendrobium hookerianum*   p.329

169 Corydalis polygalina p.287

171 Caesalpinia decapetala   p.303

173 *Cautleya gracilis*   p.393

175 *Ligularia atkinsonii*   p.254

177 *Salvia campanulata*   *p.300*

178 *Salvia nubicola*   *p.300*

180 *Pedicularis longiflora* p.376

182 *Corylopsis himalayana*   p.295

184 Oenothera biennis p.319

186 Rheum nobile   *p.348*

188 Berberis asiatica   p.230

190 Primula sikkimensis   p.351

192 Pseudognaphalium affine   p.255

193 Sigesbeckia orientalis   p.258

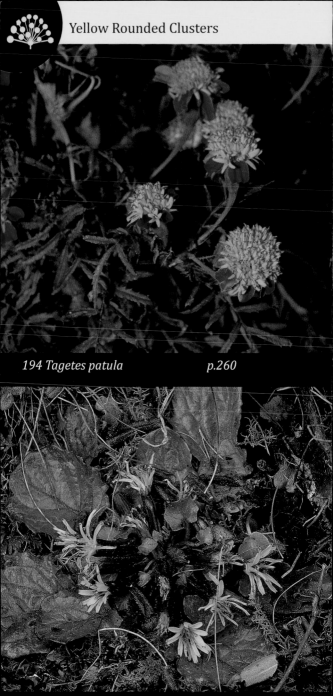

194 *Tagetes patula*   p.260

195 *Youngia depressa*   p.261

196 Asclepias curassavica   p.229

198 Edgeworthia gardneri   *p.384*

199 Rhododendron cinnabarinum   *p.275*

201 Lilium nanum   *p.310*

203 *Bombax ceiba*   p.231

205 Aeschynanthus sikkimensis p.294

206 Lonicera webbiana p.240

208 Phlogacanthus thyrsiformis   p.222

212 *Agapetes serpens*   *p.270*

214 *Amaranthus hybridus var. erythrostachys*   p.224

216 Colquhounia coccinea   *p.298*

218 *Erythrina arborescens*   p.306

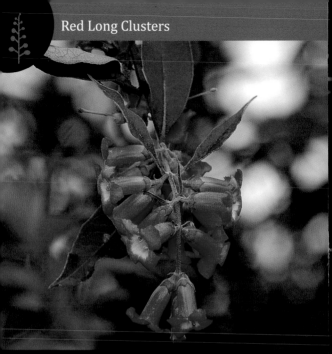

220 Buddleja colvilei   p.233

222 *Rheum acuminatum* p.347

224 Enkianthus deflexus   p.271

226 *Rhododendron cinnabarinum*   p.275

227 *Rhododendron hodgsonii*   p.277

228 Rhododendron keysii　　　p.278

229 Rhododendron thomsonii　　p.280

233 Gastrochilus acutifolius   p.331

234 Erythrina stricta   p.306

235 Duchesnea indica p.359

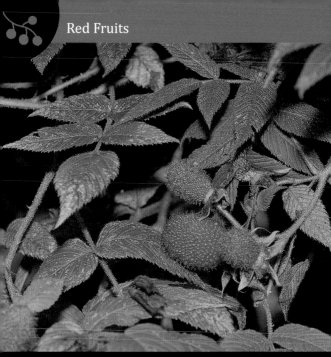

237 Rubus indotibetanus   p.366

238 Mallotus philippensis   p.284

239 *Neillia rubiflora* p.360

241 *Panax pseudoginseng*   *p.228*

242 *Sambucus adnata*   *p.240*

243 Clematis buchananiana   p.355

244 Paris polyphylla   p.384

245 Aristolochia griffithii   p.229

247 *Bulbophyllum umbellatum* p.323

248 *Paphiopedilum fairrieanum* p.333

249 Cleisostoma racemiferum   *p.324*

250 Cymbidium erythraeum   *p.326*

251 *Cymbidium hookerianum*   p.326

253 Ione cirrhata   *p.332*

255 *Vanda bicolor*   *p.336*

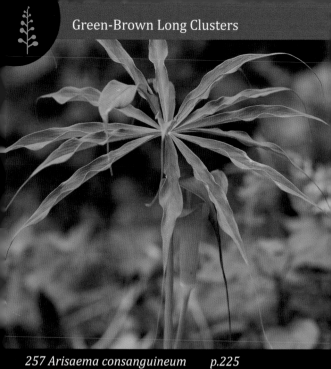

257 Arisaema consanguineum   *p.225*

259 *Arisaema nepenthoides*   p.226

260 *Arisaema speciosum var. speciosum*   p.227

261 Arisaema tortuosum   *p.227*

262 Brassaiopsis mitis   *p.228*

263 *Cannabis sativa* p.239

265 Engelhardia spicata   *p.297*

267 Megacodon stylophorus   p.291

269 Ricinus communis   p.284

271 Thysanolaena latifolia   p.342

272 Triosteum himalayanum   p.241

273 *Sapium insigne*   p.284

274 *Saurauja nepalensis*   p.223

275 *Solanum viarum Dunal*   p.380

276 *Toona ciliata*   p.317

278 *Geranium donianum*   p.292

280 *Rhododendron camelliiflorum*　　　　p.274

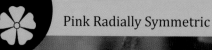

282 *Rhododendron virgatum*   p.281

284 Rubus hypargyrus   p.366

286 Schisandra grandiflora   *p.373*

287 Zephyranthes carinata   *p.225*

288 Cosmos bipinnatus   *p.250*

289 Osbeckia nepalensis   p.316

290 Pleione praecox   p.334

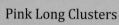

291 *Anthogonium gracile* p.321

293 *Arundina graminifolia* p.322

295 Spiranthes sinensis   *p.335*

297 *Bistorta vaccinifolia*   p.344

299 Vaccinium retusum   p.282

301 *Pedicularis elwesii* p.375

303 *Pedicularis siphonantha* p.377

305 *Clinopodium umbrosum* p.297

307 Epilobium angustifolium p.319

309 Leycestra formosa   p.239

310 Myricaria rosea   p.382

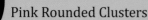

311 Osbeckia stellata p.316

312 Rhododendron arboreum var. roseum p.274

313 Rhododendron kesangiae   p.278

314 Rhododendron maddenii   p.280

315 Persicaria capitata   p.345

316 Persicaria nepalensis   p.346

317 Persicaria runcinata   p.346

318 *Androsace hookeriana*   p.349

319 *Primula gracilipes*   p.351

321 *Spiraea bella*   p.367

323 *Geranium polyanthes* p.293

324 *Luculia gratissima* p.368

325 Adenophora khasiana   p.236

326 Campanula pallida   p.236

327 *Crawfurdia speciosa* p.287

328 *Cyananthus incanus* p.237

329 *Cyananthus lobatus*   p.237

330 *Gentiana algida*   p.288

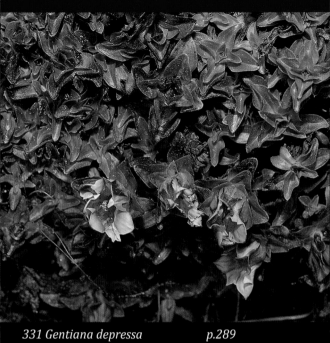

331 Gentiana depressa   p.289

332 Gentiana urnulla   p.290

333 Gentiana veitchiorum   *p.290*

334 Iris clarkei   *p.296*

335 *Lomatogonium brachyantherum*   p.291

336 *Meconopsis horridula*   p.338

337 Meconopsis simplicifolia   *p.339*

338 Nicandra physalodes   *p.379*

339 Aster diplostephioides   p.247

340 Aster neoelegans   p.248

341 *Aster vestitus*   p.248

342 *Mulgedium bracteatum*   p.254

343 Mazus delavayi   p.374

344 Mazus surculosus   p.375

345 Crotalaria occulta   *p.305*

346 Parochetus communis   *p.308*

347 Corydalis ecristata   *p.285*

348 *Strobilanthes wallichii* p.222

349 *Viola betonicifolia* p.392

350 Asyneuma fulgens   p.236

351 Lobelia erectiuscula   p.238

352 *Lobelia seguinii*   p.238

354 *Hackelia uncinata*   p.234

356 *Caryopteris bicolor*   p.389

357 *Vitex negundo*   p.391

358 Prunella vulgaris   p.301

359 Halenia ellliptica   p.290

360 Gentiana capitata   *p.288*

362 *Primula glabra* p.350

364 *Ceratostigma griffithii*   p.341

365 *Cyanotis vaga*   p.243

366 Dichroa febrifuga p.295

367 Gaultheria trichophylla p.272

368 *Clematis acutangula*   p.354

370 Polygonatum kansuense p.347

372 Erigeron multiradiatus   *p.251*

374 *Barleria cristata* p.221

379 Bulbophyllum emarginatum   p.322

381 Dendrobium aphyllum   *p.327*

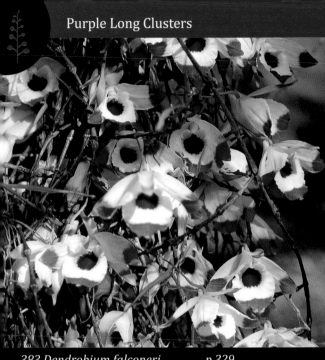

383 Dendrobium falconeri   p.329

385 *Cleisostoma williamsonii*   p.325

386 *Ione bicolor*   p.331

387 *Schoenorchis gemmata* p.335

388 *Notholirion macrophyllum* p.312

389 Campylotropis speciosa p.305

390 Indigofera dosua p.307

392 Elsholtzia strobilifera   *p.299*

394 *Cardamine griffithii* p.266

396 Corydalis leptocarpa   *p.286*

398 Thalictrum chelidonii   *p.358*

399 Verbena officinalis   *p.391*

400 Cirsium eriophoroides   *p.249*

402 Cirsium verutum   *p.250*

403 Rhododendron setosum   *p.280*

404 Rhododendron wallichii   *p.282*

405 *Primula calderiana* p.349

407 *Astragalus bhotanensis*   p.303

409 Allium wallichii   p.224

III: Description of Flowers

The flowers are described in the following format:

Photo #, Species name, Author

Dzo: Dzongkha name (if any)
Med: Traditional Bhutanese medicinal name (if any)
Eng: Common English name (if any)

Description of plant covering its habit (herb, shrub etc.), vegetative parts, flowering parts and fruits

» Habitat where the plant grows
» Elevation range of the plant
» Flowering months
» Distribution in Bhutan by administrative districts
» Notes on uses, origins, subspecies or varieties (if any)

Acanthaceae
Acanthus Family

374 Barleria cristata L.
Eng: Philippine Violet, Bluebell Barleria, Crested Philippine Violet

Hairly undershrub to 50cm. Stem wiry, much branched. Leaves elliptic 3-14x1-3.5cm, long hair on both surfaces. Inflorescence in axillary cymes. Corolla funnel shaped, 5.5-6.5cm, 5 lobes not all equal, pinkish purple, tube covered with hairs. Capsule oblong 15-17mm, glabrous.

» Common in chir pine forests, in dry valleys
» 100-2000m
» August-November
» Samdrupjongkhar, Punakha, Wangduephodrang, Mongar, Trashigang
» Easily propagated and useful as garden borders

81 Justicia adhatoda L.
Eng: Malabar Nut Tree

Shrub 1-1.5m. Stem greenish-brown, glabrescent. Leaves elliptic, 5-25 x 2-9cm, sometimes pubescent on veins below; petiole 0.5-3cm. Inflorescence short, dense, terminal and axillary spikes 2-8cm; peduncle 1-15cm. Bracts ovate to elliptic, 10-20 x 5-12mm; bracteoles oblong-lanceolate, similar to calyx lobes. Calyx 5-lobed, c 8mm, puberulent. Corolla white with purple lines, c 3cm, glabrous or pubescent, tube short and broad, upper lip hooded. Lower lip with 3 ovate lobes c 1.5cm. Anthers not exserted. Capsule woody, 2.5-4cm, pubescent.

» Secondary scrub and broad-leaved forest, often in dry valleys and near settlements, locally abundant and possibly introduced in some places
» 200-1610m
» January-April
» Chhukha, Sarpang, Samdrupjongkhar, Samtse, Punakha, Trongsa, Mongar, Trashigang.

208 *Phlogacanthus thyrsiformis* (Hardwicke) Mabberley

Shrub up to 3m. Stems erect, glabrous. Leaves often crowded near branch tips, elliptic to obovate, 11-28x2.5-8cm, shortly acuminate at both ends, glabrous; petiole 15-35mm. Flowers in a dense, uninterrupted terminal thyrse, 4-23 x 4-5cm, usually solitary, rarely 2-3; rachis pubescent. Bracts linear, c 6mm, pubescent, lobes linear. Corolla orange-brown, tubular, 20-25mm, c 8mm wide at mouth, pubescent; upper lip 6-7mm, spreading, about twice as long as deflexed lower lip. Anthers 4-5mm, shortly exserted. Capsule narrowly clavate 2-3cm.

» In sub-tropical forest and in secondary scrub, particularly in gullies and near streams
» 200-1100m
» February-March
» Samtse, Chhukha, Sarpang, Samdrupjongkhar

348 *Strobilanthes wallichii* Nees

Perennial herb 0.3-0.5m. Stems glabrous, erect from creeping woody rootstock. Leaves equal or almost equal, ovate or elliptic, 1.2-5x1-3.5cm, acute tip. Toothed margins, smooth or thinly haired, upper leaves sessile and lower ones petiolate. Flowers in opposite pairs in axils or leaf-like bracts forming small axillary 1-sided spikes, but spikes much reduced and flowers solitary in axils of leaves on main stem; bract like small leaves present. Calyx 1-1.5cm, smooth, or covered in glands or long hairs, with thin long equal lobes. Corolla blue (rarely white), smooth, 28-35mm, tube slightly inflated to above base, widening to 15mm at mouth, bent sharply below mouth. Capsules 13-19mm, glabrous.

» Abundant and locally subdominant in forest floor of moist fir and hemlock forest to open *Rhododendron* scrub
» 2200-3960m
» June-September every year
» Paro, Thimphu
» Many *Strobilanthes* flower only periodically (12 years)

209 *Thunbergia coccinea* Wall.
Eng: Scarlet Clock Vine

Vigorous twining shrub with stem climbing to 12m and then pendulous. Stem variable in surface; glabrous, pubescent or setose especially near nodes. Leaves ovate-triangular, 4-18x3-10cm, acute, cordate to hastate at base, weakly sinuate with prominent teeth, glabrescent to thinly long-haired; petioles 2-9cm. Flowers in long, pendulous, terminal racemes 10-50cm; bracts sessile, ovate, 0.5-8cm; pedicels 1-5cm. Bracteoles ovate-elliptic, sometimes falcate, dark red, 1.8-3cm, acute or apiculate, densely puberulent, especially on the margins. Calyx a minute rim. Corolla orange-red or crimson, glabrous or finely puberulent, tube widened from just above the base, 22-28mm, lobes 8-11mm. Anthers with some cells spurred and some not spurred. Capsules c 4cm, glabrous; seeds flattened, rugose.

- » Warm moist forests
- » 700-2200 m
- » July - November
- » Samtse, Chhukha, Sarpang, Samdrupjongkhar, Punakha, Trongsa, Mongar, Trashigang.

Actinidiaceae
Chinese gooseberry family

274 *Saurauja nepalensis* DC.

Tree to 6m bearing appressed ovate scales 1–1.5mm. Leaves elliptic-oblanceolate, 15-35x5-12cm, acuminate, base rounded, margins finely serrate, veins 30-35 pairs, glabrous or more often brownish tomentose beneath; petioles 2–5cm. Panicles 15–20cm. Sepals ovate, 5–6x 4mm, glabrous. Petals pink, obovate, c 10x6mm, rounded. Fruit globose, c 8mm diameter.

- » Warm broad-leaved forest
- » 1300–2100m
- » May–August
- » Chhukha, Samdrupjongkhar, Punakha, Trashigang

Alliaceae
Onion Family

409 *Allium wallichii* Kunth
Dzo: Lagop

Bulb-forming perennial strongly smelling of onion. Leaves 4-5, basal, flat, keeled beneath, to 51x0.7-2.5cm. Stem strongly 3-4-winged, 22-80cm. Umbel hemispheric, loose with many flowers, 3-8cm. Perianth red-purple, rolled backwards, tepals narrowly oblong-elliptic, acute, 5-10x1.5-3.5mm. Stamens erect; filaments 4.5-6.8mm, anthers 1.2-2mm. Ovary 2-4x2-5mm; style 2.5-5.4mm

» Conifer forest, open wet cliff-ledges and hillsides, among scrub
» 2670-4420m
» July-October
» Chhukha, Haa, Paro, Thimphu, Punakha, Bumthang, Gasa, Trashigang, Trashiyangtse

Amaranthaceae
Amaranth family

214 *Amaranthus hybridus* var. *erythrostachys* Moq.
Dzo: Memja

Erect annual with stems 30-200cm. Leaves ovate elliptic, 5-18 x2.5-9cm, glabrous, green with large purplish blotch beneath; petioles 1-10cm. Flowers in clusters densely aggregated into robust spikes, bright red. 4-15x0.8-1.2cm, male flowers uppermost, females closer to main rachis. Bracteoles c 5mm with awn-like tips. Perianth segments 5, ovate, 2.5-3.5mm, keeled; male flowers with 5 free stamens and rudimentary ovary; females with oblong ovary. Capsule circumsessile, seed c. 1.25mm.

» Cultivated and around settlements
» 2000-2850m
» July-October
» Thimphu, Paro, Mongar, Gasa, Lhuentse
» Cultivated as a grain and leaf crop. Bhutanese plants belong to **subsp.** *hybridus* var. *erythrostachys* characterised by its bright red inflorescences (becoming green when dry)

Amaryllidaceae
Amaryllis family

287 Zephyranthes carinata Herbert

Low growing bulbous perennial with hollow scape. Leaves 3-6, linear and not fully developed at flowering up to 40cm long, 2-4.5cm wide. Scape hollow 7-18.5cm. Inflorescence 1-flowered. Spathe longer than pedicel, membraneous, purplish. Pedicels 1.5-3.4cm. Perianth pink, 4.5-8.2cm, funnel-shaped. Stamens erect and joined near throat of tube, style long and filiform with a distinctly 3-lobed stigma.

» Cultivated in gardens, naturalised on waste grounds, roadsides and edges of fields
» 1200-2450m
» April- August
» Thimphu, Wangduephodrang
» Native of Mexico but now widely cultivated

....

Araceae
Arum family

257 Arisaema consanguineum Schott.

Dioecious. Plant 17-69 cm; pseudostem, cataphylls and stem with pinkish, purplish and/or brownish chequering. Leaf 1, radiate; leaflet 11-20, linear to narrowly oblanceolate (1-5cm). Peduncle shorter than leaves. Spathe: tube 3-6cm; blade arching over spadix, oblong-ovate, margins narrowly auriculate at base, 3-6.5x1.3-4.5 cm, greenish or greenish-yellow, sometimes striped purplish outside, sometimes tinged purplish towards apex, abruptly acuminate into drooping, filiform-caudate tip (5-18cm). Appendix narrowly club-shaped 1.5-3.5x0.16-0.8 cm, just exceeding spathe tube, smooth, greenish or yellow, stripe short (0.2-0.5 cm), usually bearing several, ascending, filiform neuters. Synandria dense, sessile, yellowish. 4-loculed, locules opening by apical pores. Fruiting peduncle recurved.

» Open or disturbed forest (Blue pine, Oak and Chestnut forest)
» 1400-2900
» May-July
» Chhukha, Haa, Thimphu, Punakha, Trongsa, Bumthang

258 Arisaema jacquemontii Blume
Dzo: Tou
Eng: Jacuemont's Cobra Lily

Dioecious perennial 13-54cm. Pseudostem, petioles and peduncle pale green and unmarked. Leaf palmate with 5-7 leaflets with central leaflet narrowly oblanceolate to elliptic with outer leaflets narrower. Spathe pale green with narrow whitish stripes, margins and sometimes whole blade flushed dark purplish; 2.5-6.5cm; blade arching over spadix, oblong triangular and narrowing into an upright thin tail 2.5-6cm.

» Open grassy places, among rhododendron and juniper and edges of forests
» 2290-4270m
» June-August
» Haa, Thimphu, Trongsa, Bumthang, Mongar, Gasa, Trashiyangtse

259 Arisaema nepenthoides (Wall.) Mart.
Eng: Cobra Lily

Perennial herb 29-100cm; pseudostem, petioles and peduncle with large pinkish and brownish to blackish chequered blotches; sometimes flowering before leaves are produced. Cataphylls, brownish, with pinkish and dark blotches. Leaves usually 2, palmate with 5 (sometimes to 7) leaflets, dark green, glossy above; central leaflet 6-20x1.5-6.5cm. Petiole 7.5-20cm. Peduncles usually exceeding leaves. Spathe; tube 3-8cm; blade arching over spadix, oblong-ovate, with two spreading, rounded, basal lobes, greenish pinkish, brownish (occasionally blood purple) with broad, pale stripes, sometimes also with dark blotches. Appendix cylindric, tip rounded, greenish or pinkish. Fruiting peduncle erect.

» Edges and banks of wet broad-leaved, hemlock/ rhododendron, oak/pine, beside streams
» 1830-3440m
» February-May
» Chhukha, Sarpang, Samdrupjongkhar, Haa, Paro, Thimphu, Punakha, Gasa, Wangduephodrang, Trongsa, Bumthang

260 *Arisaema speciosum* var. *speciosum* (Wall.) Mart. ex Schott

Perennial herb. 1 leaf divided into three leaflets with narrow red margins; central one lanceolate to elliptic; outer leaflets oblong-lanceolate, base strongly asymmetric, 12-36.5x5-21cm. Petiole 19-55cm, irregularly transversely striped with pale green and reddish-brown. Peduncle 2.5-21cm, much shorter than petiole. Spathe; tube 4-10cm, with broad white stripes; blade arching over spadix, oblong-lanceolate, drooping tip, 8-21.5x4-9.5cm, shiny, bronze-coloured, purplish or chocolate brown. Appendix swollen, 3-7cm (without tail), widest (8-9mm) just above base, curving above and coming out from tube and gradually drawn out to a thin flagellum (to 50cm). Fruiting peduncle erect.

» Margins of broad-leaved (oak and subtropical) forests.
» 460-3050m
» March-June
» Chhukha, Sarpang, Thimphu, Punakha, Trongsa, Gasa

261 *Arisaema tortuosum* (Wall.) Schott.
Dzo: Jag

Herbaceous plant 40-200cm; cataphylls, psuedostem and petioles variously blothched with pinkish, grey, dark brownish or purplish. Leaves 2-3, well spaced along the pseudostem, pedate with 5-7 leaflets; peduncles longer than leaves. Spathe tube1.5-4.5cm long; blade spreading horizontally, oblong lanceolate, 4-11.5x1.5-4cm, green, yellowish-green or creamy yellow, not striped. Spadix rising in a curved manner, greatly exceeding the spathe, smooth, green, bluish-green or yellowish, sometimes purplish at base. Male or female flowers may be borne on different plants; incase monecious, male section of spadix usually exceeding female.

» Broadleaved and subtropical forest, especially at edges or disturbed areas, along road or trails, stream sides
» 150-3050m
» (March-)May-June
» Chhukha, Sarpang, Samdrupjongkhar, Thimphu, Punakha, Trongsa, Gasa

Araliaceae
Ginseng family

262 Brassaiopsis mitis C.B. Clarke

Tree to 6m, spiny on main stem. Leaves palmately 7-12 lobed, suborbiclar in outline, to 60x60cm, lobes divided 2/3 to base, linear lanceolate, acuminate, margins toothed, smooth above, sparsely stellate below; petioles c.60cm, densely bristly at apex. Panicles racemose, 40cm, main axis shortly prickly; peduncles 10-20cm; umbels c. 5cm diameter. Flowers creamy; petals 3mm.

» In broadleaved forests
» 1830-2350m
» May-July
» Trongsa, Mongar, Gasa
» Foliage lopped for fodder

241 Panax pseudoginseng Wall.
Eng: Ginseng

Stems up to 75cm, erect, bearing a whorl of 3-7 palmate leaves; petioles 2.5-12cm; leaflets 3-6, ovate or lanceolate, 3.5-129x1-7cm, acuminate, base rounded or cuneate, margins serrate or deeply incised-pinnatfied, sparsely hirsute along veins on both surfaces. Male umbels 1.5cm diameter; female umbels 3cm diameter. Petals white. C 2mm. Fruits scarlet, 4mm diameter.

» In coniferous forest
» 1500-3650m
» May-September
» Sarpang, Samdrupjongkhar, Haa, Thimphu, Trongsa, Trashigang
» An important species in traditional medicine. The typical subsp. *pseudo-ginseng* with short rhizomes and carrot-like roots, and flattish seeds 5-8mm long x 2-2.5mm thick

Aristolociaceae
Birthwort family

245 *Aristolochia griffithii* Duchartre
Eng: Griffith's Birthwort

Woody twiner or climber. Leaves heartshaped, 6-15x5-9cm, sparsely pubescent on both surfaces, 7-9 veins at base. Flowers zygomorphic, solitary and hanging on a pubescent pedicel 2-4cm. Perianth S-shaped; folded tube 4-6.5cm, green with purple veins, strongly inflated at bend 3-4cm broad; limb funnel shaped 6-9cm across, yellowish with dark purple veins outside, coarsely warted and brownish purple inside. Fruit oblong, 12-18x1.5-2.5cm.

» Cool broad-leaved, evergreen oak and fir forests
» 1800-3000m
» April-May
» Chhukha, Thimphu, Punakha, Gasa, Trongsa, Mongar, Trashigang

Asclepiadaceae
Milkweed family

196 *Asclepias curassavica* L.
Eng: Scarlet Milkweed, Blood Flower

Perennial herb, becoming woody at base. Small to large herb, sometimes shrubby to 1m tall. Leaves lanceolate to oblong-lanceolate, 5-15 x 0.6-4 cm, apex acute, base cuneate, usually glabrous; petiole short, 0.2-1.2cm, glabrous. Flowers in umbels of 7-12, Corolla orange to red, corraline coronal scales and gynostegium bright yellow to orange. Peduncle 2-4cm long; pedicel 8-20mm, both puberulent. Calyx lobes c 3x0.5mm. Corolla lobes 7-8x2-3mm. Gynostegium column c 2.5mm long. head c 3mm long. Stigmatic head c 2.5mm broad. Follicles 5.5-8xc 1cm. Pale grey. Seeds c 6x 3.5mm.

» Cultivated and weedy
» Flowers all year round
» 250-1350m.
» Punakha, Samtse, Trashigang, Trashiyangtse
» A pan tropical weed from tropical America

Balsaminaceae
Balsam family

162 Impatiens cristata Wall.
Eng: Crested Balsam

Annual herb to 70cm, but often only 20-30cm, pubescent; stems usually branched. Leaves ovate to elliptic or elliptic-oblanceolate, 3.8-15x1.4-5.5cm. Inflorescence of 1-3 (sometimes 4) flowers, pale creamy white to yellow, reddish brown spots in throat. Bracts midway along pedicels. Dorsal petal 14-18 x 18-24mm with a prominent keel-like crest above; lateral petals united, 18-28mm; lower petal constricting into a curved a filiform spur 8-18mm. Capsule cylindrical, 37-42mm

» Sunny or semi-shaded moist habitats, particularly in open forest, along pathways or close to habitation
» 1500-2500
» June-October
» Chhukha, Thimphu, Bumthang, Trongsa, Trashiyangtse

Berberidaceae
Barberry family

188 Berberis asiatica DC.
Dzo: Kepai Tsang
Eng: Asiatic Barberry

Evergreen shrub 1-3m, yellowish stems and spines 5-10mm. Leaves leathery and obovate 3-6 x 1.2-3cm, acute or rounded tip with sharp point at apex, and gradually narrowing to base, margins without spiny teeth, and veins much branching above. Racemes short at flowering (1cm) and elongating in fruit (4cm). Flowers with 6 petals and 6 sepals similar, yellow and sometimes tinged red. Berries ellipsoid about 10x7mm, red becoming black.

» Dry valleys and hillsides
» 1400-2300m
» April-May
» Haa, Thimphu, Punakha, Trongsa

189 *Berberis praecipua* Schneider
Dzo: Kepe Tsang

Evergreen shrub 1-3m, stems grooved, yellowish. Leaves elliptic, 2-4 x 0.5-2cm tapering to pointed tip and base, margins more or less inrolled, with spiny teeth on margins, veins prominent underneath. Flowers in clusters of 5-15 with pedicels 1-2.5cm. Sepals and petals similar and yellow, with inner sepals 5-5.5 x 2-3.5cm, petals, 4.5-5 x 3mm, Berries obovoid, reddish, 8-10x 3-4mm.

» Dry open hillsides and margins of coniferous forests
» 2350-3650m
» April- June
» Haa, Thimphu (common), Gasa

183 *Mahonia napaulensis* DC.
Eng: Nepal Mahonia

Unarmed shrub 1-3 m tall. Stem leafy near apex. Leaves coriaceous unevenly 1-pinnate, rachis articulated at each leaflet node. Flowers yellow in narrow fascicled racemes. Sepals usually in 3 series of 3, yellow. Petals 6 in 2 series of 3. Berries ellipsoid, 8 – 12 x 5 – 7mm, blue-black, glaucous, style 0.5 – 2mm.

» Forest margins
» 1525 - 3000m
» April
» Chhukha, Thimphu, Gasa, Trongsa, Mongar, Trashigang

....

Bombacaceae
Bombax family

203 *Bombax ceiba* L.
Dzo: Pema Geysar
Eng: Silk Cotton Tree, Red Cotton Tree

Large tree to 30m; branches whorled, spreading horizontally; trunk buttressed at base, often bearing large conical spines. Leaves +- clustered towards branch ends, with 5-7 leaflets; petiole 8-22 cm; leaflets elliptic, 9-20 x 4-6.5cm, caudate-acuminate, base cuneate, margins entire, glabrous; petiolules 1-2.5cm. Flowers appearing before leaves, solitary, axillary, borne towards branch ends; pedicels short stout. Calyx green, 1.5-3cm, with 3-5 unequal round lobes, silky hairy within. Petals crimson, thick, narrowly oblong-obovate, 7-11 x 2-4.5cm, stellate-pubescent, densely so outside. Stamens 3-5cm, shortly united at base. Style 4-6mm; stigma of 5 linear lobes c 5mm. Capsule ellipsoid, 10-15cm long, thickly white woolly within; seeds numerous.

» Found on silty soil close to rivers, native and cultivated
» 200-1300m
» January-February
» Chhukha, Sarpang, Punakha
» Wood used to make tea boxes and matches. Bark produces a useful gum and other part of the plant have medicinal use. The cotton from the capsule is used as stuffing for mattresses, pillows, etc.

....

Buddlejaceae
Butterfly bush family

78 Buddleja asiatica Loureiro
Dzo: Kang Shing Chuwa
Eng: White Butterfly Bush

Shrub to 5m. Leaves narrowly lanceolate, 6-15 x 1-4cm, acuminate, base cuneate; margins minutely dentate, closely white stellate-pubescent or tomentose beneath, glabrous to stellate-pubescent above; petioles 3-10mm with stipular line between opposing petioles. Panicles dense, spike-like, terminal and axillary, 5-20cm, not fragrant. Calyx 2-3mm, stellate-pubescent, lobes triangular, short. Corolla white, sometimes violet, tube 3-4 x 1-1.5mm, stellate-pubescent outside, wooly inside; lobes orbicular, 1.5mm. Stamens inserted near middle of tube. Capsules ovoid, compressed, 3-5 x 1.5-3mm.

» In scrub on river banks, open hillsides and margins of subtropical and warm broad-leaved forests
» 200-1500m
» January-March
» Samtse, Chhukha, Sarpang, Samdrupjongkhar, Punakha, Trongsa, Mongar, Trashigang, Trashiyangtse.

220 Buddleja colvilei Hook. f. & Thomson
Eng: Butterfly Bush

Shrub or small tree 2-8m. leaves elliptic-oblanceolate, 6-20 x 1.5-5.5cm, acuminate , base attenuate, margins shallowly serrate, glandular and sparsely to densely stellate hairy especially beneath; petioles 0-8mm; stipules reduced to line between opposing petioles. Panicles 7-20cm, terminal and axillary , branches cymose, lax, 3-flowered not fragrant. Calyx 5-7mm, glandular and subglabrous to densely stellate-tomentose, lobes short. Corolla wine-red, tubular-companulate, tube 15-22mm, 6-10mm diameter at mouth, glandular and sparsely stellate hariy outside, sparsely long-haired within. Capsules broadly ellipsoid, 10-16 x 5-8mm.

» Among shrubs on open hillsides and margins of hemlock and mixed forest
» 2100 - 5000m
» June-August
» Thimphu, Punakha, Trongsa, Bumthang, Mongar, Trashigang, Gasa, Lhuentse
» An ornamental species because of its flowers

322 Buddleja crispa Benth.
Eng: Himalayan Butterfly Bush

Deciduous shrub. 1.5-5m, densely stellate tomentose. Leaves ovate 3-7x1.5-3cm, base heart-shaped or truncate, sometimes decurrent on petiole, margins toothed, both surfaces covered in densely whitish wooly hair. Panicles appear before leaves. Corolla pinkish-purple with orange throat. Capsule ellipsoid, 5-6mm.

» Among scrub in blue pine forest, dry hillsides and dry roadsides
» 2000-2500m
» April-June
» Chhukha, Haa, Paro, Thimphu

Boraginaceae
Borage family

353 Cynoglossum furcatum Wall.
Dzo: Chima, Cimba
Eng: Indian Hounds Tongue

Biennial herb with stout rootstock. Stems 25-100cm, erect, unbranched below but much branched when flowering, with dense soft hair. Basal leaves withered by the time of flowering. Stem leaves many, lower ones with short petioles, upper leaves without periole and clasping stem, shape is more or less narrowly elliptic or oblanceolate both sides covered in short fine hair. Inflorescence branched, with ultimate branches 5-9cm, furcate (forked) at 30-70° angle; upper branches densely hairy. Calyx lobes covered in fine stiff hairs. Corolla deep blue with violet tinge 4-5mm long. Nutlets ovate, 2-2.5mm covered in barbed bristles.

» Roadsides, riversides, warm broad-leaved and ever green forests
» 1200-3600m
» April-October
» Chukha, Sarpang, Haa, Thimphu, Punakha, Trongsa, Mongar

354 Hackelia uncinata (Bentham) Fischer
Eng: Hooked Stick Seed

Stems erect or ascending 30-60cm. Leaves densely hairy on lamina beneath as well as on veins broadly elliptic narrow pointed with rounded or shallow heart shaped base and with 2-3 pairs of incurved lateral veins arising from near the base of the blade. Flowers pale blue, to 1.3cm, with rounded overlapping corolla-lobes and with a raised usually yellow ring of blunt scales, borne in lax branched clusters

» Open slopes and in forest
» 3050 - 3963m
» June - July
» Bumthang

355 *Trigonotis microcarpa* (DC.)

Weak herb, perennial, rootstock sometimes creeping. Stems erect to 17-35cm, usually branched above with moderate to sparsely covered in appresed hairs. Leaves ovate to rounded or tapering acute with distinct pointed tip; base obtuse to squared off, upper surface densely covered in dense very short hair (0.5-0.3mm), lower surface with less hair, midrib and veins raised on lower surface. Inflorescence at top of flower with many flowers and coiling to one side. Corolla powder or sky blue, c. 2.5mm with yellow/orange throat, 5 lobes. Nutlets tetrahedral, brown c. 1mm.

- » Damp or wet areas, often wooded river banks
- » 1500-2745m
- » May-September
- » Punakha, Trongsa, Bumthang, Trashigang

....

Cactaceae
Cactus family

142 *Opuntia vulgaris* Miller
Dzo: Gawairinga Tsang
Eng: Prickly Pear

Sub-erect or sprawling shrub 2-4m; trunk spiny or smooth; branch segments obovate, flattened, 10-30x5-12cm; areoles whitish wooly with a few brown barbed bristles; spines 1-2 per areole, 2-6cm, terete, pale grayish with brown tip. Leaves subulate, 2-3mm. Flowers 5-7cm diameter; perianth segment bright yellow, outer tinged wtih red. Fruits obovoid, 5-7x2-4cm, reddish, spineless but with numerous barbed bristles on areoles.

- » Hillside in dry valleys
- » 250-1,500m
- » April-June
- » Chhukha, Punakha, Wangduephodrang, Trongsa
- » Native of South America naturalized in Bhutan. Formerly used as a host for cochneal insects. Fruit edible

Campanulaceae
Bellflower family

325 *Adenophora khasiana* (Hook. f. & Thomson) Feer

Perennial erect or suberect herb. Stems 40-75cm, subglabrous, branched or not. Leaves alternate, sessile, ovate-elliptic to elliptic, 4-6.5x1.6-2.7cm, margins saw toothed, with very little hair. Inflorescence in spike-like, sometimes branched. Flower lax. Calyx 5-lobed, lobes linear-lanceolate, 5-8.5mm, margin toothed, without hair. Corolla oboconical-campanulate, 12-19mm, pale blue to lilac, divded to half or less; 5 lobes broad ovate to oblong, up to 5.5mm. Capsule subglobose, c 7x5mm.

» On banks, exposed slopes, open woodland, roadsides.
» 1981-2591m
» July-October
» Thimphu, Trongsa, Trashigang, Gasa, Trashiyangtse.

350 *Asyneuma fulgens* (Wall.) Briquet

Erect herb 25-38 cm and stem smooth or with hair. Leaves lance-like 25-60x6-18mm, almost without stalk, and margin toothed. Bracts linear up to 11mm. Flowers few and arranged in spike like fashion, calyx narrow and almost long as corolla. Corolla 6-8.5mm, pale blue with 5 thin oblong and slightly spreading lobes. Capsules obovoid splitting laterally near apex.

» Grassy areas and among shrubs and roadsides of blue pine forests.
» 1219-3048m
» June – September
» Chhukha, Thimphu, Punakha, Trongsa, Bumthang, Mongar

326 *Campanula pallida* Wall.

Somewhat shrubby herb covered with stiff hair. Stems erect, 15-58cm, lateral branches spreading-erect. Leaves sessile, elliptic, (8-)12-37(-50) x 2-16mm, with stiff upward pointing hair, veins prominent on lower surface, base wedge-shaped to gradually tapering, margins, serrated-rounded teeth. Flowers 1-2 at apex and tips of branches; pedicels up to 2cm. Calyx lobes triangular, 3.5-6.5mm, usually with small teeth on margin. 1/2 - 1/3 as long as corolla. Corolla campanulate to tubular campanulate, 8-14mm, pale blue or blue to purple; lobes ovate-oblong, 3-5.5mm. Capsule obovate to subglobose, 3-5x4-7mm, dehiscing at base.

» Open rocky outcrops, mountain slopes (sometimes among shrubs), sandy turf, stream shingles, cultivated areas
» 1850-3950m
» (April), June-September, (November)
» Samdrupjongkhar, Haa, Thimphu, Punakha, Wangduephodrang, Trongsa, Bumthang, Trashigang, Lhuentse

328 *Cyananthus incanus* Hook. f. & Thomson

Low growing perennial herb. Stems prostrate, 3-16cm, covered in soft white hair. Leaves sessile, lanceolate, elliptic or spathulate, 4-9x1.8-3.5mm, appressed hairs above and white soft hair below with margins curled in. Flowers terminal solitary, calyx tubular, 5-9mm, more slightly glabrous or densely white or yellowish brown hairs outside, 5 lobes narrow tirangular 2-3.5mm, always hairy inside. Corolla tubular campanulate, 13-28mm, deep blue to violet, rarely white, throat densely hairy; lobes oblongish, 7-14mm. Capsule ovate.

» On banks and open grassy hillsides
» 3290-4877m
» July-October
» Haa, Paro, Thimphu, Gasa, Trongsa, Bumthang, Lhuentse

329 *Cyananthus lobatus* Wall. ex Benth.
Eng: Trailing Bellflower

Low growing perennial herb. Stems trailing on the ground, 10-40cm, subglabrous to long-haired. Leaves cuneate-spathulate, 10-32x5-17mm, with 3-5 lobes at apex, sometimes with subsidiary lobing, with little appressed hairs above, and wooly below. Pedicel 8-30mm, densely brown-black villous. Calyx broadly tubular, 13-20mm; lobes triangular, 4-5.5mm, densely brownish-black haired. Corolla broadly funnel-shaped, 31-40mm, blue, rarely white; lobes broad obovate, 12-17mm. Capsule ovate-acuminate, more or less equal to calyx.

» Open grasslands, banks or hillsides, in turf, peat, sands, gravel, among rocks, among shrubs or forest glades.
» 3200-4900m
» June-October
» Paro, Thimphu, Trongsa, Trashigang, Gasa, Bumthang, Lhuentse, Trashiyangtse

351 *Lobelia erectiuscula* H. Hara
Eng: Upright Lobelia

Erect herb from 30-80cm with sparse fine hair. Leaves sessile and serrated, 3.7-15.5x1-3cm. Flowers in unbranched erect raceme. Irregular flowers with 2 lips- one lip with two lobes and the other with three lobes. Corolla is mauve or violet blue with white markings in throat.

» In grassy areas in *Fir* & *Juniper* forests or among bamboo
» 2286-4267m
» July to September
» Haa, Thimphu, Punakha, Wangduephodrang, Trongsa, Mongar, Trashigang, Gasa

352 *Lobelia seguinii* H. Lév. & Vaniot
Eng: Seguin's Lobelia

Sparsely hairy herb. Stems erect 0.6-1.3m, puberulent. Leaves alternate, sessile, lanceolate to linear-lanceolate, 7.5-16x1-4cm, margins toothed. Flowers in terminal, sometimes branched racemes, spreading, bending downward to twisting upside down. Calyx 15-18mm; lobes linear, 10-13mm, toothed. Corolla 22-24mm, 2-lipped, 2-lobed lip divided to base, 3 lobed lip, not divided, blue or violet. Capsule erect or deflexed, oblong-ellipsoid c 11x8mm.

» Oak forest margins, moist grassy hillsides
» 1950-2600m
» August-October
» Samdrupjongkhar, Thimphu, Punakha, Gasa, Trashiyangtse

Cannabaceae
Hemp family

263 Cannabis sativa L.

Dzo: Kenam
Eng: Hemp, Marijuana

Erect annual herb 1-1.5m. Leaves with 3-9 sometimes to 11 narrowly elliptic or lanceolate leaflets, each 4-18x0.3-1.5cm, toothed margins; petioles 1-7cm. Male flowers in short pendulous panicles 1-5cm long, perianth of 5 free segments, 5 stamens. Female flowers sessile, crowded in short leafy spikes of 2-3cm, perianth unlobed. Achenes ovoid, 3-3.5mm, greenish brown.

» Streamsides and waste grounds
» 300-3000m
» June-August
» Widespread - Chhukha, Sarpang, Paro, Thimphu, Trongsa, Bumthang, Trashigang.
» Used as source of fibre and oil and also for intoxicating resin
» Two subspecies occur: subsp. *sativa* is common in Bhutan and yields fibre and oil, with taller, elongate sparsely branched stems, with long, hollow internodes; subsp. *indica* yields greater quantities of resin especially on young leaves and inflorescences; usually a smaller plant, much-branched and with short, solid internodes.

Caprifoliaceae
Honeysuckle family

309 Leycestra formosa Wall.

Eng: Himalayan Honeysuckle, Flowering Nutmeg, Himalayan Nutmeg, Pheasant Berry

Shrub 2-5m. Arching hollow stems. Leaves opposite, ovate-acuminate 4-13.5-2-6.5cm, rarely toothed or lobed, lower surface whitish, pertiole 5-12mm. Small white or pink flowers on long pendulous racemes with purple bracts below each flower. Red or purple berries

» In shrubbery in hemlock or fir forests
» 1524-3658m

» June-August
» Thimphu, Punakha, Wangduephodrang, Bumthang, Trashigang

163 *Lonicera quinquelocularis* Hard.
Eng: Translucent Berry Honeysuckle

Erect shrub with hollow pith. Young branches are purple becoming tan, with soft hair. Leaves, opposite, ovate to elliptic, 4-5.5x2-2.5cm, with soft hair above pale long matted hair below; petioles 6-8mm. Flowers two lipped. Corolla white to yellow, tube 5-6mm, with stamens extending beyond petals. Fruit free, whitish, translucent, ovoid, 2.5cm, calyx persistent.

» Common in roadside shrubs and disturbed places, stream sides in blue pine forests
» 2100-2600m
» April-June
» Common in Thimphu and Paro

206 *Lonicera webbiana* Wall. ex DC.

Shrub up to 4m. Leaves broadly lanceolate, 6-11x2-3.5cm, with few hairy with glands, up to 7 pairs of prominent veins. Paired flowers emerging from axils on penduncles 2-4cm long, corolla distinctly two lipped and crimson in colour (sometimes yellowish).

» Damp grounds along streams and in birch, rhododendron and mixed conifer thickets
» 2450-3840m
» April- June
» Paro, Thimphu, Bumthang, Gasa

121, 242 *Sambucus adnata* DC.

Shrubby herb up to 1.5m. Compound leaves, 12-30cm, with 1-4 pairs of leaflets with serrate margins, upper 1-2 pairs connate with rachis. Upper surface hairy on midrib and main veins, lower surface similar with sparse brownish hairs. Flowers in pubescent, umbelliform corymbs. Corolla rotate, 2-2.5mm, cream or white to pink, lobes 1.5-2mm. Fruits are round red berries, 4.5x3mm..

» Exposed hill slopes and clearings in mixed rain forests and blue pine forest

- » 305-3962m
- » June-September
- » Chhukha, Haa, Thimphu, Wangduephodrang, Bumthang, Gasa, Trashiyangtse

272 *Triosteum himalayanum* Wall.

Coarse erect herb. Stems 45-60cm, simple, long-haired with both eglandular and glandular hairs. Leaves opposite joined at base around stem, entire, sinuate margins, obovate to oblong, 5.5-14.5x3.1-9cm, surface as stem. Flowers in terminal spike 3-6cm. Calyx lobes 0.5-1mm. Tubular, bilabiate corolla 11-14mm, curved, gibbous at base, green outside and blotches of purple/red inside, lower lip deflexed. Berry c 11.5mm. Seeds c. 8x4mm

- » In open or cleared spruce/fir forest often in damp ground
- » 3048-3962m
- » May-June
- » Haa, Paro, Thimphu, Bumthang

105 *Viburnum cotinifolium* D. Don
Eng: Smoketree-Leaved Viburnum

Deciduous shrub, 2-5m. Leaves ovate to broadly ovate, 4.8-12.5x3.8-9.3cm, margin toothed, upper surface hairy, lower surface more dense and whitish hair, petiole 6-17mm. Flowers in umbelliform corymbs. Calyx 4-4.5mm, 5 lobes 0.5-1mm. Corolla more or less campanulate, 5.5-6.5mm, white tinged pink outside, 5 lobes 1-2mm. Drupe oblong-ellipsoid, black, 7-10x5-6mm.

- » Blue pine and conifer/Rhododendron forests, often at forest edges
- » 1524-3720m
- » April-June
- » Haa, Paro, Thimphu

106 *Viburnum erubescens* DC.
Eng: Reddish Viburnum

Deciduous shrub, 1.5-4m. Leaves elliptic to narrowly oblong elliptic 3.7-9.5 x 2-5.2cm, sharply or gently to narrowing to tip, base more or less wedge shaped, toothed margins, upper surface smooth or very thin flat hair. Flowers in small hanging clusters, with peduncle 8-37mm, smooth or hairy.

Corolla tubular to bellshaped 8.5-12mm, pink or white tinged pink on lobes, lobes 3-3.5mm. Stamens joined at upper part of tube. Drupe ellipsoid, purplish black, 6.5-8.5 x 4.5-6mm.

» Broadleaved conifer/Rhododendron and evergreen oak forests, sometimes in degraded areas
» 1402-3962m
» April-May
» Chhukha, Samdrupjongkhar, Punakha, Trongsa, Mongar, Trashigang

107 *Viburnum grandiflorum* Wall. ex DC.
Eng: Himalayan Viburnum

Deciduous shrub or small tree, 1.5-4m. Leaves obovate or elliptic to narrow elliptic, 4.2-10x1.5-5cm, toothed margins, petioles 12-28mm. Flowers appearing before leaves in sessile corymbs. Calyx 3.5-4.2mm, 5 lobes. Corolla, pale pink to rose pink, tubular campanulate, 12-15mm; 5 lobes broadly rounded, 3.5-4.5mm.

» Conifer/Rhododendron forest, stream banks, damp grassy slopes
» 2743-3810m
» March-May, September
» Haa, Paro, Thimphu, Bumthang, Mongar, Lhuentse

108 *Viburnum nervosum* D.Don.
Dzo: Ola Sima

Deciduous shrub up to 6m. Ovate leaves tapering to tips and heart-shaped base and toothed margins. Veination very prominent. White flowers arranged in corymbs usually appearing when leaves are young. White flowers in sessile corymbs. Corolla flat 5-7mm, 5 lobes 4-6mm. Drupe ellipsoid, purplish 7-9x4-5mm.

» Conifer and rhododendron forests. Sometimes degraded areas
» 2743-3962m
» April-June
» Haa, Thimphu, Punakha, Trongsa, Mongar

Caryophyllaceae
Carnation family

26 Arenaria polytrichoides Edgeworth & Hook f.
Eng: Sandwort

Perennial herb forming dense hemispherical cushions. Cushion 5-10cm tall. Leaves linear lanceolate 3.5-4 x 1-1.25mm, gradually narrowing to aristate point, recurved, base sheathing, sessile, margins thickened. Flowers terminal, sessile at first, pedicels lengthening up to 4mm in fruit. Sepals oblong-elliptic, 2.5x1.5mm, obtuse, glabrous. Petals 5, white, obovate, c. 4x1.75mm, narrowed at base. Stamens 10.

»   On mountain rocks
»   3900-4570m
»   June – July
»   Thimphu, Gasa, Bumthang, Trashiyangtse

27 Stellaria vestita Kurz
Eng: Hairy Chickweed

Weak greyish herb covered in soft short hair, prostrate up to 50cm. Leaves ovate 0.6-3x0.3-1 cm, tapering to tip and rounded base, sessile. Flowers few in loose cymes. Sepals longer than petals c4mm. 4 or 5 petals white divided almost to base. Capsules ovoid almost as long as sepals.

»   Among shrubs and margins of disturbed ground
»   1400-2750m
»   April-July
»   Chhukha, Haa, Punakha, Trongsa, Trashiyangtse

....

Commelinaceae
Spiderwort family

365 Cyanotis vaga (Lour.) Roem. & Schult.
Eng: Spiderwort

Perennial herb. Stems decumbent, much branched, 6-65cm. Basal leaves in bulbous forms long (to 40cm); stem leaves lanceolate to linear-lanceolate, tapering gradually form base to apex, 2-8.5x0.4-0.7cm, decreasing in size upwards, with scattered hairs on both surfaces. Flowers in curved cyme, at ends of stem or betwen leaf axils, subtended by leaf-like spathes. Corolla pale blue, lower half tubular, 6.5-8mm, c2,5mm wide. Staminal filaments sticking out long from corolla with bluish hairs (sometimes white); anthers oblong, notched, yellow. Capsule 3-lobed, truncate, 2.5-3x1.5-2mm.

»   Very common on rocks, pasture, banks and slopes, in open or in scrub or pine forest
»   910-3100m
»   June-October
»   Chhukha, Thimphu, Punakha, Trongsa, Bumthang, Mongar, Trashigang, Gasa, Trashiyangtse

....

Compositae
Sunflower family

90 *Ageratina adenophora* (Spreng.) R.M. King & H. Rob.

Herb or subshrub, 0.4-2m. Stems more or less erect, branched, purplish to brown, densely glandular pubescent. Leaves trowel shaped, blades 2-7x1.5-5.5cm, 3 veined at base, margins coarsely toothed, sub-glabrous above, glandular pubescent below, petioles slender 0.8-3cm. Capitula c50-60 discoid flowers, in a dense terminal and axillary corymbs. Corollas white, tubular campanulate, 3.5-4mm. Achenes 1.5-2mm, glabrous; pappus bristles c 10-12, caducous.

»   Forest roadsides, cultivated areas
»   750-2050m
»   January-June
»   Chhukha Sarpang, Punakha, Trongsa
»   Native of Mexico, now a weed in most tropical areas of the world

72 *Ainsliaea aptera* DC
Eng: Wingless Ainsliaea

Subscapose perennial herb. Stems 6-120cm, sparsely hairy. Leaves simple, alternate, mostly associated with the root, blade ovate, 4 -9 x 3 -7cm, acute, cordate, prominently dentate, subglabrous above, sparsely pubescent beneath, petiole winged, to 13cm. Flowering in autumn, capitula small or subsessile, drooping, borne singly or in small fascicles, discoid. Phyllaries ovate to linear lanceolate, 1-11x1-2mm. Fully developed corollas white or purplish, cylindric, tube 3-7.5mm, limb 6-9mm. Achenes c5.5mm pappus 7-8mm.

» In deciduous and coniferous forests
» 2000-3100m
» September-December
» Chhukha, Haa, Thimphu, Punakha, Trashigang

91 *Anaphalis contorta* (D. Don) Hook. f.
Dzo: Chukarp
Eng: Twisted Pearly Everlasting

Perennial herb, woody at base. Stems 15-40 cm tall erect or decumbent. Numerous narrow leaves, 1-5cm long up to 0.5cm wide, with recurved margins, sessile. Fine whitish hair on leaves but more densely on lower surface, 1 vein. Rounded capitula of flowers with shiny white papery involucral bracts arranged in dense corymbs.

» Open slopes, scree and roadsides
» 2150-4400m
» February, July- November
» Chhukha, Haa, Paro, Thimphu, Punakha, Trongsa, Mongar, Bumthang, Gasa

92 *Anaphalis margaritacea* (L.) Benth. & Hook. f.
Dzo: Daningon
Eng: Pearly Everlasting

Herb 30-80cm with greyish stems covered in fine hair. Leaves narrow and without stalk, with three veins, smooth or little hair and dark green above but covered in fine greyish or brownish hair below. Flower heads in dense clusters to diffuse corymbs. Flower heads whitish to yellowish surrounded by numerous white bracts and less than 1cm in diameter.

» Forest clearings, roadsides, rock crevices etc.
» 900-4500m
» July- December
» Paro, Thimphu

93 *Anaphalis nepalensis* var. *nepalensis* (C. B. Clarke) Ridley

Herbaceous plant sometimes with arching stolons. Stems sparsely or densely covered in whitish wooly hair, 10- 50cm tall. Leaves variable in shape, lower leaves oblong, elliptic to spathulate 1-10 x 0.3-2.3cm, tapering to base, 1 or 3 veined, whitish hairy on both surfaces, but more densely below or sometimes yellowish to cinnamomeous below, petiole up to 4.5cm; upper leaves usually narrower and sessile. Capitula 1-15, in corymbs, with white shiny papery involucral bracts.

» Forest margins, open grassland, road and trailsides
» 2400-4265m
» June - October
» Thimphu, Punakha, Trongsa, Bumthang, Mongar, Gasa, Trashiyangtse
» var. *monocephala* has solitary capitula, or rarely 2-4 together, lower leaves smaller, often sessile and usually only 1 veined

44 *Aster ageratoides* Turcz.
Eng: Whiteweed Aster

Perennial somewhat shrubby herb. Stems 0.3-2m, finely pubescent above. Leaves ovate-elliptic, 4.5-10x1.5-2cm, with few coarse teeth, pinnately veined but with superficially 3-veined with 1 pair of veins near base more prominent, usually finely pubescent and glandular beneath. Capitula in lax corymbs, involucres c6mm diameter. Ray flowers 10-20, corolla tube 2-3mm; ligules usually white, sometimes pale pink or mauve, 7-10mmx1.5-3mm. Disc corollas yellow, 5-6.5mm, lobes often glandular. Achenes obovoid, 2.5-3x0.75-1mm, sparsely silky pubescent, seomtimes glandular; pappus whitish.

» Forest margins, clearings, among shrubs
» 1800-3650m
» June-November
» Paro, Chhukha, Thimphu, Wangduephodrang, Punakha, Gasa

45 *Aster albescens* (DC.) Wall. ex Hand.-Mazz.
Eng: Fading Himalayan Aster

Erect shrub; stems 0.5-2m, sparsely pubescent intermixed with glands, rarely white tomentose. Leaves ovate-lanceolate, 3-10x0.8-2.5cm, acute or acuminate, cuneate at base, sessile or shortly petiolate, entire or finely serrate, sparsely pubescent beneath and sometimes bearing a few glands. Capitula usually numerous, in terminal corymbs; involucres c 5mm diameter; phyllaries usually c 20, imbricate, linear-lanceolate, 3.5-4.5x0.5mm, green or purplish at tip, pubescent or tomentose towards base. Ray flowers 12-30; corolla tube c 2.5mm; ligules 4-4.5x0.6-1.2mm, blue, mauve in early to mid summer and fade to white later in season. Disc corollas yellow, 4.5mm. Achenes 1.75-2.5x0.5mm, sparsely pubescent, often glandular at apex; pappus brownish, 3.5-4mm, simple.

» Open slopes, blue pine forest
» 1750-3600m
» May - September
» Chhukha, Haa, Thimphu, Trongsa, Bumthang, Trashiyangtse

339 *Aster diplostephioides* (DC.) C.B. Clarke

Erect perennial herb. Stems 15-40cm surrounded at base by layer of leaf remains, glandular pubescent above. Leaves alternate. Basal leaves lanceolate or oblanceolate, 6-13x1.3-2cm, sometimes toothed margins, glandular or sparsely pubescent; cauline leaves olong or linear, decreasing in size above. Capitulum solitary, radiate, involucre 17-22mm diameter, phyllaries in two rows, oblong-lanceolate, 10-12x3-4.5mm, blackish glandular and bearing long white hairs especially towards base. Ray flowers more or less numerous in 1-2 rows, corolla tube 1.5mm; ligules mauve or blue, 20-30x1.25-2.5mm. Disc corollas blackish purple, fading to orange, 5mm, teeth glabrous. Achenes obovoid, 3-3.5x1-1.5mm, glandular and whitish pubescent; pappus white.

» Grassy slopes, screes, forest openings
» 3200 - 4730m
» June - September
» Haa, Paro, Thimphu, Gasa, Bumthang, Lhuentse, Trashiyangtse

340 Aster neoelegans Grierson

Erect stolon-forming perennial. Simple stems 40-100cm. Leaves oblanceolate or narrowly spathulate, 2.5-7x0.4-1cm, acute or obtuse, attenuate to sessile base, entire, finely pubescent. Capitula 1-5; involucre c 8-13mm diameter, 3-4 seriate; phyllaries more or less oblong to linear 4-8x1-1.5mm, sparsely appressed pubescent. Ray flowers 30-40, ligules white, mauve or blue violet, 7-12mm x1mm. Disc corollas yellow 4-5mm. Achenes obovoid, 2.5-3mm, sparsely pubescent, with few glands at apex, pappus whitish, 4-5mm. simple.

- » Marshy ground, meadows, forest clearings, open hillsides
- » 2450-3200m
- » May-September
- » Haa, Thimphu, Punakha, Trongsa, Bumthang, Gasa

341 Aster vestitus Franch.

Erect perennial; Stems 60-130cm, densely glandular, usually mixed with spreading eglandular hair. Leaves elliptic lanceolate, 2.5-6.5x0.45-1.5cm, acute tip, rounded base, sessile, with a few small teeth, glandular pubsescent on both surfaces. Capitula, radiate, more or less numerous, in terminal corymbs; involucres c8mm diameter. Ray flowers 20-30; corolla tube 1.5mm; ligule white mauve or blue-violet, 10x2mm. Disc corollas yellow 4.5mm. Achenes obovate, 2.5 x1mm; pappus white, simple, as long as corollas.

- » Open banks, forest margins
- » 2350-3200m
- » August-October
- » Haa, Thimphu, Trongsa, Bumthang, Gasa

46 Bidens pilosa L.
Eng: Blackjack, Beggars Tick, Spanish Needle, Cobbler's Pegs

Herb 20-80cm with smooth or slightly hairy stems. Compound leaves with usually three leaflets and rarely up to 7 leaflets; leaflets with toothed margins. Capitula radiate, 5-6 white ray flowers and yellow central disc. Achenes linear, 6-11 x c0.8mm, blackish, glabrous below, sparsely setose above.

- » Fields, roadsides and among scrub.

- » 150-2400m
- » April – December
- » A weed in all districts

94 *Chromolaena odorata* (L.) R.M. King & H. Rob.
Eng: Siam Weed

A smelly herbaceous perennial. Erect or scrambling 1.5-3m, branchlets crisp pubescent. Leaves opposite, ovate triangular, toothed, 3-veined near base, 4-10x3-6.5cm, coarsely serrate near the broadest part, sparsely pubescent on upper surface, pubescent and sessile glandular beneath. Capitula discoid, c 30 flowered, cylindrical campanulate, numerous in more or less compact corymbs. Corollas, white or mauve, 5.5mm. Achenes 4mm

- » Roadsides, forest clearings and plantations
- » 200-1450m
- » August-December
- » Samtse, Chhukha, Sarpang, Punakha, Wangduephodrang
- » Native of South America, widely naturalised in India and occurs in most warmer districts of Bhutan

400 *Cirsium eriophoroides* (Hook. f.) Petr.
Eng: Woolly Thistle

Perennial herb 60-120cm. Leaves ovate-elliptic in outline, acuminate, with numerous lobes tipped with spine to 15mm, araneous on both surfaces but more densely beneath, upper surface occasionaly sparsely setulose; lower leaf blades to 45x15cm, narrowed to petiole to 15cm; upper ones 9x4cm, rounded at base, sessile. Capitula solitary at branch ends. Involucre 30-50mm diameter; phyllaries acuminate, 40-50x2-3mm, densely cottony. Corollas 30-50mm, dark purple, limb 15mm including lobes 5.5mm. Achenes obovoid, 5-6mm; pappus c25mm, brownish.

- » Hillsides, grassland, screes and river banks
- » 3100-4730m
- » June-October
- » Thimphu, Trongsa, Bumthang, Gasa

401 *Cirsium falconeri* (Hook.f.) Petrak
Eng: Falconer's Thistle

A very spiny perennial herb 0.5-1.5m. Stems sparsely pubescent at least above and often arraneous. Leaves covered in dense bristles to almost smooth above, white hairy beneath, base broadly clasping stem; lowest leaves 1-2 times pinnatisect, oblanceolate in outline c20-40x5.5-20cm, with 7-12 pairs of leafy primary segments, spiny on tips and margins; upper leaves smaller, ovate-lanceolate in outline, cut deeply and irregularly from sides. Capitula discoid, at branch ends, usually solitary, sometimes in cymes of 2-4. Involucre 12-25mm diameter, phyllaries lanceolate to linear, sparsely hairy, outer and middle ones often spiny. Flowers pale to dark purple; corolla tube 10.5-19m; limb 10.5-18.5mm including lobes 5- 7.5mm, tapered at base to abruptly campanulate. Achenes obovoid, dark brown, 6-7mm, pappus 15.5-23mm, brownish.

- » Open hillsides, forest clearings, roadsides
- » 2745-4265m
- » July - October
- » Thimphu, Trongsa, Bumthang, Gasa, Bumthang to Trashiyangtse
- » Very variable species

402 *Cirsium verutum* (D. Don) Sprengel

Spiny herb 45-200cm, sparsely pubescent. Leaves pinnately divided, lanceolate-elliptic in outline 12-20x4-5cm, tapering to spine 8-12mm, lateral segments 8-12 pairs with spines 5-10mm, hairless above and hairless to cottony below, base clasping stem. Flower capitula in tight racemes, involucre 1-1.5cm diameter, phyllaries greenish, outer tapering to spine, corollas purple 17mm. Achenes obovoid, 4.5mm, pappus 16mm dirty white.

- » Sides of cultivated areas, ditches
- » 1500-2100m
- » April-May
- » Thimphu, Punakha

288 *Cosmos bipinnatus* Cavanilles
Eng: Cosmos, Mexican Aster

Erect annual herb 0.5-1.5m tall, almost smooth to stiffly puberulous. Leaves opposite doubly pinnatisect resulting in a lacy foliage with thin segments (5-30x1mm). Capitula solitary on long peduncles, radiate, paleate. Ray flowers usually 8, ligules obovate, upto 30x18mm, with broad shallow teeth at apex, white rose or purplish pink. Disc corollas c5.5mm. Achene 6-10mm, beak 1-6mm, pappus awns absent or present.

» Grassy places, roadsides, cultivated grounds and disturbed areas
» 2300-2400m
» July-October
» Thimphu, Paro, Bumthang, Trashigang and districts mainly above 2000m
» Native of southern North America

151 *Dubyaea hispida* (D. Don) DC

Perennial herb. Stems 10-50cm, covered in coarse stiff hair. Leaves alternate, acuminate, and toothed margin; lower leaves simple to lobed with 1-4 pairs of rounded lateral lobes, lanceolate to oblanceolate in outline, 7-12x2-5cm, sessile, with lobes base, petiole to 15cm; upper leaves ovate to linear lanceolate, to 10-4cm, sessile. Inflorescence more or less corymbose with 1-15 capitula. Capitula ligulate, 6-15mm across, cernous; peduncles up to 10cm covered in black stiff hair. Phyllaries lanceolate 8-20x2-5mm, blackish stiff hairs. Corolla yellow, tube 9mm, ligules 13x2.5mm. Achenes brown, 9.5mm, pappus dirty white.

» Open grassy banks and forests
» 2750-4370m
» July-October
» Haa, Paro, Thimphu, Punakha, Bumthang, Mongar, Gasa
» Extremely variable in leaf and habit

372 *Erigeron multiradiatus* (DC.) Clarke
Eng: Himalayan Fleabane

Erect perennial herb, with simple stems sparsely covered in hair and glandular higher up. Leaves variable in shape, with basal ones oblanceolate if present 5-11x0.7-1.5cm, acute tip and tapering to broad petiole, sparsely pubescent on both surfaces, upper leaves oblanceolate to oblong, 3-7x 0.7-3cm acute or acuminate, narrowed or rounded at base, sessile. Capitula usually solitary; involucre 12-22mm diameter. Flowers dimorphic, ray flowers 120-200, 2-3 seriate; ligules mauve red to purple-blue, 8-15mm long, Disc corolla yellow or purplish. Achenes oblong or narrowly ovoid, minutely pubescent, pappus brownish.

» Open grassy slopes among shrubs or boulders, on cliffs and rocky slopes in wet pine forests
» 3050-4800m
» May- September
» Haa, Thimphu, Punakha, Trongsa, Bumthang, Gasa, Bumthang, Lhuentse, Trashiyangtse

48 *Galinsoga parviflora* Cavanilles
Dzo: Jaga Ima, Jaga Suju
Eng: Quickweed

Herbaceous annual 10-60cm. Stem with short soft hair above. Leaves ovate-lanceolate with rounded base and slightly toothed margin and three veined at base, sparse hair on surface. Flower stalk with short hair without glands. Flower heads about 4mm high with 5 white ray florets per head and yellow disc florets.

» Waste areas, disturbed soils, cultivated areas
» 900-2450m
» March-December
» One of the most common dry-land weeds in Bhutan above 1000m
» Introduced weed species, originally from South America

47 *Galinsoga ciliata* (Rafinesque) Blake

Very similar to *G. parviflora*. Distinguished by hairs on flower stalks with some bearing glandular heads.

» Roadsides
» 1800-2200m
» March-December
» Common
» Introduced weedy species from the Americas

147 *Helianthus annus* L.
Dzo: Nyeem-Gang-Shar
Eng: Sunflower

Erect, coarse annual herb. Stems 1-3m, more or less unbranched. Leaves simple ovate, 10-40x5-35cm, acuminate, base cordate, toothed margins, petioles up to 15cm. Capitula large, radiate, solitary or few in open corymbs. Disc 3-6cm diameter at flowering, paleae lanceolate, 9-13cm, 3 toothed, center tooth elongate. Ray flowers c 20-35, corolla tube 2-3mm, ligules yellow 45-60x16-20mm. Disc corollas 6-9mm. Achenes at flowering time c6mm, pubescent.

» Cultivated and near settlements
» 1980-2370m
» June - September
» Native to North America

155 Hippolytia gossypina (Hook.f &Thomson) Shih

Plant 4-10cm. Leaves of sterile shoots c 7 x 3mm, appressed and +- scarious below, lobes usually oblong and obtuse. Leaves of flowering stems often larger, spreading from base. Capitula 3.5-5mm diameter. Phyllaries 4.5-6mm, sparsely hairy. Corollas 2.5-4mm. Achenes 2mm.

» Sandy screes and rocky gullies
» 4100-5200m
» July-September
» Gasa, Trongsa, Bumthang, Trashiyangtse

148 Inula hookeri C.B. Clarke
Eng: Hooker's Inula

Coarse elongate herb. Stem 0.6-1.5m, loosely wooly at first. Leaves, simple, alternate, elliptic-lanceolate, 8-15x2.5-4.5cm, margins minutely denticulate, pubescent and short glandular on both sides, but more dense below. Capitula few in terminal corymbs, sometimes single on long axillary peduncles, radiate. Involucre 18-30mm diameter, phyllaries to 15x1mm and covered in shaggy brown hair. Tube of ray flowers 5-7mm, ligule 18-45x1mm, yellow, with long soft hair at base. Disc corollas 5-6.5mm. Achenes 1.5mm, pappus white, shorter or equal to corolla.

» Hillsides, forest clearings, coniferous and wet-broadleaved forest, riverside scrub on gravel
» 2450-4300m
» August-October
» Samdrupjongkhar, Haa, Thimphu, Paro, Punakha, Trongsa, Bumthang, Mongar, Gasa, Lhuentse

39 *Leontopodium jacotianum* Beauverd
Eng: Edelweiss

Perennial stoloniferous, mat forming herb. Stems 6-28cm, greyish (greyish-yellow) covered in soft matted hair. Leaves 7-25mm, subobtuse to acuminate; rosette leaves linear, strap-shaped to spathulate or oblanceolate, 1-3mm wide; stem leaves lanceolate to strap-shaped or linear with margins recurved, 1-5mm wide. Flowering stems 2-25cm. Capitula discoid, 4-9, all female or predominantly male or female flowers usually densely crowded; radiating bracts 8-25x2.2-7mm, densely covered in whitish wooly hair forming a star shaped pattern exceeding the flower heads. Corollas 3-3.5mm. Achenes pubescent

- »   Rocky hillsides, apline pastures
- »   3800-5500m
- »   June-October
- »   Haa, Paro, Thimphu, Trongsa, Gasa, Lhuentse, Trashiyangtse

175 *Ligularia atkinsonii* (Clarke) Liu

Erect perennial herb 47-90cm. Stems glabrescent below, sparse hair above, denser and sometimes mixed with white woolly hair in inflorescence. Basal leaves, liver shaped to triangular to ovate, 70-150x70-140mm, pointed to obtuse tip, prominently arrow-shaped, margins toothed, smooth or pubescent on veins below. Leaves on stems 2-3 and much reduced. Capitula yellow, 10-50 in a narrow raceme, hanging when fruiting, bracts below capitula linear. Achenes oblong c5.5mm, pappus white (yellowish) 5.5-8mm reaching middle of corolla.

- »   Streamsides, meadows, marsh, turf on top of hill-top
- »   2300-4400m
- »   July-September
- »   Thimphu, Haa, Bumthang
- »   Can be difficult to tell apart from *L. fischeri.*

342 *Mulgedium bracteatum* (Hook. f. & Thomson ex C.B. Clarke) C. Shih

Perennial herb. Stems erect, 20-80cm, covered in stiff coarse hair. Leaves obovate-elliptic, 3.5-11x1-4cm, tapering to tip, narrowed and base almost clasping stem, margins toothed, sparsely pubscent. Inflorescence sparse, racemose or paniculate, wth prominent toothed bracts; capitula ligulate, usually 10-20; involucre 5-9mm diameter. Corolla tube 5-8mm, ligule 13.5-15x2.5-3mm, pale mauve to blue or violet. Achene narrowly ellipsoid, 5.5mm, pale brown, 3-7 ribbed on each side, beak 4mm, brownish, pappus 7mm, white.

» In forest, on stony slopes and among scrub
» 2130-3650m
» September - October
» Thimphu, Gasa

49 *Myriactis wallichii* Lessing

Annual herb 10-60cm, stems covered in finely apressed hair. Leaves ovate-elliptic 5-16 x 1-6cm, acute tip and tapering towards a narrow petiolate base. Flower heads more or less hemispherical 7-10mm diameter, ray flowers in 2-5 series, whitish; ligules pinkish white; achenes often 2.5 x 1mm.

» Forests, clearings, roadsides
» 1500-3650m
» July-October
» Thimphu district

192 *Pseudognaphalium affine* (D. Don) Anderberg
Dzo: Meto Kapa

Annual herb up 10-40cm with whitish soft hair on stems, often branched from base. Leaves narrow lance-like, alternate and entire with whitish wooly hair or both surfaces. Flower heads globular and glistening yellow 3mm across in dense rounded solitary clusters. Achenes 0.5mm, papillae sparse; pappus as long as corollas.

» Common weed on roadsides and cultivated areas.
» 1050-4900m
» March-December
» Chhukha, Sarpang, Samdrupjongkhar, Thimphu, Trongsa, Mongar

95 *Saussurea gossipiphora* D. Don.
Med: Jagoid Sugpa

Rhizomatous, 30-70cm; stems erect, pubescent at least above, surrounded at base by dead leaves. Lower leaves oblanceolate, 15-30x2-5cm, +- acute, long-tapering to broad semi-amplexicaul petiole, dentate, puberulous (to sparsely tomentose); uppermost leaves membranous, 8-15 x 3-13cm, concave, loosely surrounding inflorescence, whitish or pale green. Capitula 4-11 in compact corymbs. Involucre 8-15mm diameter; phyllaries mostly lanceolate, purplish-black, 10-20 x 2-4mm, acuminate, sparsely pubescent. Corolla 1-17mm, including lobes 4-5.5mm. Achenes oblong, 5-6mm; pappus double, inner 11-14mm, outer scabrid, 3-5mm.

» Screes, hillsides in open or among scrubs, wet gullies
» 3950-5000m
» July-September
» Thimphu, Gasa, Trongsa, Bumthang

73 *Saussurea obvallata* (DC.) Edgeworth.

Rhizomatous, 30-70cm; stems erect, pubescent at least above, surrounded at base by dead leaves. Lower leaves oblanceolate, 15-30 x 2-5cm, +- acute, long-tapering to broad semi-amplexicaul petiole, dentate, puberulous (to sparsely tomentose); uppermost leaves membranous, 8-15 x 3-13cm, concave, loosely surrounding inflorescence, whitish or pale green. Capitula 4-11 in compact corymbs. Involucre 8-15mm diameter; phyllaries mostly lanceolate, purplish-black, 10-20 x 2-4mm, acuminate, sparsely pubescent. Corolla 1-17mm, including lobes 4-5.5mm. Achenes oblong, 5-6mm; pappus double, inner 11-14mm, outer scabrid, 3-5mm.

» On damp screes, rocky hillsides, rich pastures, peaty soils, etc.
» 3660-4880m
» July-September
» Thimphu, Trongsa, Gasa, Bumthang, Lhuentse, Trashiyangtse

373 *Saussurea sughoo* C.B. Clarke

Perennial herb without a stem. Leaves, narrowly oblanceolate in outline, pinnately divided, deeply on basal side, shallowly towards apex, 10-23x1.5-5cm, sparsely pubescent above, white hairy below. Capitulum discoid, solitary, base tightly sheathed by base of all the leaves. Involucre 12-20mm across, phyllaries lanceolate, 23-28mmx5mm, apex curved back. Corolla purplish or violet, 24mm including lobes.

Achenes obovoid, 5mm, ribbed; pappus double brownish.

» Alpine grasslands, among alpine scrub
» 3650-4880m
» October
» Paro, Thimphu

149 *Senecio laetus* Edgeworth
Dzo: Uma Elama

Rhizomatous perennial herb. Stems 45-150cm. Leaves alternate. Radical leaves usually absent at flowering time, with long, dentate, and often winged petioles; lower and mid-stem leaves lyre shaped and pinnately divided, oblanceolate in outline, 10-25x1.5-6.5cm, sessile, glabrous above, hairy beaneath; upper stem leaves oblong in outline, 8-10x1.5-3cm, irregularly divided, sessile and clasping base. Capitula radiate, numerous, in terminal corymbs, involucre 3.3-4mm in diameter, on slender peduncles. Ray flowers 11-20, ligules yellow, 7-12x2-4.5mm. Disc flowers numerous, yellow, tublar campanulate. Achenes obovoid, 2mm, glabrous, pappus 3mm, whitish, reduced or absent.

» Fields, open spaces, grassy banks, roadsides
» 2150-3950m
» May-September
» Paro, Thimphu, Trongsa, Wangduephodrang, Gasa, Bumthang

150 *Senecio scandens* Buch.-Ham. ex D. Don
Eng: Climbing Senecio

Perennial herbaceous plant. Stems scrambling, strongly bending in zig-zag fashion, 1.5-5m, sparsely pubescent at first. Leaves ovate or triangular, 4-13x1.5-5cm, toothed or pinnately divided with 1-6 pairs of lateral lobes, smooth on both surfaces; petiole 1-2cm. Capitula radiate, in loose spreading corymbs. Ray flowers 8-10, corolla tube 3mm, ligule 5.5x1.2mm, yellow. Disc flowers numerous, yellow. Achenes oblong, 2.5-3mm, pubescent; pappus 5.5-7mm, white.

» Roadsides and climbing over shrubs
» 1100-3800m
» April-December
» Samtse, Chhukha, Samdrupjongkhar, Thimphu, Trongsa, Bumthang, Trashigang, Gasa

There are two varieties of *S. scandens*:

var. *scandens* with leaves subentire or dentate without lobes at base is more common;

var. *incisus* with pinnatifid leaves with 1-4 lobes at base, is rarer and known only from Thimphu, Trongsa and Gasa

193 *Sigesbeckia orientalis* L.
Eng: St. Paul's Wort

Stems up to 1.5cm, purplish, spreading whitish pubescent. Leaves ovate-triangular, 6-15x3-10cm, acuminate, long attenuate at base, variously toothed, usually with 1-3 pairs of larger lateral teeth or lobes, pubescent on both surfaces. Capitulum, excluding outer phyllaries, 5mm diameter. Outer phyllaries oblonceolate, 8-10x1-1.5mm; inner phyllaries oblong, 4-5x1.5mm. Ray flowers 5; corolla tube 1mm, pubescent, sometimes persistent around achenes. Achenes 3-4mm.

» Waste ground near habitation, roadsides and weed of cultivation
» 300-2450m.
» March-December
» Samtse, Chhukha, Thimphu, Punakha, Sarpang, Trashigang

153 *Sonchus asper* (L.) Hill
Eng: Prickly Sow Thistle

Annual herb 15-120cm, smooth stem or with glandular hairs above. Leaves simple or deeply divided with sharp prickly margins, and rounded base clasping stem, 5-25 x3-8cm. Inflorescence of 1-several flower heads, Flower heads dandelion like with yellow ligulate flowers which are longer towards margin of capitula. Mature flower heads covered in white feathery pappus. Achene obovate-ellipsoid, strongly compressed and ribbed.

» Roadsides and cultivated lands
» 1800-2700m
» February- September
» Thimphu, Paro, Bumthang
» Leaves can be eaten

154 *Sonchus oleraceus* L.
Eng: Smooth Sow Thistle

Similar to *S. asper* but leaves, simple or lyrate (pinnately divided but terminal lobe rounded and larger), and pointed base clasping stem. Achenes narrowly obovoid, less compressed, not winged, and 2 grooves on each side.

» Roadsides, open ground, cultivated areas
» 1950-2450m
» March- November
» Thimphu, Punakha, Trashigang

176 *Soroseris hookeriana* Stebbins.

Dwarf rosulate rhizomatous perennial, with thick often hollow stems 2-30cm; scale leaves few or absent. Leaves lanceolate to oblanceolate or linear, 4-13 x 0.3-3.5cm, shallowly pinnatifid to deeply pinnatisect, at least when well developed (when length of blade is more than 4 x width, when shorter sometimes simple, dentate), long attenuate at base; lobes entire (rarely with 1 broad and 2 minute teeth); petiole 0-6cm. Inflorescence convex or elongate (to 16cm). Bracts usually densely hirsute at least at base. Involucre 2-3 mm diameter; inner phyllaries 8-12.5mm, hirsute (very rarely subglabrous), innermost 2.6-4mm wide. Corolla 12-18mm; tube 3-6.5mm; ligule yellow, 7-12mm, with small regular teeth. Anthers dark (very rarely yellowish with whole flower lacking cyanic pigments). Pappus white, sooty or stramineous, usually with bluish tips, 6.5-13mm.

» Among boulders and on screes
» 3650-4720m
» July-September
» Haa, Thimphu, Trongsa, Gasa

50 *Tagetes minuta* L.
Eng: Mexican Marigold

Plant 0.3-2m; stem usually simple, erect, short branched above. Leaves 5-16cm; leaflets 4-5 pairs, 10-7-x1.5-9mm, acuminate, attenuate at base, serrate, with rounded oil glands near margin at base of each tooth, others scattered near midrib. Capitula in compact corymbs. Involucres cylindrical, 9-10 x 1.5-2mm; phyllaries 3, bearing lenticular oil glands. Corollas lemon yellow. Ray flowers, corolla tube 3.2-5mm, hairy; ligule usually 2-lobed, 1.5-2.2 x c 2.4mm.

Disc flowers 2-3; corolla 4-4.5mm. Achenes 5-6.5mm; pappus awns to 3.2mm.

- » River banks and cultivated ground
- » 200-2350m
- » February-October
- » Chhukha, Wangduephodrang, Punakha, Thimphu
- » Native of South America now widespread weed of warmer countries

194 *Tagetes patula* L.

Strongly smelling glabrous annual. Stem 0.2-0.7m, Leaves opposite, 3-8cm, pinnate with leaflets narrowly elliptic in 3-6 pairs, serrate and gland dotted. Capitula solitary at branch ends; peduncles gradually swollen. Involucres 7-12mm diameter. Ray flowers 7-10 in single form, numerous in double forms, tube 8-9mm; ligule 10-13x10-11mm, yellow or deeper red. Disc corolla tube and throat 9-10mm; lobes 3-4.5mm.

- » Cultivated
- » 1200-2350m
- » February - October
- » Widespread
- » Native of Mexico, now widely cultivated.

152 *Taraxacum mitalii* Soest
Eng: Dandelion

Acaulescent herb. Leaves basal 40-85x6-20mm, margins deeply lobed and pointed back, oblanceolate in outline; lateral segments 2-4 pairs, entire, with 1-2 narrow teeth from broad base or 1-3 denticles. Scapes 16-55mm. Capitula many flowered, ligulate. Involucre 7-11mm diameter with 2 rows of phyllaries; outer phyllaries 14-19 or more, 4-8x1.2-2.5mm, callose tip; inner phyllaries 9.7-15mm, callose to slightly corniculate tip. Flowers white to yellow or reddish; stigmas greyish-green. Achene body squamate-spinulose above; body and cone 4.5-4.7mm; beak 7-8.5mm; pappus 5-5.5mm

- » Short grass, roadside
- » 3050-3500m
- » April-May
- » Paro

»   *T. mitalli* is very similar to *T. parvalum* (*T. officinale*) but can be differentiated by leaf lobes and number of phyllaries. T. parvulum has leaf lobes that are often entire, and outer phyllaries number 8-13.

51 *Tricholepis furcata* DC.

Perennial herb with stems 60-260cm minutely rough with fine short hair. Leaves simple alternately arranged, elliptic to lanceolate, 5-15x1-4.5cm, sub-sessile, finely toothed margins, upper surface minutely roughened, pale soft hairy beneath. Capitula solitary at branch ends, discoid. Involucre campanulate 1-2cm across; phyllaries numerous, blackish, very narrow with long recurved hair-like points, 5-25x0.1-1.2mm, barbellate; receptacle convex with many fine linear scales c 8-10mm. Corollas white or yellow, tube 7.5-8.5mm; throat scarcely dilated, 7.5-8.5mm; lobes 5-6.5mm. Achenes oblong-obvoid, c6mm, pale, smoth. Pappus many seriate, capillary, white, to 19mm.

»   Fields and dry hillsides
»   1525-3650m
»   August-November
»   Thimphu, Paro, Punakha, Trongsa, Mongar, Trashigang

195 *Youngia depressa* (Hook. f. & Thomson) Babc. & Stebbins

Perrenial herb without a stem, and leaves forming a basal rosette. Leaves oblong, ovate or orbicular, 1.5-5 x 1-4cm, rounded or weakly heart-shaped at base, margins entire or obscurely toothed, sparsely pubescent at junction with petiole; petiole to 5cm, pubescent. Capitula numerous, clustered on top of leaves, approx 15-flowered; peduncles 3-10mm densely pubescent. Involucre cylindrical, 3-5mm diameter, green or crimson.

»   Grassy slopes
»   3050-4700m
»   August-October
»   Thimphu, Paro, Gasa, Trongsa, Bumthang, Lhuentse, Trashiyangtse

Convallariaceae
Lilly of the valley family

Maianthemum oleraceum (Baker) La Frankie

64 var. *oleraceum*
Eng. Chinese False Solomon's Seal

Rhizome forming herb with stems 21-152cm, sometimes slightly zigzag and hairy above. 8-12 leaves on stem arranged alternately, lanceolate, gradually tapering to point or with with tail-like tip, base rounded, smooth above with tiny hairs on lower surface, petiole very short, less than 7mm. Inflorescence a many branched panicle 4-23cm long. Flowers white, sometimes flushed pink or mauve, outer tepals oblanceolate to elliptic 2.3-4mm wide, inner ones elliptic to broadly elliptic 4.5-7.5 x 3.2-5mm. Ovary round with 3 lobes 1.4-2mm diameter, style 3 lobed, stamens 6. Berry pale mulberry-coloured to 8mm diameter.

» Fir and rhododendron forest (edges and clearings, ravines and streamsides)
» 2130-3700m
» May - August
» Chhukha, Haa, Thimphu, Punakha, Bumthang, Trongsa, Trashigang, Gasa, Lhuentse
» Can be eaten as vegetable

221 var. *acuminatum* (Wang & Tang) Noltie
Flowers deep wine red to blackish; Inflorescence laxer, axis zigzag, pedicels longer.

» Fir forest – at higher altitudes than the type variety.
» 2740-3700m
» Paro, Thimphu, Punakha, Trongsa, Trashiyangtse

M. purpureum is similar but has inflorescence in a cylindric raceme (without branches), flowers dark red, purplish or reddish outside and whitish or pale greenish inside.

Convolvulaceae
Morning glory family

285 *Ipomoea purpurea* (L.) Roth
Eng: Morning Glory

Herbaceous annual twiner. Stems with short appressed hairs and longer stiffer hair. Leaves heartshaped, 2.5-15x2.5-12cm, usually unlobed but sometimes 3-lobed, hairy. Inflorescence of axillary cymes with 1-5 flowers, peduncles 3-18cm. Pedicels 8-15mm. Sepals oblong lanceolate, 8-16mm. Corolla funnel shaped 4-6cm long and to c 8cm across, hairless; tube white or pink; outer corolla white, deep pink, red or purple. Capsule globose, hairless, straw coloured.

- » Cultivated in gardens and a local weed of maize and other crops, roadsides
- » 250-2370m
- » May-October
- » Native of America, now widely cultivaed in tropical and subtropical countries as ornamental, can be very invasive weed

369 *Ipomoea turbinata* Lagasca & Segura
Eng: Purple Moonflower

Extensively climbing, nearly glabrous, herbaceous annular twiner with milky juice. Leaves ovate to orbicular, 7-18 X 6-15cm, acuminate, base cordate, glabrous beneath but with some bristles long the main vein above. Inforescence an axillary 1-few flowered cyme; peduncle muricate, 3-12cm. Pedicel 10-20 mm, much thickened in fruit, broadened near apex. Sepals sub-equal; outer ones oblong to ovate, 6-7mm (excluding awn), attentuate into thick patent to reflexed awn 4-6mm; inner ones 7-8mm, obtuse or emarginate, wtih 4mm awn. Corolla opening at night, pale bluish-purple to white, narrowly infundibular to salverform, 5-7.5cm, glabrous; tubes 3-6cm.

- » Climbing in dense broad-leaved forest
- » 150 -1,220m
- » February – October
- » Samdrupjongkhar, Trashigang

Cornaceae
Dogwood family

30 Benthamidia capitata (Wall.) H. Hara
Dzo: Pheytse Shing
Eng: Himalayan Strawberry Tree, Evergreen Dogwood

Shrub or tree 2-10m. Leaves elliptic-oblong or elliptic, 5-11 x 2.1-4.1cm, acute or acuminate, base cuneate, more or less densely appressed-hairy, hairs medifixed; petiole 0.7-1.1c. Inflorescence 0.8-1.5 cm diameter; bracts obovate to suborbicular, 3.5-6.3x2.3-4.3cm, white to yellow. Calyces adnate in inflorescence. Petals yellowish, almost oblong, c 2mm. Stamens almost equaling petals. Fruiting heads 2-3cm in diameter, pendent, red, succulent.

» Moist broad-leaved forest, pine forest, occassionaly on hillside
» 1830-2900m
» May-July, October
» Chhukha, Samdrupjongkhar, Thimphu, Punakha, Gasa, Trongsa, Bumthang, Mongar, Lhuentse, Trashigang, Trashiyangtse.
» Fruit pulp edible. Attractive horticultural species.

277 Toricellia tiliifolia DC

Tree or shrub, 2.5–5m. Leaves broadly ovate or orbicular, 9–19x8.4–18.5cm, usually acute, base cordate, margin conspicuously serrate-dentate, tomentose on margin and veins especially on upper surface, otherwise usually glabrous; petiole 3.5–13cm. Male and female panicles 12-32cm. Male fowers reddish-green, c 3.5mm long; petals oblong, c 3mm; stamens shorter than petals. Female flowers c 2.5mm; styles c 1mm. Fruit c 6x5mm, glabrous; black when ripe.

» Warm broad-leaved forest
» 1000 – 2150m
» April
» Chhukha, Punakha, Trongsa, Mongar

Coriariaceae
Coriaria family

215 Coriaria napalensis Wall.

Dzo: Limphu Shing, Nimbo

Eng: Tanner's Tree

Shrub 1-2.5 m. Leaves elliptic or ovate, 3.5-10x2-8 cm, acute, base rounded or shallowly cordate, glabrous, 3-5 - veined at base. Flowers in racemes upto 10 cm, borne in clusters from the axils of the fallen leaves; pedicels upto 7mm; bracts oblanceolate, c 3mm. Sepals ovate, c 1mm, rounded. Petals minute at first, later broadly elliptic, 3-5x2 mm, reddish, turning black in fruit. Filaments c 3mm; anthers c 1.5 mm, crimson. Carpels c 0.75mm; styles linear, thickish, c 2 mm. Achenes ovoid, 2-2.5x1.5 mm surrounded by persistent fleshy petals.

» Steep dry shrub covered forest
» 1220-3200m
» April-May
» Chhukha, Haa, Thimphu, Trongsa, Bumthang, Mongar, Trashigang, Trashiyangtse.
» Wood use as firewood

Cruciferae
Mustard family

65 Capsela bursa-pastoris (L.) Medikus.

Dzo: Bura Zey

Eng: Shepherds Purse

Erect herb 10-50cm with simple hairs on stem. Basal leaves in rosette and deeply divided 3-10x0.6-3cm. White flowers arranged on a raceme with flowers maturing from bottom. Petals 2.5x1.25mm. Pods heartshaped with notch at tip, 6-7mm long.

» Weed of roadsides and alpine meadows
» 1980-3960m
» March - July
» Sarpang, Thimphu, Trongsa, Mongar, Trashigang
» Leaves can be eaten

66 *Cardamine flexuosa* With.
Eng: Wavy Bittercress

Slender annual or biennial herbs. Flexuose (zig zag) stems 20-35cm. Basal leaves few, hardly forming rosette; stem leaves leaves compound with leaflets ovate or sometimes 3-4 lobed, terminal leaflet is larger. Flowers few to numerous with small white petals around 3mm long, 6 stamens and pods thin about 2cm long and 1mm thick.

- »   Moist soils, streamsides
- »   500-2500m
- »   January-June
- »   Samtse, Sarpang, Thimphu, Trongsa, Trashigang

394 *Cardamine griffithii* Hook. f. & Thomson

Herb with stems 20-60cm, smooth and angular grooved. Leaves 1.5-9cm with 3-5 pairs of leaflets with lower most pair clasping against stem, margins entire or irregularly sinuate. Racemes with few white or purplish flowers, petals obovate, 8-9x3-3.5mm.

- »   Streamsides
- »   2000-3800m
- »   May-July
- »   Paro to Bumthang, Gasa to Trashiyangtse

395 *Cardamine macrophylla* Willdenow
Eng: Large-Leaved Bittercress

Herb 45-150cm with stems initially covered in fine hair. Leaves 5-25cm with 2-7 lateral leaflets that are coarsely toothed. Few to numerous purplish flowers on pedicels 1-2cm long. Thin pods 3-4.5cm x 0.3cm

- »   Shady and damp areas of forests
- »   2440-4100m
- »   May - July
- »   Haa to Trashigang, Gasa to Trashiyangtse

67 *Lepidium virginnicum* L.
Eng: Virginia Pepperweed

Erect herb 40-60cm, with very short, fine hair on stems. Lower leaves oblanceolate 4-7 x 0.75-1.5cm, margin coarsely toothed, upper leaves thin and long more or less not toothed. Small flowers arranged in branched racemes, white petals barely longer than the sepals. Pods broadly ovate or orbicular, 3-3.5 x 3mm, apex rounded and broadly notched.

» Weed of roadsides and farmland
» 2250-2500
» May-June
» Thimphu, Paro, Punakha, Trashigang

68 *Nasturtium officinale* Brown
Eng: Watercress

A marshland herb with stems 10-30cm, erect or spreading with white roots emerging from lower nodes. Leaves, pinnately compound with lateral leaflets elliptic 3-20 x 2-10mm; terminal leaflet ovate-cordate, 5-20 x 5-15mm. Small white flowers in racemes. Petals 5x2mm. Pods straight, more or less cylindrical with ridges from seeds, 10-12 x 1.75-2mm, somewhat upwardly curved, spreading horizontally.

» Streams, ditches
» 2200m
» April- June
» Thimphu
» Edible as salad plant

....

Cucurbitaceae
Cucumber family

146 *Thladiantha cordifolia* (Blume) cogniaux;
Eng: Himalayan Goldencreeper

Climbing herb. Cordate leaves 8.5-17x6.5-12cm, toothed margins, rough hair on above and softly below, petioles to 7cm. Flowers yellow, bell shaped with spreading lobes. Male flower peduncles 7cm long, oblong bracts, calyx lobes linear-oblong, 10mm, corolla lobes ovate, joined below middle. Female flowers without bracts, ovary ellipsoid and densely hairy. Fruit oblong 2.5-3x1.5-2cm.

» Warm broadleaved forests
» 1500-2300m
» April-September
» Chhukha, Sarpang, Samdrupjongkhar, Punakha, Trongsa, Trashigang

Cuscutaceae
Dodder family

79 *Cuscuta reflexa* Roxb
Eng: Giant Dodder

Twining parasitic herb with little or no chlorophyll. Stems slender reddish or light to dark brown, 0.5-1.5mm thick, branched. Inflorescence a short lax raceme of up to 12 flowers. Calyx lobes 5, much shorter than corolla tube. Corollas creamy white and sweetly scented, 5-7mm; lobes obtuse, erect, finally reflexed. Stamens 5 with anthers slightly exserted from corolla tube, stigmas 2 unequal, thick, divergent or erect. Capsule globose-conical, 1-3 x 23mm, dehiscing irregularly.

» Scrambling on shrubs in scrub and at margins of secondary subtropical and warm broadleaved forests, road sides.
» 600-2700m
» February to October
» Samtse, Thimphu, Punakha, Trongsa, Mongar, Gasa.
» Can be a damaging weed in Citrus plantations.

....

Dipsicaceae
Teasel family

408 *Acanthocalyx nepalensis* (D. Don) M. Cannon

Perennial herb to 50cm. Leaves forming rosettle on sterile shoots. Basal and stem leaves linear to linear-lanceolate, 4-27x0.6-1.7cm; upper stem leaves sometimes narrowly ovate up to 5cm; margins spiny; petiole sheath to 7cm. Bracts ovate-acuminate, spiny on margins, usually hiding calyx. Flowers sessile, capitate, sometimes in 1-2 whorls below head. Calyx 8.5-10.5mm, spiny. Corolla tubular, with 5 spreading lobes (almost equal), 20-22mm, pink to rosy purple with darker ring in throat; tube slightly to strongly curved, widening at throat to 3.5-4.5mm; lobes 2-3mm.

» In damp or marshy areas and dry ground on cliffs, in clearings of juniper/Betula and cleared Picea forest.
» 2434-4572m
» May-August
» Haa, Paro, Thimphu, Bumthang, Gasa, Lhuentse

111 *Dipsacus inermis* Wall.
Eng: Spineless Teasel

Perennial erect herb with stems 32-100cm and covered in stiff short hair often with prickles. Basal and mid stem leaves pinnately divided, 11-21 x 4.5-9cm, margins toothed. Upper leaves simple and lance like with toothed margins, lower leaves deeply lobed almost to the middle. Flowers in round heads, hairy and white or cream. Corolla tubular to obconical, 8-11mm.

» Open hillsides and among shrubs.
» 1219-3658m
» August-September, December
» Haa, Thimphu, Trongsa
» A variable species.

112 *Pterocephalodes hookeri* (Clarke) Mayer & Ehrendorfer

Thick fleshy tap-root. Leaves forming rosette at base, linear-oblong, 4-22 x 1-4.3cm, margin conspicuously lobed, rarely entire, villous on both surfaces, lobes obtuse, flowering stem 14-36cm, leafless, densely hairy. Involucral bracts ovate-acuminate up to 15mm. Bracteoles linear-oblanceolate, +- equaling flowers. Involucel c 2.5mm, densely hairy, apex +- undulate. Calyx disc-like at base with c 20 setate, disc c 0.5mm, setae up to 10mm. Corolla tubular-obconical, 11-14mm, white or cream, tube 8-11mm; lobes obtuse, subequal. Fruit elliptic, c 4.5 x 1.8mm.

» Among shrubs or on open grassy hillsides
» 3048-4877m
» August-October.
» Thimphu, Gasa, Bumthang

....

Elaeagnaceae
Oleaster family

34 *Elaeagnus parvifolia* Wall. ex Royle
Dzo: Bji
Eng: Autumn Olive, Small Leaved Olive

Spiny shrub, 1-5m. Leaves narrowly oblong-elliptic to elliptic, 1.7-6.4x0.9-2cm, lower surface silver-white, densely scaly, upper surface almost without hair. Flowers 1-3 in leaf axils on young shoots. Calyx 12-14mm, constricted above ovary, breaking at constriction as fruit develops, lobes 4 spreading, white to greenish yellow, densely scaly. Petals absent. Fruit ellipsoid, 6.5-8x4.5-6mm.

» Roadsides, stream banks in dry valleys, among scrub or blue pine forest.
» 1100-3200m
» March-June
» Chhukha, Haa, Thimphu, Punakha, Trongsa, Mongar, Trashigang
» Fruits edible, foliage lopped for fodder.

....

Ericaceae
Heath family

212 *Agapetes serpens* (Wight) Sleumer
Eng: Himalyan Lantern, Creeping Agapetes

Pendulous epiphytic shrub, 0.5-1.5m; shoots covered with bristly hairs. Leaves leathery, borne in one plane, ovate-lanceolate, 1-1.5 x 0.5-0.7cm, apex subacute, base rounded, margins recurved, remotely serrulate or subentire, subsessile. Flowers solitary, axillary; pedicles 0.7-1.5cm, glandular-hairy. Sepals lanceolate, 0.8-1cm, glandular-hairy. Corolla tubular, 2-3 x 0.5-1cm, red with darker markings, lobes 3-5mm. Anthers 6-9mm; apical tubes 12-15mm, not spurred. Berries globose, 10-12mm, 5-winged.

» Common on trees and sometimes on rocks in warm broad-leaved, evergreen oak, and *Quercus griffithii/ Rhododendron arboreum* forest
» 1720-2130m
» February-May
» Chhukha, Sarpang, Samdrupjongkhar, Punakha, Trongsa and Trashigang

31 *Cassiope fastigata* (Wall.) D. Don.
Eng: Himalyan Heather

Erect shrub 15-30m. Leaves ovate-oblong, 3-5x1-2mm, with membranous, white, ciliate margins. Pedicels 2-6mm, woolly. Sepals elliptic, tinged red, 2-4mm, margins papery and ciliate. Petals white. Filaments glabrous or long-haired.

Capsule globose 2-4 x 2-3mm.

» Seen on grassy mountain sides, river banks and Juniper/Rhododendron scrub.
» 3650-4750m
» May-September
» Thimphu, Trongsa, Bumthang, Gasa and upper Trashiyangtse.

224 *Enkianthus deflexus* (Griff.) Schneider
Eng: Himalayan Red Bells

Shrub or small tree 3-6m. Leaves ovate-elliptic, 3-5 x 1.5-2.5cm, apex acute to acuminate, base acute, pubescent beneath when young; petioles 5-10mm. Inflorescence 8 - 12 flowers; pedicels slender, 2-4cm. Sepals triangular, 2-3mm. Corolla 8-12 x 6-10mm, greenish, often tinged pink or orange, with red veins. Filaments and anthers hairy; spurs c 1mm. Capsule globose, 5-7 x 4-6mm.

» Seen with evergreen oak, spruce and hemlock forest.
» 2300-3660m
» May-June
» Haa, Thimphu, Punakha, Trongsa, Bumthang, Gasa, Lhuentse.

61 *Gaultheria fragrantissima* Wall.
Dzo: Chamze Kam, Chamze Ngedub
Eng: Wintergreen

Shrub 2-3m; branches glabrous. Leaves ovate-lanceolate, 4-13x2.5-5cm, apex acute, base cuneate, lateral veins 2-4 pairs; petioles 5-9mm. Racemes 10-30 flowered, 3-7cm, pubescent; pedicels 2-5mm; bract at base c 3mm; bracteole c 1mm, remaining near apex of fruiting pedicels. Sepals triangular, acute, c 1.5mm. Corolla barrel-shaped, constricted towards apex, 3-5x2-4mm, white, sometimes greenish-white, lobes minute. Stamens 10; anthers with 4 spurs c 0.5mm. Capsules 5-8x3-5mm, surrounded by enlarged fleshy calyx.

» Road side banks in warm broad-leaved and evergreen oak forest
» 1700-2500m
» March-June
» Samdrupjongkhar, Thimphu, Punakha, Trongsa, Mongar, Trashigang.

367 *Gaultheria trichophylla* Royle.
Eng: Himalayan Snowberry

Prostrate dwarf shrub with creeping leafless stems and short, erect, bristly leafy shoots 3-9cm. Leaves elliptic-oblanceolate, 5-10 x 2-3mm, apex subacute, base cuneate, margins ciliate, cilia c 0.5mm, otherwise glabrous; petioles 1mm. Flowers solitary, axillary; pedicels 2-4mm; bracteoles ovate, 1.5mm. Sepals triangular, 3mm. Corolla broadly campanulate, slightly constricted at apex, 3-5 x 2-4mm, whitish pink, lobes 1mm. Stamens 10; anthers with 2 apical spurs. Capsule 6-9 x 5-8mm, surrounded by enlarged fleshy calyx, deep blue when ripe.

» Seen on cliffs, screes and rocky stream sides.
» 2900-4270m
» May-June
» Thimphu, Trongsa, Mongar, Bumthang, Trashigang, Gasa, Lhuentse

75 *Lyonia ovalifolia* (Wall.) Drude.
Dzo: Zentu Shing
Eng: Oval Leaved Staggerbush

Deciduous or semi-evergreen shrub or tree 2-10m. Leaves ovate, 4-15x1.5-6cm, apex acuminate, base rounded to cordate; petioles 5-15mm. Racemes c 40-flowered, 3-16cm with leaf-like bracts 1.5-4cm at base. Sepals triangular, 1.5-2.5mm. Corolla cylindric, 8-12 x 2.5-5mm, white, sometimes tinged pink towards apex, pubescent. Filaments hairy towards base; anthers with 2 spreading, basal spurs c 0.5mm. Capsule globose 2.5-4.5 x 3.5-6mm; seeds 1mm.

» Margin of and clearings in Oak and Blue pine forest.
» 1500-2600m
» May-August
» Chhukha, Thimphu, Punakha, Trongsa, Mongar, Trashigang, Gasa, Lhuentse, Trashiyangtse

76 Pieris formosa (Wall.) D. Don
Dzo: Khepsi Meto

Evergreen shrub or tree 1-5m. Leaves elliptic or oblanceolate, 5-12x1.5-3cm, leathery, apex acuminate, base cuneate, margins toothed; peioles 3-15mm. Flowers in racemes which are aggregated into panicles 6-15cm long. Sepals triangular, 3-5x1-2mm. Corolla urn-like to cylindric, 5-10x3-7mm, white sometimes tinged pink. Stamens hairy especially towards base. Style slightly impressed into apex of ovary. Capsule ovoid to globose, 3-6x4-7mm; seeds c3mm.

» River banks, scrub, Blue Pine forests.
» 1830-3960m
» February-June
» Chhukha, Thimphu, Punakha, Trongsa, Mongar, Trashigang, Gasa, Lhuentshe, Trashiyangtse
» Poisonous

96 Rhododendron anthopogon D. Don
Dzo: Dali Meto
Eng: Dwarf Rhododendron

Small erect aromatic shrub 15-60cm, much branched; branchlets scaly with short and long-stalked lacerate scales, these later becoming bristles. Leaves ovate, 1-3 x 0.7-1.5cm, rounded, shortly mucronate, base rounded, sparsely scaly above, densely (usually brown) scaly beneath with closely overlapping, lacerate scales; petioles 2-5mm. Flowers 5-10 in dense subcapitate racemes; pedicels short, 2-4mm. Calyx deeply 5-lobed, lobes ovate 3-4mm, scaly and with ciliate margins. Corolla salver-shaped, 5 lobed, white, pink or yellow, tube 6-10mm, lobes 4-7mm, glabrous outside, densely white long-haired in tube. Stamens usually 5-8. Ovary scaly. Capsule 4-5mm, enclosed in calyx.

» Open hillside, rocky slopes and cliff ledges
» 3650-4700m
» May-August
» Haa, Thimphu, Punakha, Trongsa, Bumthang, Trashigang, Gasa, Trashiyangtse

225 Rhododendron arboreum Smith
Dzo: Eto Meto

Shrub 1-2m or tree up to 15m, young shoots with fine hair. Leaves elliptic-oblanceolate, 7-17 x 2 -5cm, lower surface densely matted white, silvery or fawn tomentose, (sometimes obscured by loose red-brown tomentum) or loosely whitish or fawn floccose; petioles 8-15mm. Racemes compact, 10-20-flowered; pedicels 5-10mm, hairy and glandular. Calyx 1-2mm. Corola tubular-campanulate, 3-4.5cm, 5-lobes, bright red, pink or more rarely white, with darker spots and nectar pouches. Stamens 10. Ovary white tomentose. Capsules slightly curved, 1.5-2.5 x 0.7-0.9cm. A very variable species.

» Evergreen Oak, Blue pine, Hemlock and Fir forest
» 3048-4267m
» March-May
» Chhukha, Sarpang, Thimphu, Punakha, Trongsa, Bumthang, Mongar and Trashigang
» Wood is uesful for timber and firewood.

312 Rhododendron arboreum var. roseum Lindley
Dzo: Eto Meto

Leaves lower surface closely matted cream or fawn colour. Corolla tubular-campanulate, 3-4.5cm, 5 lobes, pink or crimson, rarely white with darker spots and nectar pouches. Very similar to subsp. arboreᴜ.n, which has closely matted, white or silvery beneath and flowers red.

» Blue pine, Hemlock and Fir forests
» 1370-3960
» April-May
» Chhukha, Sarpang, Thimphu, Punakha, Trongsa, Bumthang, Mongar, Trashigang

280 Rhododendron camelliiflorum Hook. f.

Shrub 1-2m, often epiphytic; young shoot scaly. Leaves elliptic or oblanceolate, 5-8(-10) X 1.5-3 cm, acute, base rounded or broadly cuneate, subglabrous above, densely brown scaly beneath. Flowers white tinged with pink, deep wine red, open bell shaped, 1.6-2.4 cm, fleshy terminal flowers, 1-2 flowers per raceme. Capsule ovoid-oblong 10-12 mm, scaly, on short thick pedicel.

» Found on trees and cliff ledges in evergreen oak and

Hemlock forest.
» 2540-3400m
» June-July
» Chhukha, Thimphu, Punakha, Trongsa, Bumthang, Mongar and Trashigang, Trashiyangtse

97 *Rhododendron campylocarpum* Hook. f.

Aromatic shrub 2-4m or small tree to 6m; branchlets thinly covered with stalked glands. Leaves ovate-elliptic, 4-9x2.3-5cm, rounded or apiculate, bases shallowly cordate, whitish and without hair below; petioles 1-2cm, with stalked glands. Racemes 5-13 flowers; pedicels 1-4cm, with stalked glands. Calyx a 5-lobed glandular cup 1.5-2mm. Corolla campanulate, 3-3.5cm, 5-lobed, pale yellow, sometimes with a red basal blotch. Stamens 10. Ovary densely covered with stalked glands; style glandular at base, glabrous above. Vapsules 2-3x0.5cm, strongly curved.

» Hemlock and Fir/Rhododendron forests,
» 3050-4200m
» May-July
» Haa, Paro, Thimphu, Punakha, Bumthang, Mongar, Trashigang, Gasa, Lhuentse

199, 226 *Rhododendron cinnabarinum* Hook. f.
Eng: Cinnabar Rhododendron

Shrub or small tree 2-6m. Branchlets densely scaly. Leaves narrowly to broadly elliptic, 6-11x2.5-4cm, rounded or subacute with mucronate point, base rounded, densely scaly beneath, glabrous or scaly above; petioles 1-1.5cm, scaly. Racemes terminal, compact, 2-6 flowered; pedicels 6-13mm, Calyx small, cup-shaped with short rounded lobes upto 1mm, scaly. Corolla fleshy, tubular-companulate or companulate, 2.5-3.5cm, usually orange-yellow, some times reddish or purple. Stamens 10; filaments hairy towards base. Ovary scaly. Fruits cylindric, 8-12mm.

Subsp. *cinnabarinum*, leaves, glabrous above except when young, corolla 3-3.5cm with narrow tube

» Fir/Rhododendron, Hemlock and Blue Pine forests,
» 2750-3200m
» April-July
» Haa, Thimphu, Punakha, Trongsa, Mongar Trashigang
» leaves reported to be poisonous

Subsp. *xanthocodon,* distinctly persistantly scaly above, corolla more broadly campanulate 2.5-3cm. Red flowered plants are subsp. *xanthocodon* var. *breviforme.*

» Fir and Hemlock forests and in Juniper/Rhododendron scrub,
» 2900-4100m.
» May-July
» Haa, Thimphu, Punakha, Trongsa, Mongar Trashigang
» Leaves reported to be poisonous.

98 Rhododendron dalhousiae var. *rhabdotum* (Balfour f. & Cooper) Cullen

Shrub 1-4m with young shoots scaly and sparsely bristly. Leaves elliptic to obovate 10-17x2.5-7cm with rounded apex or with pointed tip, densely reddish scaly beneath. Racemes of 2-3 flowers with pubescent pedicles, corolla funnel-campanulate with 5 lobes, 9-11cm white or creamy, with or without a red line from base to apex on each lobe. 10 stamens which are pubescent on lower part.

» Growing on trees and rocks in warm and cool broad-leaved forests.
» 1500-2300
» April - July
» Chhukha, Punakha, Trongsa, Trashigang

var. *dalhousiae* has corolla 7.5-9cm and creamy wihout red lines.

99 Rhododendron falconeri Hook. f.
Dzo: Khangley Meto

Large shrub or tree 5-15m; bark smooth, branchlets thinly brown tomentose. Leaves broadly elliptic-obovate, 15-35 x 7-17cm, dark green and rugose above, thickly brown tomentose beneath (rough to touch) with long-fimbriate hairs, obscuring lower fine white tomentum; lateral veins 12-17 pairs, weakly prominent and thinly tomentose; petioles stout, 3-4.5cm, +- tomentose with white and brown indementum. Racemes dense, subglobose, 12-16cm diameter, 15-20 flowered; pedicels 3-5.5cm, glandular. Calyx a minute cup 1-2mm. Corolla fleshy, obliquely campanulate, 4-5cm, 8-10-lobed, white, creamy or yellow with purple blotch at base, rarely tinged pinkish; nectar-pouches absent. Stamens 12-16. Ovary densely glandular and thinly to thickly tomentose. Capsules straight, c 3.5 x 1.2cm.

» Cool broad-leaved, Hemlock/Rhododendron forest
» 2500-3200m
» April-May
» Thimphu, Punakha, Trongsa, Mongar, Trashigang

100 *Rhododendron griffithianum* Wight

Shrub or tree 2-10m, bark grey, papery, shoots smooth. Leaves oblong-eliptic, 9-20x3-7cm, tip bluntly acute or with small pointed tip, base rounded, smooth beneath. Racemes 3-5 fragrant flowers. Corolla funnel shaped, 6-8cm long with 5 lobes, pure white or tinged pink. Stamens 13-16, filaments smooth. Ovary and style with glands. Capsules stout 2.5-3.5 x 1.2-1.7

» River Banks, ravines and cliffs in cool broadleaved and evergreen oak forests.
» 1800-2590m
» April-May
» Chhukha, Haa, Thimphu, Punakha, Trongsa, Mongar, Gasa, Trashiyangtse

227 *Rhododendron hodgsonii* Hook. f.

A large shrub or tree 5-15m with smooth peeling bark. Leaves broadly elliptic ovate, 15-35x7-11cm, rounded tip with small blunt point and rounded base, dark green and white to pale brown with fine frilly cup-shaped hairs below, 12-15 pairs of lateral veins (not prominent). Racemes dense and globe like 12-16 cm diameter with 15-20 flowers. Corolla pinkish-red to purple with 7-8 lobes. Capsules narrow, curved

» Firs/Rhododenron and Hemlock forests
» 2900- 3690m
» April -May
» Haa, Thimphu, Trongsa, Bumthang, Trashigang, Gasa, Trashiyangtse
» Can be mistaken for *R. kesangiae* which has rounded buds scales, very prominent lateral veins, white or silvery surface without cup-shaped hairs, pink flowers and nectar pouches.

313 Rhododendron kesangiae D.G.Long & Rushforth

Dzo: Tala

Tree 8-15m, bark rough, young shoots often closely white floccoses, leaves broadly elliptic to almost obovatge, 20-30x10-16cm, apex rounded, with small pointy tip, base rounded or wedge-shaped, silvery white beneath with hair, very prominent lateral veins, 12-15 pairs. Racemes dense 15-25 flowered; calyx a minute rim 1-2mm. Corolla campanulate 3-4.7cm, pink. Stamens usually 16. Ovary densely glandular, sometimes also thinly tomentose. Capsules 3.5-4x0.9-1cm curved.

» Amongst Rhododendrons and bamboos in Fir and Hemlock forests.
» 2890-3450m
» April-May
» Chhukha, Thimphu, Punakha, Trongsa, Bumthang, Mongar, Lhuentse, Trashiyangtse.
» Endemic to Bhutan. Can be confused with *R. hodgsonii*. *R. kesangiae* has very prominent lateral veins, white or silvery surface below without cup-shaped hairs, pink flowers and presence of nectar pouches.

228 Rhododendron keysii Nuttall

Shrub 1.5-6m; shoots densely scaly. Leaves elliptic, 6-9 x 2-3cm, acute, subacute or rounded and finely mucronate, base rounded or cuneate, densely scaly beneath, sparsely scaly above; petioles 7-11mm. Racemes axillary, often several close together, each 2-5-flowered, flowers pendulous; pedicels slender, 5-8mm, scaly. Calyx minute, with short spreading lobes 0.5mm. Corolla tubular, 1.5-2.5cm, orange-red or crimson, becoming paler towards 5 short, weakly spreading, yellowish or greenish lobes. Stamens 10; filaments pubescent in lower half. Capsules cylindric, 1cm.

» Spruce, Hemlock and Fir forest, and in Juniper/ Rhododendron scrub
» 2600-3500m
» May-September
» Thimphu, Punakha, Trongsa, Bumthang, Mongar, Trashigang

101 *Rhododendron lanatum* Hook. f.

Shrub 1.5-4m. Leaves coriaceous, obovate, 6-10 x 2-5cm, obtuse with short mucro, base cuneate to rounded, glabrous above except for pale tomentum on midrib, thickly chocolate-brown or pale brown tomentose beneath; petioles stout, 0.8-1.5cm, densely whitish tomentose. Racemes short, 4-8-flowered; pedicels 1-2cm, tomentose. Calyx minute. Corolla campanulate, 5-lobed, 3-4.5cm, yellow, often red-spotted within. Stamens 10; filaments pubescent at base. Ovary red-brown tomentose. Capsules slightly curved, c 2.5 x 0.8cm.

» Fir/Rhododendron forest
» 3500-4260m
» May-June
» Haa, Thimphu, Punakha, Trongsa, Gasa, Trashiyangtse

144, 281 *Rhododendron lepidotum Wall*. ex G. Don
Med: Dali Meto
Eng: Pink Scaly Rhododendron

Aromatic subshrub 15-60cm with scaly brachlets and leaves. Leaves obovate to elliptic 5-15mm long with scales on both surfaces and petioles missing or only 1mm. 1-2 terminal flowers on slender scaly pedicels up to 2.5cm. Corolla campanulate (bell shaped) red pink, purple, white or yellow and often spotted. 10 stamens.

» Open mountainsides, moraines, riverbanks, juniper/ rhododendron scrub, and openings in fir forests
» 2400-4570m
» May-July.
» Common
» var. *album* has white flowered plants.

This is the most common dwarf rhododendron and differs from;

» *R. nivale* which has very short pedicels up to 1mm.
» *R. fragariiflorum* has 2-3 flowered racemes with pedicels 7-10mm and larger funnel shaped corollas.
» *R. pumilum* has leaves without scales above and funnel shaped corollas eternally long-haired.

314 *Rhododendron maddenii* Hook. f.

Shrub 1-4m with scaly branchlets. Leaves elliptic, oblanceolate or obovate 7-14x2.5-6cm with acute tip and base wedge-shaped, scaly and red brown beneath and smooth above, petioles 5-15mm. Racemes umbel-like with 2-5 fragrant flowers. Calyx cup-shaped, divided nearly to base to 5 rounded and fringed lobes. Corolla funnel-bell shaped, 5 lobes, white, pinkish-white or pink throughout, and with yellow blotch at base of tube 6-8cm long, tube scaly outside. Stamens 17-25.

»   On rocks and cliffs in evergreen oak forests and in Rhododendron arboreum scrub
»   1800 - 3000m
»   May- July
»   Chhukha, Gasa, Bumthang, Wangduephodrang, Trongsa, Trashigang

403 *Rhododendron setosum* D. Don

Compact and strongly aromatic subshrub 10-60cm; young shoots densely scaly and spreading-bristly. Leaves oblong-obovate, 9-13x3-6mm, rounded, truncate or shallowly retuse, base rounded, conspicuously scaly with yellowish scales above and red-brown scales beneath, apex, margins and base of midrib beneath bristly; petioles c1mm. Racemes dense, 2-5flowered; pedicels 3-8mm, scaly and pubescent. Calyx deeply 5 lobed, lobes ovate-elliptic, 4-7mm, pale to deep purple, deeply 5-lobed, glabrous outside. Stamens 10, sticking out of corolla, pubescent towards base. Ovary pubescent and scaly. Capsules oblong-ovoid, c5mm.

»   Open mountain slopes and valleys.
»   2770-4800m
»   June-August
»   Haa, Paro, Punakha, Trongsa, Bumthang, Gasa

229 *Rhododendron thomsonii* Hook. f.
Dzo: Khempa Meto

Shrub 1.5-5m. Leaves, broadly elliptic or suborbicular, round apex with minute apiculate at tip, base round or hear-shaped, 4-8-10x3.5-6cm, smooth below with maybe few glands. Raceme of 3-8 flowers. Calyx cup-shaped with shallow lobes. Corolla tubular campanulate 3.5-5cm, 5 lobed, deep crimson, ovary without hair. Capsule, curved.

- » Fir forests and open hillsides with secondary bamboo.
- » 3050-4000m
- » April-July
- » Haa, Thimphu, Trongsa, Bumthang, Trashigang, Gasa
- » A very variable species.

102 *Rhododendron triflorum* Hook. f.

Evergreen or semi-deciduous shrub 1-5m. Branchlets minutely scaly. Leaves ovate to lanceolate 3.5-6.5cm x 1.5-3cm with pointed tips and rounded base, green and smooth above, pale green or whitish below with minute scales. Racemes of 2-3 flowers; pedicels 7-12mm and scaly. Corolla strongly zygomorphic, open and funnel shaped, 2-3cm, pale yellow, and somtimes reddish brownish blotched within. Stamens 10.

- » Coniferous forests
- » 2300-3600m
- » April- June
- » Haa, Paro, Thimphu, Punakha, Gasa, Bumthang, Mongar, Trashiyangtse

282 *Rhododendron virgatum* Hook. f.

Shrub 0.4-1.3m; young shoots scaly. Leaves oblong or oblong-elliptic, 2.5-7.5x1-2cm, acute or mucronate, base wedge-shaped, without hair above except for few scales on midrib, red brown scaly beneath; petioles 3-6mm, Flowers 1-2 in upper leaf axils; pedicels 3-6mm. Calyx of 5 rounded lobes 1.5-2mm, sparsely scaly and ciliate. Corolla funnel-shaped, usually pale pink, 2.0-3.5cm, sparsely pubescent and scaly outside. Stamens 10; filaments pubescent towards base. Ovary densely scaly; style pubescent and with few scales near base. Capsules c1cm, scaly.

- » Blue pine and evergreen oa forest, usually around wet places.
- » 1900-3000m
- » April-May
- » Haa, Paro, Thimphu, Punakha, Trongsa, Bumthang, Gasa

404 *Rhododendron wallichii* Hook. f.

A shrub to small tree1.5m-4m or small tree to 6m tall. Leaves leathery but thin, elliptic, 7-11x 3-5cm, slightly pointed tip, and base rounded or slighly heart-shaped, smooth above, but lower surface, sparsely dirty brown hair (rough to touch) becoming smoother when older. Racemes of 5-10 flowers, corolla lilac or pink mauvish 3-4cm, with five lobes. 10 stamens. Capsules weakly curved.

» Fir and Rhododendron forests, and in Juniper/ Rhododendron scrub
» 2750-4260m
» April-May
» Haa, Thimphu, Punakha, Trongsa, Bumthang, Trashigang, Gasa.
» Similar to *R. campanulatum* which has lower surface of leaves covered in more dense brown hair that is smooth to touch. Corolla white or pink with reddish spots.

299 *Vaccinium retusum* (Griff.) Hook. f. ex C.B. Clarke

Epiphytic shrub 1-2m; young shoots pubescent. Leaves obovate, 15-25x7-10mm, tip rounded and notched, margins recurved, entire, without hair; petioles 1-3mm. Racemes 10-20 flowered, 2-5cm, pubescent; pedicels 2-5mm; bracts elliptic, 6-10mm deciduous; bracteoles 3-5mm. Sepals triangular, 0.5mm. Corolla barrel-shaped, constricted towards apex, 3-5x3-4mm, white sometimes pink; lobes deep pink, minute. Tubular anther tips c1mm; dorsal spurs c 0.5mm; filaments hairy. Fruits c 3x4mm.

» Wet broad-leaved and coniferous forests.
» 2130-3050m
» April-June
» Trongsa, Mongar, Gasa

300 *Vaccinium nummularia* Hook. f. & Thomson ex C.B. Clarke

Similar to *V. retusum* but smaller, 0.5-1m; young shoots rough with bristly hairs; leaves elliptic often broadly so, 5-15x5-10mm, base rounded, margins sparsely ciliate, subsessile; racemes 8-15 flowers, condensed; pedicels 4-7mm; corolla 3-7x2-4mm; tubular anther tips 1-1.5mm.

- » On wet rocks and trees in evergreen oak and Hemlock/ Rhododendron forests.
- » 2,400 - 4,000 m
- » April-June
- » Thimphu, Punakha, Trongsa, Mongar, Gasa

....

Euphorbiaceae
Spurge family

230 Euphorbia griffithii Hook. f.
Med: Durjit

Perennial herb with erect annual stems 40-80cm with simple or few branches in upper parts, upper leaves and inflorescence reddish especially when dry. Leaves simple and narrow, arranged alternately on stems with uppermost in a whorl each subtending an umbel ray. Rays 2-4.5cm, smooth and each with a whorl of 3-4 orange or red bract, enclosing a cyathium.

- » Clearings among scrub in blue pine, oak and conifer/ rhododendron forests.
- » 2300-3500m
- » May- August
- » Chukha, Haa, Paro, Thimphu, Trongsa, Bumthang
- » The common variety *griffithii* has smooth hairless leaves; var. *bhutanica* has leaves softly hairy beneath.

231 Euphorbia pulcherrima Willd. ex Klotzsch
Eng: Poinsettia

Shrub 2-3m with stout branches. Leaves alternate; lower leave, green, ovate 13-20x7-13cm; upper leaves bright red, elliptic, 5-12x2-4cm; Flowers in solitary cyathia. Cyathia green, with yellow ring-like gland on one side.

- » Cultivated in gardens and roadsides.
- » 230-1500m
- » April-May
- » Chhukha, Wangduephodrang, Punakha
- » Native of tropical America, cultivated as ornamental.

238 Mallotus philippensis (Lamarck) Mueller
Dzo: Theshom

Small evergreen tree 5-19 m. Leaves coriaceous, ovate, acuminate, base rounded or cuneate, strongly three veined at base, minutely tomentose below, mixed with numerous minute red glands.

» Sub-tropical and warm broad-leaved forest among dry scrubs in hot dry valleys
» 300-1600 m
» October-December
» Samtse, Chhukha, Punakha, Trongsa, Trashigang,
» Red gland from capsule used to prepare a red dye.

269 Ricinus communis L.
Med: Denrog
Eng: Castor Oil Plant.

Glabrous evergreen shrub to 2m or tree to 5m. Leaves orbicular in outline, 10-30cm long, palmately deeply 5-10-lobed, coarsely toothed margins; petioles 7-15cm. Flowers in terminal panicles with females upper most. Male flowers clustered, c 1cm diameter, sepals 3-6, petals absent, stamens many, filaments united in bunches. Female flowers with 2 sepals, 3 styles spreading, covered in small bumps. ovary globose, densely prickly. Capsules 3 lobed, softly prickly, 3-seeded.

» Waste grounds in towns and villages.
» 200-3000m
» January-March
» Chhukha, Thimphu, Punakha, Trongsa
» Often cultivated for seed oil used in lamps and sometimes medicinally as castor-oil. Seeds poisonous. Probably native to tropical Africa.

273 Sapium insigne (Royle) Hook. f.
Dzo: Sho Shi

Robust glabrous deciduous tree 7–12m, branches stout, with large leaf scars. Leaves ovate elliptic 10–25x6–11cm, acuminate, base cuneate, margins serrulate, minor veins reticulate beneath; petiole 4–8cm; stipules lanceolate, 1.5mm, fimbriate. Dioecious; flowers spikes terminal, erect, rigid, males 15–20cm, deciduous, females stouter, 7–15cm. Male flowers minute, green, sessile in clusters of

10 in axil of bract, calyx 2-lobed, stamens 2. Female flowers solitary, subsessile, calyx 2-lipped, ovary ovoid, styles short, recurved. Fruit subglobose, glossy, dark crimson, fleshy c 8mm diameter, dehiscing to leave bristle-like vascular strands between the 2 ovoid seeds 5 – 6mm.

» Among scrubs in dry valley
» 460 – 1400m
» January – April
» Sarpang, Punakha, Trongsa

....

Fumariaceae
Fumitory family

347 Corydalis ecristata (Prain) D.G. Long

Slender herb with 1-3 simple stems 10-15cm. Basal leaves few, soon withering, twice divided into threes, 2-3cm diameter, on slender petioles 3-6cm. Leaflets obovate, entire or bluntly toothed. Stem leaf solitary, bract like, 0.5-1.5cm, deeply divided into linear segments. Flowers 2-4 in terminal umbel subtended by deeply toothed bracts. Pedicels slender 1-2cm. Petals blue, upper 13-22mm, including spur 6-16x2.6-3mm, deflexed at tip; upper lip hooded and subacute, not or very narrowly crested; lower lip long and sticking out 4-8mm beyond upper, spathulate, 8-13x6-11mm, limb flat, suborbicular, obtuse or shallowly 3-lobed. Capsules ellipsoid, c 7x2mm.

var. *ecristata*; Upper petal 13-18mm, including short spur 6-10mm, weakly deflexed at tip.

» Alpine pasture, screes, cliff ledges and in Juniper/ Rhododendron scrub.
» 3650-4880
» June-September
» Punakha, Trongsa, Gasa, Lhuentse

var. *longicalcarata*; Upper petal 18-22mm, including long spur 11-16mm, strongly deflexed at tip.

» Alpine screes, turf slopes, Juniper/Rhodo. scrub.
» 3200-4500m
» May-July
» Haa, Paro, Thimphu

C. cashmeriana looks similar to *C. ecristata* but it has has more stems, umbels denser with 4-6 flowers, upper lip on flower has crest c0.5mm broad, lower lip rhombic shape, and only extends out 1-3mm beyond upper lip.

168 Corydalis juncea Wall.
Eng: Himalayan Corydalis

Slender simple-stemmed herb 8-30cm, borne on a dense cluster of elongate tubers. Basal leaf usually solitary, biternate or trifoliate, on long petiole 8-20cm; leaflets variable, sometimes simple, elliptic, more often deeply palmatisect, up to 3.5cm across, with linear to obovate segments, petiolules 1-3cm. Stem leaf usually solitary, linear, 0.5-1.5cm, entire. Racemes 5-20-flowered. Bracts linear. Bracts linear, entire, up to 2cm. Pedicels equaling or exceeding bracts. Upper petal 9-10(-12)mm, including short, broad spur c 3.5 x 2mm, keel broadly crested. Lower lip deflexed, crested.

» Alpine turf and scree slopes
» 3600-4600m
» June-September
» Thimphu, Trongsa, Bumthang, Paro

396 Corydalis leptocarpa Hook. f. & Thomson

Diffuse herb 15-40cm, with several stems arising from a cluster of slender fibrous roots. Basal leaves biternate (twice divided into triplets), 5-8 x3-5cm, petioles 5-9cm, terminal and lateral segments, ovate elliptic, up to 2x1cm, rounded teeth, pale beneath. Racemes 2-6cm, 5-8 flowers. Petals purple or mauve, sometimes whitish, outer pair crested, upper 26-30mm, including spur 13-15 x 3-3.5mm with tip deflexed. Capsules linear, 20-30 x 1.5-2mm.

» Damp streamsides and shady ravines in warm and cool broadleaved forests.
» 1000-2500m
» March-June
» Chhukha, Samdrupjongkhar, Haa, Thimphu, Punakha, Gasa, Trongsa, Mongar, Trashigang.

169 Corydalis polygalina Hook. f. & Thomson

Herb with slender stem 8-30cm, sometimes with short axillary shoots. Basal leaves pinnatisect or ternatisect. Stem leaves are similar but shorter petiole or sessile. Yellow flower with spur half the length of entire flower. Flower in racemes of 5- 20 flowers.

» Alpine screes and gravel, along valley bottom
» 3650-4880m
» June - September
» Thimphu, Gasa, Trongsa, Lhuentse
» A variable species, especially its leaves.

170 Corydalis thyrsiflora Prain.
Eng: Broad Spur Corydalis

Flowers yellow, borne in a widely branched Inflorescence with few or many dense terminal clusters carried above the leaves. Distingiushed by its short broad capsule 5-7mm with a curved style as long. Flowers 12-15mm; spur broad, blunt, about half as long as the flower, straight or slightly down-curved. Leaves hairless, somewhat glaucous, three times cut into oblong to linear usually pointed segments 5-10mm long; stems branched, 15-30cm.

» Among scree
» 3000-4300m
» July-August
» Thimphu, Gasa, Trashiyangtse

....

Gentianaceae
Gentian family

327 Crawfurdia speciosa Wall
Eng: Showy Gentian Vine

Leaves membranous, glabrous, elliptic to ovate, 3-11 x 0.8-6cm, base attenuate or rounded, almost cordate, margins minutely denculate, glandular; petioles 0.5-1.2cm, glandular. Pedicels 0.5-14.5cm. Calyx tube truncate, 10-15mm, lobes lanceolate, 1-4 x 0.5-2mm, acute, reflexed, attached below rim of tube. Corolla blue or mauve, tube campanulate, 15-40mm; lobes triangular, 4-6 x 2-6mm, acuminate. Stamens 13-17mm, attached at middle of corolla tube. Ovary ellipsoid

20-23mm; style 7-10mm; stigma 1.5-3mm. Fruit ellipsoid, 25-30 x 6-10mm; stipe elongating to 20-30mm.

- » Climbing over shrubs by path and over bamboo in forest clearings
- » 2130-3810m
- » April-August
- » Punakha, Trongsa, Bumthang, Trashigang, Trashiyangtse, Gasa

330 *Gentiana algida* Pallas
Eng: Arctic Gentian

Erect perennial to 15cm. Stems to 15cm tall. Leaves linear, basal leaves 15-100 x 1-8mm, forming a long papery sheath 3cm; stem leaves 15-35x2.5-5mm, apex rounded, margin finely glandular-serrate. Flowers terminal and axillary, solitary or in 3-4 flowered cymes. Calyx tube 9-15mm; lobes unequal (1 short, 4 long), linear-lanceolate, 3-8x1-3mm. Corolla campanulate, creamy white, striped and spotted dull green or slaty blue; tube 3-4.5cm; lobes ovate. Filaments attached less than halfway up corolla tube, winged. Capsule ellipsoid, 12-20x4-5mm, protruding from corolla; stipe elongating to 30mm.

- » On scree and damp grassy slopes
- » 4260-5030m
- » August-October
- » Lhuentse

360 *Gentiana capitata* D. Don

Small erect annual herb 3-17cm with single stem and leaves clustered under flower head. Leaves ovate 6-30x3-15mm with short sharp tip. Flowers in capitate heads and sometimes in axillary branches. Corolla pale blue or sky blue and calyx margins transluscent.

- » Open hillsides, roadsides and rivesides.
- » 1370-3660m
- » February – June, occasionally October
- » Samdrupjongkhar, Thimphu, Punakha, Trongsa, Mongar, Gasa

331 *Gentiana depressa* D. Don

Mat forming perennial low lying herb with stems up to 4cm. Leaves in dense squarish rosettes, 9-24x4-12mm, mid vein prominent. Flowers solitary at end of each stem. Calyx tube 8-13mm, lobes unequal. Corolla bright blue or violet inside, lower half greenish-white, spotted purple, outside dull purple; tube urn shaped, 22-29mm, lobed broadly ovate or oblong, 2-3x3-4mm, acute or rounded, margins toothed.

» On cliffs, gravelly hill slopes, open area.
» 3350-3660m
» August-October
» Paro, Thimphu

361 *Gentiana elwesii* Clarke

Erect perennial to 35cm. Stems unbranched, ridged, glandular. Basal leaves ovate to lanceolate, 12-35x2-10mm; stem leaves elliptic or oblong, 16-20x5-12mm, margins glandular, mid-vein prominent. Flowers in cymes of umbels or solitary flowers. Corolla tube white at base, sometimes flecked blue, deep blue above, 22-24mm; lobes triangular 12x2-3mm. Filaments 11-15mm, widening at base, winged, attached less than half way up corolla tube; anthers 1.5-2mm. Capsule ellipsoid, 13-15x4-5mm.

» In grassy meadows among dwarf rhododendrons.
» 3660-5100m
» July-September
» Haa, Thimphu, Trongsa, Bumthang, Gasa, Lhuentse, Trashiyangtse

28 *Gentiana robusta* Hook.f

Perennial herb with stems 10-30cm. Basal leaves 5-50x1-3.5cm; stem leaves 2.5-7.5x0.5-1.3cm. Flowers in terminal clusters, many flowered; calyx tube 1-1.5cm; lobes unequal, very small, narrowly triangular, 2 longer than others; corolla creamy white with dark stripe at base, sometimes with green markings; tube 15-25mm; lobes ovate, 2-3x2.5-3mm, obtuse; filaments attached near middle of corolla tube, 7-9mm; anthers 2-2.5mm.

» Alpine meadows
» 4570-5200m
» August-September

332 *Gentiana urnulla* H. Smith

Rosette- or mat-forming perennial to 4cm tall. Stems prostrate, elongated, covered with small leaves, ending in square shaped rosette of larger, slightly fleshy leaves. Stem leaves obovate, 4-9x5-8mm; upper leaves closely overlapping, broadly obovate, 13-18x13-18mm. Flowers in terminal clusters. Calyx tube white, papery, 11-13mm. Corolla papery, white or blue-violet with dark stripes and spots on upper part; tube widely cylindrical, 15-30mm; lobes ovate, mucronate. Filaments attached less than halfway up corolla tube, 4-10mm, winged, widening at base; anthers 3-4mm. Capsule ellipsoid. 18-23 x 7-9mm, protruding from corolla on long stipe 10-40mm.

» On scree slopes
» 4570-4880m
» July-October
» Haa, Gasa

333 *Gentiana veitchiorum* Hemsley

Trailing procumbent perennial herb. Flowering stems up to 8cm long. Young shoots forming central rosette of linear leaves, often longer than stem leaves, 12-20x1-2mm; stem leaves elliptic to linear lanceolate, 6-20x1-2mm. Flowers terminal, solitary. Calyx tube 11-14mm, membrane truncate; lobes linear lanceolate, 8-11x1mm. Corolla deep blue, streaked yellow-green tube 30-50mm, very narrowly funnel-shaped; lobes ovate, 4-6x3-4mm, acute with pointed tip, 1-2x5-6mm.

» Open alpine grasslands.
» 3350-5030m
» August - October
» Paro, Thimphu
» Differs from *G. ornata* which has wider funnel shape corolla which suddenly constricts above the calyx. Lobules between corolla flowers are almost as large as lobes.

359 *Halenia ellliptica* D. Don
Med. Chaktig

Erect herb up to ·90cm. Leaves elliptic or ovate, 0.7-5.5 x 0.4-1.5cm, membraneous, upper mostly sessile, lower with short petiole, 0.5-1cm. Flowers in axillary cymes, forming loose terminal panicle; corolla, mauve, blue to blue, campanulate with spurs at base of petals, 2.5-8mm Capsule ovoid-ellipsoid, 7-9 x 3-5mm, enclosed by persistent calyx and corolla.

» Open hillsides, sandy peat, coarse turf, forest clearings, below cliffs and on marshy ground at roadside.
» 1829-4877m
» May - September
» Haa, Thimphu, Punakha, Wangduephodrang, Trongsa, Bumthang, Trashigang, Gasa, Trashiyangtse

335 *Lomatogonium brachyantherum* (C.B. Clarke) Fernald

Small decumbent or acending annual herb. Stems up to 14cm. Basal leaves ovate elliptic 6-15x15.3mm, stem leaves elliptic 4-7x1-2mm. Flowers solitary, terminal on long pedicel 10-60mm. Calyx 5 lobes, elliptic or lanceolate, unequal, 4-6 x2.5-4mm, fimbriate double glands or flaps at base sometimes very prominent.

» Among small shrubs on dry hillsides, alpine grasslands.
» 3800-4300m
» August - September
» Paro, Thimphu, Trongsa

267 *Megacodon stylophorus* (Clarke) H. Smith

Perennial herb to 2cm tall. Leaves broadly elliptic or ovate, 10-26 x 4-13.5cm, acute; petioles on lower leaves 1-3cm. Calyx tube 0.6-1.6cm; lobes lanceolate, 1.2-2.5 x 0.6-1.5cm. Corolla tube 1.5-3cm; lobes ovate, 2.5-5 x 1.5-3cm. Filaments 1-1.5cm, attached halfway up corolla tube; anthers oblong, 1-1.2 x 0.2-0.3cm. Ovary 1-1.5 x 0.2-0.5cm; style 0.8-1.5cm; stigma 2-3 x 1.5-2mm. Fruit 4 x 1cm, splitting in half when mature.

» Grassy areas, meadows in *Fir* and *Rhododendron* forest.
» 3048-4267m
» June-August
» Thimphu, Bumthang, Mongar, Trashigang, Trashiyangtse

29 *Swertia bimaculata* (Siebold & Zuccarini) Clarke
Eng: Double Spotted Swertia

Annual or biennial herb to 70cm. Stems rounded or square. Leaves broadly elliptic or ovate, 2.5-12x1-4.5cm, pointed tip and narrowing towards base to a broad petiole. Flowers branching to flat topped cluster. Calyx tube 1-1.5mm with unequal lobes. Corolla tube 1-1.5mm, lobes 5 divided almost to base, white or greenish yellow, spotted dark purple or black, with two greenish glands per lobe. Capsule ellipsoid 10-15 x 4-6mm

- »   Warm to cool broadleaved forests, on road sides
- »   1520-3660m
- »   February - October
- »   Chhukha, Trongsa, Punakha, Trashigang, Gasa

....

Geraniaceae
Geranium family

278 *Geranium donianum* Sweet

Erect, stout herb, usually muched branched, 10-30cm tall. Basal leaves suborbicular, 2.5-4.5cm across, lobes deeply incised into long linear segments with acuteish tips; petioles 4-18cm; stipules linear lanceolate, acute, 4-8mm. Peduncles 3-8.5cm, 2-3 flowered. Pedicels 1-6.5cm. Sepals 8-10mm with pointed tip 0.5mm. Corolla deep pink-purple, 2.8-3.6cm across, not reflexed. Fruit including beak 2cm.

- »   Fir and juniper forests.
- »   2400-4100 m
- »   June - October
- »   Haa, Paro, Thimphu, Trongsa, Gasa, Bumthang, Trashiyangtse
- »   Similar to *G. nakaoanum* which differs in its smaller size and 1-flowered peduncles.

279 *Geranium nakaoanum* Hara

Erect or decumbent slender little branched herb, 6-20cm. Leaves mostly basal, suborbicular, 1.5-3.0cm across, divided into 7-9 obovate lobes, the apex of the lobes deeply 3-toothed, sparsely pubescent; petioles 2-17cm, subglabrous or with short bristle-like hairs; upper leaves usually on shorter petioles; stipules oblong-lanceolate, 3-4mm, free. Peduncles

4-15cm, each bearing one flower. Pedicels slender 1.5-6.5cm. Sepals 5-7mm, with mucro 0.5mm. Corolla bright pink-mauve, 2.5-3.5cm across.

» Grassy mountain slopes.
» (2500-)3350-4200
» May-July
» Thimphu, Bumthang,
» Can be confused with *G. donianum,* which has larger leaves and 2-flowers/peduncle, corolla 3-3.6cm across.

35 *Geranium nepalense* Sweet
Eng: Nepal Geranium

Sprawling to decumbent herb, little to much branched, 9-40cm tall. Basal leaves heart-shaped, 1.5-4.5cm across, deeply divided into 3-5 ovate to rhombic lobes, unequally toothed, pubescent; petioles 5-8cm, very pubescent, upper leaves on shorter petioles. Peduncles 2-6cm, 2 flowered. Pedicels wihtout gland 8-18mm. Sepals 4-5mm. Corolla white with dark veins at base, or bright rose with darker veins, 13-15mm across. Fruit including beak 13-18mm.

» Warm and cool broadleaved and blue pine forests.
» 1400-3000m
» February-July
» Chhukha, Sarpang, Samdrupjongkhar, Haa, Thimphu, Trongsa, Bumthang, Mongar, Trashigang, Trashiyangtse.

323 *Geranium polyanthes* Edgeworth & Hook. f.
Med. Bonga Karpo

Erect or low lying herb with little branches, 17-35cm. Basal leaves roundish, 3.5-7.5cm across, divided into 5-7 oblong or obovate lobes, each lobe with teeth, sparsely hairy, petioles 10-15cm with glandular hair. Upper leaves on shorter petioles, stipules ovate 5-8mm. Peduncles 3-10cm each with a loose to dense umbel of 3-10 flowers, subtended by sessile leaf-like bracts. Pedicels, slender 3-15mm. Corolla pinkish purple 1.5-2cm across with 5 petals. 10 stamens with white or pink filaments. Fruit 5 lobed capsule 2-2.5 cm.

» Damp ground in fir and juniper forests.
» 2900-3600m
» June-September
» Thimphu, Punakha, Trongsa, Bumthang, Mongar, Gasa

Gesneriaceae
African violet family

205 Aeschynanthus sikkimensis (C.B. Clarke) Stapf
Eng: Sikkim Blushwort

Shrub 1m, stem spreading, laxly branched. Leaves opposite fleshy, elliptic, faintly penninerved, 7-11.5x1.3-4.5 cm, long-acuminate, base cuneate, margins entire; petiole 6-12 mm. Flowers several, clustered at tip of stem later overtopped by new growth. Bracts linear-lanceolate, 2-5x0.8-1.5 mm. Flowers scarlet in colour. Fruits c 10-20 cm long.

» Epiphytic or on rock-faces in broad leaved and mixed deciduous evergreen forest.
» 1200 - 2000 m
» May–July
» Samdrupjongkhar, Mongar, Gasa

397 Didymocarpus albicalyx Clarke

Sappy perennial herb. Stems 3-32cm long, hairy, often with gland-tipped hairs. Leaves broadly elliptic to ovate or suborbicular, sometimes unequal in size, largest pair (or 3) usually well above base, 1-3 pairs of smaller leaves above, 2.7-20 x 2.4-14cm, base cordate or rounded, margins doubly toothed, upper surface pubescent, lower surface hairs may be confined to veins, often with gland-tipped hairs; petioles 0.4-10cm. Flowers usually many in spreading cymes 5-13cm long, pedicels c6-15mm long, gland-tipped hairs on peduncles and pedicels. Calyx usually pale, rarely purplish and then leaves purplish below, glabrous or nearly so, campanulate, 2-3mm long, lobed nearly to base. Corolla glabrous, shades of purple, 1.4-2cm long, limb very oblique, lobes rounded. Anthers bearded, Capsule without a stipe, 13-22 x 1.8-2.5mm

» Moist shady mossy rock faces and earth banks, occasionally tree trunks in broadleaved and bamboo forests.
» 1200-2745
» June-September
» Chhukha, Sarpang, Thimphu, Punakha, Trongsa, Wangduephodrang, Trashigang, Gasa

Hamamelidaceae
Witch hazel family

182 Corylopsis himalayana Griff.

Shrub or small tree to 7m, shoots stellate-tomentose. Leaves ovate, palmately 7-9-veined at base, with 7-10 pairs of close, parallel lateral veins above, veins prominent and tomentose beneath; petioles 1.5-2cm; stipules elliptic 1.5-2cm, acute, cordate. Spikes 2.5-5cm, fragrant. Lower bracts (bud scales) ovate, 1.4-1.7cm, glabrous; upper (floral) bracts ovate, 5-6mm, tomentose. Calyx lobes triangular, 0.8mm. Petals yellow, obovate, 7-9mm. Capsules 5-6mm diameter.

» Among shrubs on open hillside, and margins of cool-broad leaved forest.
» 1800-2560m
» February-April
» Chhukha, Samdrupjongkhar, Haa, Thimphu, Trongsa, Trashigang, Trashiyangtse
» Sometimes cultivated as ornamental shrub.

....

Hydrangeaceae
Hydrangea family

366 Dichroa febrifuga Loureiro
Dzo: Hindo Nam, Hogena, Dhoom
Eng: Blue Evergreen Hydrangea

Shrub 1-3m. Leaves, opposite, elliptic-oblanceolate 12-15 x 3.5-7cm, acuminate, base cuneate or attenuate, margin serrate, sparsely pubescent on both surfaces; petioles 1 - 3.5cm. Calyx including acute lobes 3- 4mm. Petals elliptic 5-6 x 1.5-2.5mm, pale blue, becoming reflexed. Stamens 5-6mm purplish. Styles 3-5, c 3mm, thickened at apex. Berries subglobose 6-8mm diameter, intense metallic blue.

» Margins of warm broadleaved and evergreen oak forests
» 1000-2300m
» May-November
» Samtse, Chhukha, Sarpang, Punakha, Trongsa, Mongar, Trashigang, Trashiyangtse
» The shoots and bark of the roots are used to prepare febrifuge (anti-fever medication).

Hypericaceae
St. John's wort family

141 Hypericum hookerianum Wight & Arn.
Eng: St. John's Wort

Bushy shrub 1-2m. Leaves lanceolate, 2.5-7x1-3cm, tapering to tip, base rounded, pale green beneath, translucent lines and dots present, petioles 2-4mm. Flowers sometimes solitary but often in 3-9 flowered cymes, 4-7cm diameter. Sepals erect (not spreading), obovate or suborbicular, 7-10x5-8mm, usually rounded. Petals obovate, 2.3-3x2-2.5cm. Stamens in 5 bundles, 7-10mm long. Capsules ovoid, c 1.5cm.

- » Moist forests, especially cool broad-leaved and Fir forests.
- » 1800-3300m
- » June-August
- » Samdrupjongkhar, Thimphu, Punakha, Wangduephodrang, Trongsa, Bumthang, Trashigang

....

Iridaceae
Iris family

334 Iris clarkei Hook.f.
Dzo: Cema, Dhem

Rhizome forming herbs. Leaves on lower part of stem in fan-like rosettes, linear 24-75x0.6-1.5cm, shiny on upper surface and greyish below. Flower stem solid, exceeding leaves to 25-90cm, sometimes simple, usually with one branch. Flowers 9cm diameter, with two perianth whorls, 3 outer spreading and recurved petal-like "falls" and three inner erect petal-like "standards" fused into a corolla tube. Fall blades deflexed, dark blue to purple, with white or greenish-yellow markings at base, not bearded. Capsules oblong-trigonous, abruptly contracted at top and bottom 3-5.5cm, opening at top. Seeds flattened, D-shaped (5-7mm long) or round (4-5mm diameter), flanged, dark brown.

- » Marshy meadows, swamps in clearings in conifer forests.
- » 2280-4270m
- » June-August

» Chhukha, Haa, Thimphu, Punakha, Bumthang, Mongar, Gasa
» Dried leaves used as fodder for yaks and horses.

Juglandaceae
Walnut family

265 *Engelhardia spicata* Blume.

Tree 8-20m. Leaves 25-40cm, leaflets ovate oblong, 8-18 x 3-6.5cm, obtuse or subacute, base rounded, oblique, often unequal, petiolules 2-10mm, glabrous or pubescent beneath, petioles 3-7cm. Male catkins 4-10cm, each flower composed of 6-10 almost sessile anthers on short side of branch c 2mm. Female catkins 6-10cm, bracts c 5 mm in flower. Fruiting catkins 15-40 cm, nut ovoid, 5-6mm, mid lobe of bract largest, oblanceolate, 2- 4.5 x 0.6 -1.2cm.

» Sub-tropical and warm broad-leaved forest
» 500-2100m
» April-May
» Sarpang, Thimphu, Punakha, Mongar, Trashigang.
» Flowers and fruit highly ornamental.

Labiatae
Mint family

305 *Clinopodium umbrosum* (M. Bieb.) C. Koch

Ascending herb. Stems 18-40cm, hairy. Leaves ovate, 1.6-4 x 0.8-2.5cm, acute, rounded base to broadly wedge-shaped, serrated margins, sparsely hairy. Inflorescence of remote verticillasters of 10-20 flowers, in axils of upper leaves. Calyx, bilabiate, tubular, curved, distinctly ribbed, hairy, 5-6mm long, 5 teeth of which upper 3 are triangular and lower 2 sububulate and slightly longer. Corolla pink, mauve or purplish, 7-8mm long, bilabiate with upper lip notched at tip, lower lip slightly longer in 3 broad lobes. Nutlets 0.9x0.6mm

» Open screes, roadsides, damp banks and among shrubs
» 200-3660m
» May-September.
» Samtse, Chhukha, Thimphu, Punakha, Gasa, Trongsa,

Bumthang.

» Weed of apple orchards and buckwheat crops. Leaves fragrant when crushed.

69 *Colebrookea oppositifolia* Smith.

Shrub 1.5-3 m, softly pubescent throughout, often sericeous on young growth. Leaves elliptic to ovate-elliptic, 10-18x3.5-7.5cm, acuminate, base cuneate, margins crenulate to serrulate, whitish tomentose beneath; petiole 1-4cm, spikes 1.5-11cm, arranged in a panicle, becoming dull pink and plumose in fruit. Calyx 0.6-0.8mm; teeth hairy, lengthening in fruit to 4.5-5.5mm. Corolla whitish 1.5-2mm. Stamens 4, exserted by c 1.5; anthers 1-celled. Nutlets c 0.5mm long, usually only 1 developing, dispersed within calyx.

» Among shrubs on bank of stream, secondary scrub, edge of cultivation.
» 200-1220m
» December-February
» Samtse and Chhukha

216 *Colquhounia coccinea* Wall.
Eng: Himalayan Mint Scrub

Large aromatic, sprawling or scandent shrub. Stems branched, 1.5-5m, soft matted hairs. Leaves ovate to elliptic, 3.6-13-2.4-7.2cm, base rounded, margins toothed, both surfaces hairy, lower surface often rust coloured or whitish; petiole 0.6-2.5cm. Inflorescence of 6-8 flowered whorls in axils of upper leaves, sometimes crowded to form a spike. Calyx 8-10mm, densely whitish hairs. Corolla bilabiate with curved tube, upper lip entire, lower lip 3 lobed, orange red-25-30mm.

» Dry places, dry scrub, open oak forests, edges of cultivation, roadsides.

Very variable species in density of leaf hair and length of corolla. There are two varieties:

var. *coccinea*: Leaf hair sparse, lower surface green, margins saw-toothed.

» 1980-2700m
» July, November, January
» Samdrupjongkhar, Haa, Thimphu, Paro

var. *mollis*: Leaf hair dense, lower surface rust coloured or whitish, margins with small rounded teeth.

» 1580-2560m
» May-November
» Common around Thimphu and Punakha

70 *Elsholtzia fruticosa* (D. Don) Rehder
Eng: Shrubby Mint

Shrub 1-5m. Stems covered with very short fine hair. Leaves lance like and sessile and toothed margins with fine hair on both surfaces. Cream coloured flowers on spikes 3-11cm long and 1cm thick with fine hairs.

» Open hillsides among shrubs and roadsides or in spruce and juniper forests
» 2130-3505m
» August-October
» Paro, Thimphu

392 *Elsholtzia strobilifera* (Benth.) Benth.

Annual herb, 6-38cm. Stems erect, with or without branches. Leaves ovate, not more than 3cm long, narrowly tapering to base but with petiole from 1/3 to equal to the length of the leaf blade, margins toothed, pubescent. Spikes cylindrical, 1.2-4cmx0.5-0.8cm, hairy, with connate bracts overlapping and completely concealing calyces. Corolla sublabiate or bilabiate, 2.5mm, mauve or violet. Nutlets obovoid.

» Roadsides and trail sides, in pine, spruce and open firs forests, among bamboo.
» 2130-4170m
» September - November
» Thimphu, Punakha, Trongsa, Gasa, Trashiyangtse

393 *Phlomis tibetica* Marquand & Shaw
Eng: Tibetan Jerusalem Sage

Herb from 7-100cm with light to moderate hair on stems. Basal leaves ovate with heartshaped base, and toothed margins, and hairy surface. Upper leaves on stems smaller and few. Inflorescence of 1-5 whorls around stems, and bracts thin and long with dark brown hairs. Flowers pink, purple or dark red, 16-25mm; upper lip 5-10mm, densely pale or dark brown villous inside; lower lip5-6mm. Nutlets ellipsoid c. 4x2mm.

» Open alpine meadows and grassy slopes, sometimes, among shrubs, moist scree, gravel river beds.
» 3500-4725m
» May - September
» Haa, Paro, Thimphu, Bumthang, Gasa, Trongsa, Trashiyangtse
» Can be mistaken for *P. bracteosa* which has broader bracts and white hairs on bracts and upper lips of corolla.

177 Salvia campanulata Bentham

Robust, glandular, perennial herb. Stems erect, 40-75cm, with glandular hairs above, tomentose to glabrescent below. Leaves at base ovate to ovate-oblong, 13-24.5x5-11cm, dentate, upper surface sparsely to densely pubescent; lower surface sparsely to densely tomentose and with numerous sessile glands; petiole 8-20cm; stem leaves similar, often smaller and with shorter petiole, sometimes sessile. Inflorescence branched. Verticillasters distant, 2-6-flowered. Calyx campanulate, 11-15mm, usually flushed dull red-purple especially on upper lip, densely glandular-hairy, in fruit up to 20mm. Corolla yellow, often with brownish or purple marking on upper lip, 22-28mm; tube c 8mm diameter at throat, narrower within calyx; upper lip straight, 6-10mm; lower lip subequal in length, deflexed. Nutlets obovoid, c 4 x 3mm

» In clearings in *Fir/Rhododendron* forest and moist oak forest
» 2430-4270m
» June-September
» Thimphu, Punakha, Trongsa, Bumthang, Gasa, Trashiyangtse.

178 Salvia nubicola Sweet
Eng: Himalayan Yellow Sage

Perennial sticky herb with erect stems 50-130cm covered in stiff glandular hairs. Leaves arrowhead shaped with rounded teeth on margins. Pale yellow flowers 2-3cm long with light purplish mottling on upper lips and streaks on lower lip; arranged in whorls of 2-6 flowers which are spread apart.

- » Shrubs and dry forest margins.
- » 2440-2600m
- » August - October
- » Paro, Thimphu
- » Strongly lemon scented when bruised.

179 *Salvia roborowskii* Maxim.

Erect annual herb. Stems 8-72cm, covered in glandular and pubescent stiff hair. Leaves simple, triangular-ovate, 1.5-5.4x0.8-4.2cm, acute tip, base truncate to heart shaped, irregularly toothed on margins, upper surface sparsely hairy, lower with densely glandular hair. Inflorescence of more or less distant verticillasters, 2-6 flowers per verticillaster. Calyx 6-9mm covered in dense, stiff glandular hair. Corolla pale yellow or cream; 12-17mm; tube straight; upper lip c.4.5mm

- » Weed of barley fields, open slopes.
- » 3840-4270m
- » July -September
- » Gasa, Paro
- » Foliage lemon scented.

71 *Stachys melissaefolia* Bentham
Eng: Bee Leaf Stachys

A smelly erect herb 25-120cm often with slender branches and covered with soft hair. Leaves ovate 2-7x1.3-3.4cm, with base rounded or heart-shaped and toothed margin, with upper surface with hair and lower surface with dense white hair. Flower mauve or pink with darker blotches 12-15mm, upper lip is entire and smaller than lower lip, which has three lobes with middle much larger.

- » Open grassy banks and meadows among shrubs, blue pine forest.
- » 2130-3800m
- » June-September
- » Haa, Thimphu, Trongsa, Wangduephodrang, Bumthang

358 *Prunella vulgaris* L.
Eng: Common Self Heal

Perennial herb. Stems 5-32cm, long-haired to subglabrous. Leaves elliptic-lanceolate, 1.5-5x0.7-1.8cm, margins entire or toothed, hairy on both surfaces; petiole up to 1.7cm.

Flower purple in whorls on dense terminal spike 2-4 x 2cm. Calyx 8-9mm, tube c 3.5mm; teeth of lower lip triangular, c 3.5mm. Corolla deep purple or sometimes white, 10-12mm; upper lip c 3.5mm. Nutlets c 1.6-1mm.

» Sandy places, damp meadows, open grass, roadsides.
» 1370-3960m
» May-August
» Chhukha, Paro, Thimphu, Trongsa, Wangduephodrang, Bumthang, Gasa

---

Lardizabalaceae
Lardizabala family

36 *Holboellia latifolia* Wall.
Dzo: Enterobjay
Eng: Sausage Vine

Twining shrub. Leaves ovate-elliptic, 4.5-13x1.5-7cm, acute or acuminate to a fine tip, base rounded or cuneate, glabrous, margins entire; petioles upto 4 cm. Racemes 3-12 cam bearing 3-7 flowers. Sepals green or purplish, elliptic or ovate, usually narrower in male flowers, 10-15x3-6mm, brorder in female flowers 10-16x5-7mm. Male flowers with stamens 8-15mm; pistil lobes linear, c 1.5mm. Female flowers with oblong-ellipsoid carpels 8-10mm; staminodes ovoid 1-1.5mm. Fruiting carpels ellipsoid, 6-10x3-4cm, red; seeds ovoid, blackish, compressed, 8x6mm, glossy.

» Found in forest margins, especially in cool broad-leaved forest.
» 1880-2900m
» April-June
» Chhukha, Samdrupjongkhar, Trashigang, Haa, Trongsa.
» Flowers fragrant. Fruits edible

Leguminosae
Pea family

407 Astragalus bhotanensis Baker

Prostrate or sprawling herb, stems 20-100cm with fine white hair flat against stem. Pinnate leaves 7-15cm, with 13-20 leaflets ending in a terminal leaflet, stipules 10-15mm. Flowers 10-20 in dense cluster, with peduncle 7-17cm. Calyx with blackish hairs, tube 5-6mm and narrow teeth 2-2.5mm. Petals purplish 10-13mm, standard petal obovate-spathulate c 5mm broad, wings oblong 4 x 1.5mm sometimes pale or white, keel ovate. Pods, narrowly ovoid 1.5-2 x 0.4-0.5cm, inflated, smooth with 20-30 seeds.

» Roadsides and cultivated ground.
» 2100-3100m
» April-June
» Haa, Thimphu, Trongsa

52 Bauhinia variegata L.
Eng: White Purple Orchid Tree

Erect shrub or tree 2-12m. Leaves broadly ovate with heart shaped base 5-18x5-18cm, and apex divided into two 1/3 length of leaf, veins 9-11. Flowers axillary or terminal appearing before leaves. Petals elliptic, 4-5x2-3cm, on claws c 1.5cm, white or pink, posterior one purple, 5 fertile stamens, 4.5-5cm, pods15-20x2-3cm.

» Warm and subtropical forests.
» 250-1500m
» February-April
» Chhuka, Sarpang, Punakha, Trongsa, Trashigang
» Originally possibly a native of China, widely cultivated and naturalised throughout warm and subtropical areas. Bark, leaves and flowers are used medicinally.

171 Caesalpinia decapetala (Roth) Alston
Dzo: Tatse Tsang, Tsangi Meto
Eng: Mysore Thorn, Cat's Claw

Climber or shrub. with recurved spines. Leaves, 10-35cm, twice pinnate compound with 3-10 pairs of leaflets. Flowers on erect racemes 15-30 cm. Petals yellow sometimes with red veins, upper one suborbicular, 7-8mm, borne on claw

6-0.6mm, other petals obovate, 14-15 x 10-12mm. Stamens c15mm, lanate to middle. Pods oblong, 6-10x2.5-3cm, woody, narrowly (2-3mm) winged along dorsal suture, sharply beaked with style remnant c 0.75cm; seeds 4-9.

»   Along shrubberies near streams, open dry slopes.
»   1200-1850m
»   May-September
»   Punakha, Mongar, Trashigang, Trashiyangtse

172 Cassia fistula L.
Eng: Golden Shower Tree

Deciduous tree, 10-20m. Leaves 15-40cm, leaflets 3-4(-8) pairs ovate, 7-15x4-7cm, acute, base rounded, glabrous but grayish pubescent beneath at first, petiolules 4-5mm; stipules deltoid 1-2mm, deciduous. Raceme axillary, pendent, 10-40cm, pedicels 4-6cm. Sepals elliptic 8-10x4-5mm, becoming reflexed. Petals yellow, obovate, 2-3x1-1.5cm. Stamens 10, longest 3 with filaments 3cm, 4 medium-sized with filaments 8-10mm and 3 smaller stamens with filaments 5-6mm and poorly developed anthers. Style as long as longest stamens. Pods terete, 20-60x1.5cm, woody, indehiscent, black, transversely septate into many chambers. Seeds ovate, 12-13x7mm, glossy, brown with a darker line from hilum to top of seed on one side.

»   On dry hillside
»   300-1200m
»   May-June
»   Chhukha, Sarpang, Trashigang, Trashiyangtse

160 Cassia occidentalis L.

Shrub 1-3m. Leaves 10-20cm, pinnately compound with 3-5 pairs of leaflets, ovate 3-12x1.5-4cm, ciliate and minutely glandular pubescent beneath; petioles 3-6cm with globose or ovoid gland very close to base; racemes axillary, 4-10 flowered, bracts ovate 4-5mm, acute, deciduous. Sepals 5, subequal, obovate. Petals 5, subequal, elliptic or obovate 10-15x5-7mm, yellow or orange. Stamens 9-10, unequal, 2 much larger than rest, 4 medium sized and 3-4 very small; pods linear 10-12x0.7-1cm, brown with pale band on both sutures.

»   River banks and waste ground.
»   200-1450m

» May-September
» Chhukha, Punakha, Wangduephodrang
» Possibly South American in origin, now a pan tropical weed. Dried seeds, ground to powder make a good substitue for coffee, but can also be toxic in large doses.

389 *Campylotropis speciosa* (Schindler) Schindler

Shrub 1-2m. Leaves pinnately trifoliate, smooth above with pressed hairs below, petioles 0.5-3cm, stipules lanceolate 5-6mm. Many flowers in racemes 5-12cm long. Petals purplish 8-10mm with standard folded over wings and keel. Pods elliptic, 7-8x3-4mm with brownish hairs.

» Open Banks, margins of forests, roadsides.
» 2400-2500m
» September - October
» Thimphu, Punakha, Trongsa, Trashigang

345 *Crotalaria occulta* Bentham

Annual up to 60cm, with densely pressed hairs when young. Leaves simple, elliptic oblanceolate 3-6x1-2cm, margins entire. No stipules. Flowers on lax terminal racemes with 5-20 flowers. Calyx covered with flat dense hair and divided into 5 teeth almost to base with upper pair broader than lower three. Petals blue-violet as long as calyx teeth. Pods without hair.

» Roadsides, open ground.
» 2330m
» September-October
» Samdrupjongkhar, Thimphu

217 *Delonix regia* (Hooker) Rafinesque
Eng: Flamboyant, Flame Tree, Gold Mohur

Tree 10–15m. Leaves 20-60cm, pinnae 8-25 pairs, leaflets 12-25 pairs, oblong, 8-12x3-4mm, obtuse or subacute, base obliquely rounded, +- sessile; stipules 1-3cm. Racemes 8-12 flowered, pedicels 3-5cm, bracts ovate c 8x5mm. Sepals oblong-lanceolate, 20-25x7–8mm, reddish within. Petals obovate, 4-6x2.5-5cm, red, upper one streaked yellow. Stamens 3.5-4cm. Pods 30-70 x 4-6cm; seeds 20-50 oblong, 2x0.7cm, brown.

» Cultivated in gardens and on roadsides for its decorative habit and colourful flowers.
» May–June
» Upto 2000m
» Chhukha, Sarpang, Gaylegphu, Samdrupjongkhar
» Native of Madagascar.

218 *Erythrina arborescens* Roxb.

Dzo: Chhatsey
Eng: Coral Tree

Tree 5-15m. branchlets with short brown spines. Leaflets ovate, 12-20x9-16cm, acute shortly acuminate, base rounded or shallowly cordate, sparsely or densely pubescent beneath; petioles 12-25cm sometimes bearing a few spines. Flowers appearing after leaf development, racemes axillary on peduncles up to 30cm. Calyx 8-10mm, truncate or very shallowly bilabiate, sparsely brown pubescent. Standard ovate-elliptic, 3.5-4.7x1.5-2.2cm, orange-scarlet, wings oblong, 12-5mm, pale coloured, keel triangular, 15-20x10mm, whitish. Pods oblong-ellipsoid, 15-25x1.5-2.5cm, scarcely constricted between the 4-6 reniform black seeds 1.5-2x1x1.3cm.

» Warm broadleaved forests.
» 1525-2440m
» July-August
» Chhukha, Sarpang, Punakha to Trashigang.

234 *Erythrina stricta* Roxb.

Tree 6–20m, branchlets armed with whitish conical spines. Leaflets ovate, 15–20x8–20cm, acute or acuminate, base rounded, brownish pubescent at first. Flowers appearing before leaves. Calyx c 15mm deeply divided dorsally, densely brown pubescent. Standard narrowly ovate, 4.5–5.5x1.8–12cm, scarlet, wings oblong c 7x2.5mm, keel ovate-elliptic 2–2.5x0.7cm pale. Pods 10–15x1.5cm, thinly coriaceous, on stalks 1–1.5cm, 1–3 seeded, scarcely constricted; seed oblong c 1.5x0.6cm.

» Sub-tropical and warm broad-leaved forest
» 200–1450m
» Feubruary – April
» Chhukha, Sarpang, Trongsa, Trashigang

376 *Gueldenstaedtia himalaica* Baker

Low growing perennial herb with pubescent stems 2-10cm. Leaves odd-pinnate, 2-15cm, leaflets 9-17, obovate 3-10x2-7mm, with tip notched or bilobed, brownish hairs. Flowers solitary or 2-3. Peduncles 1.5-9cm. Calyx 4-5mm and 5-toothed, upper two broader, reddish. Petals, usually dark purple occasionally whitish, standard 8-10mm, rounded or bilobed, wings 7-8mm, keel 3.5-4mm. Pods c1.5cm, sparsely pubescent.

» Open hillsides.
» 2800-4250m
» May-July
» Haa, Paro, Thimphu, Bumthang, Mongar, Gasa

308 *Indigofera cassioides* Rottler ex DC.

Shrub 1.5 -4 m. Leaves pinnate, 7-15cm, leaflets 11-21 ovate elliptic 1-2.5x0.7-1.5. pubescent on both surfaces. Racemes showy 5-12 cm often on old wood and unfolding before leaves. Petals deep pink, standard obovate, 12-15x7-9mm, wings oblong 10-12x3-4mm, keel 12-15x2-3mm. Pods linear, 2.5-4.5x0.3-0.4, crimson when immature, 8-12 seeds.

» Common in warm broadleaved and chirpine forest.
» March-May
» 1200-1500m
» Chhukha, Punakha, Trashigang

390 *Indigofera dosua* D. Don

Shrub 0.3-4m, young growth spreading pale or brown hirsute. Leaves pinnate, leaflets 15-53mm, oblong or broadly elliptic, 5-35x3-8mm, obtuse or acute, mucronate, base rounded or cuneate, appressed pubscent on both surfaces; stipule narrowly lanceolate, 6-12 mm. Calyx 2mm, teeth broadly triangular. Petals pink to purple, standard broadly oblong c 9x6mm, wings oblanceolate, c8x2mm, keel as long as wings, Acute. Pods linear, deflexed, 20-335x2.5-3mm, pubescent, 10-12 seeded.

» Found in open hill sides and roadside banks.
» 1000-2000m
» April-August
» Chhukha,Sarpang, Samdrupjongkhar, Thimphu, Trashigang, Trashiyangtse

391 *Indigofera tinctoria* L.
Eng: True Indigo

Shrub 1-2m, stems sparsely appressed pubescent, not whitish. Leaves 6-10cm, pinnately compound with 7-10 leaflets, glabrous above pubescent below. Racemes erect 3-7cm, lax-flowered to base. Calyx c1.5mm, teeth triangular. Petals 3-4mm, reddish yellow to violet. Pods 12-30x2-2.5mm, deflexed but hardly upcurved, sparsely pubescent when young, 8-12 seeds.

- » 2400m
- » July-September
- » Paro, Thimphu, Mongar, Trashigang
- » Cultivated as source for indigo. Roadsides.

346 *Parochetus communis* D. Don
Eng: Blue Oxalis

Prostrate perennial herb, rooting at lower nodes. Leaves digitately 3-foliate, leaflets broadly obovate, 0.5-2.5cm long, tip rounded with a shallow notch, margins with rounded teeth, smooth above and pubescent beneath, sometimes a dark coloured band in the middle; petioles 2.5-20cm. Flowers solitary or 2 on axillary peduncles. Calyx campanulate, unequally 5 toothed, upper 2 teeth connate near apex. Petals blue; standard obovate 15-22mm, wings oblong, keel shorter than wings and slightly hooded distally. Pods 15-20x3-4mm, seeds rounded c. 1.5mm, blackish.

- » Moist places and streamsides, open slopes, cultivated areas.
- » 1500-3960m
- » March-Septmeber
- » Widespread from Chhukha to Samdrupjongkhar, and Thimphu to Trashigang

161 *Piptanthus nepalensis* (Hook.) D. Don
Eng: Evergreen Laburnum, Black Piptanthus

Deciduous shrub 1-2.5m, young shoots densely pubescent. Compound leaves with 3 leaflets; leaflets ovate-elliptic 5-8x1-2.5cm, densely pubescent below, margins entire and sessile. Flowers in short terminal racemes. Calyx bell-shaped with 5 teeth. Petals yellow 2-3cm, with standard erect c 2cm broad, brown streaks at base, wings and keel 7-8mm broad. Pods 8-12x1-2.7mm.

» Open hillsides and among scrub.
» 2300-3650m
» April-May
» Haa to Mongar including Gasa

124 *Trifolium repens* L.
Eng: White Clover

Creeping perennial herb, stems frequently rooting at nodes. Leaves digitately 3-foliate, leaflets obovate or obcordate 1-3x0.7-2cm, margins finely toothed, without hair, usually wth whitish V-shape mark on upper side. Petioles 4-16cm. Flowers in dense sub-globose heads 2-2.5cm diameter, peduncles 6-30cm. Calyx tube 2-3mm. Petals white, 7-10mm. Pods oblong, 4-5mm.

» Grassy areas and roadsides.
» 2000-2700m
» April-June
» Widespread.
» Introduced from Europe for agriculture.

....

Liliaceae
Lily family

60 *Cardiocrinum giganteum* (Wall.) Makino
Dzo: Dhoong Meto
Eng: Giant Himalayan Lily

Large hebaceous plant, stem 0.9-4 m, to 4.5 cm diameter, hollow. Basal leaves rosetted, blades ovate, deeply cordate, to 33-45x24-40 cm; petiole to 25 cm; stem leaves smaller. Inflorescence 6-25 flowered raceme. Flowers white tinged greenish outside, streaked reddish or purple inside, sweetly scented, horizontal or deflexed, trumpet shaped. Tepals narrowly oblanceolate, apex rounded or sub-acute, reflexed, saccate at base, 11-20x1.6-2.9 cm, inner broader than outer. Anthers purplish-yellow, 0.6-1.5cm. Capsule segments oblong, to 7x3.5cm.

» 1830-3660 m
» June-August
» Chhukha, Haa, Thimphu, Punakha, Wangduephodrang, Mongar, Trashigang, Gasa, Bumthang

201 Lilium nanum Klotzsch
Med: Abbikha
Dzo: Cima

Bulb 2.5-3 cm, scale lanceolate brown or yellowish. Flowers single, drooping, companulate, deep reddish-purple to lilac, inside usually paler with varying degree of darker flecking. Tepals narrowly elliptic, contracted at extreme tip, apex not reflexed, with tufts of branched hairs at base on both sides of basal nectar furrow.

» Found in meadows and grasslands; peaty hillsides; among rocks in open, by rivers or commonly among shrubs (Rhododendron, juniper, potentilla, etc.)
» 3350- 4880 m
» June–August
» Thimphu, Trongsa, Bumthang, Trashigang, Gasa, Trashiyangtse

138 Lilium nepalense D. Don
Eng: Nepal Lilly

Flower stem 46–108cm. Leaves narrowly elliptic to oblong lanceolate, narrowed to sub-acute apex, 4.5–14x0.9–2.7cm, veins 5-7. Flowers drooping, funnel-shaped, apex of tepals reflexed. Tepals yellowish-green above, dark crimson-brown below, lanceolate, contracted at extreme apex to minute, blunt tip, narrowed towards base, 8–15x1.7–3cm, inner broader than outer. Filaments 5.5–7.8cm; anthers yellow or brown, 0.8 – 1.2cm. Ovary cylindric, c, 1.2cm; style to 8cm.

» On rocks on scrubby hillside; on cliffs and rocky hillsides among bracken and shrubs
» 2130 – 2800m
» June – July
» Punakha, Trongsa

202 Lilium sherrifiae Stearn.
Dzo: Abecas

Rooting stem short (c.2.5cm), erect. Flower stem to 46cm. Leaves linear-lanceolate, to 12x0.95cm, many veined. Flowers single (occassionally 2), companulate, drooping, reddish-brown chequered with gold inside. Tepals elliptic, contracted below, apiculate apex, not reflexed, c.6cm. outer c1.6cm wide, inner c.2.3 cm wide. Filaments c.1.9cm, anthers c.1.3 cm. Ovary c.1.2 cm; style c.2.8 cm, thickened upwards. Capsule oblong in outline, 6-winged, 2-2.5x1.5cm, shortly stipitate.

» Sandy soil among willow by stream; rocky and sandy grassy hillside; damp humus-rich slope in Fir forest.
» 2740-3680m
» May-July
» Bumthang, Trashiyangtse.

23 *Lilium wallichianum* J. A. & J. H. Schultes var. *wallichianum*
Eng: Wallichianum Lilly

Bulb c. 5x4cm; scales c.20, lanceolate, to 1.5cm wide, fawn to reddish-brown, margins scarious. Flower stem 70-113cm. Leaves linear, finely tapered to apex, 10.5-20 x 0.45-0.65cm, veins 1-3. Flowers sweetly scented, white or yellowish-white, sometimes golden yellow inside, held horizontally, funnel-shaped, narrowly tubular at base, apex of tepals reflexed. Tepals 16-21cm; inner to 45cm wide; outer to 3.5cm wide, with narrowly elliptic blade, contracted at extreme apex to blunt tip, narrowed below into a claw for basal third.

» Open grassy hillsides among rocks, sometimes in open forest.
» 1220 – 2440m
» June – September
» Punakha, Wangduephodrang, Trongsa, Mongar, Trashigang, Trashiyangtse

139 *Lloydia flavonutans* Hara

Tunics whitish. Flowering stalk 6.5-26cm. Basal leaves upto 5, apex blunt, sometimes darkened, filiform, equal or shorter than flower stalk, 1-2mm wide. Leaf-like bracts 2-3. Flowers 1-3, drooping, yellow with white orange or brownish spot at base. Tepals 1-1.7cm; outer narrowly oblong, rounded, 2-4mm wide; inner narrowly rhombic, sometimes slightly contracted below rounded apex, 3.8-7mm wide. Filaments 4.3-7mm, with spreading hairs; anthers oblong, 1.6-2.4mm. Ovary 3.5-5mm, cylindric, tapered into style; style 3.7-5.5mm; stigma lobes scarcely developed. Capsule c 1.8x4 0.4cm, narrowly oblong to clavate, splitting only at apex to form 3 subacute points.

> » 3050-4880m
> » May-July
> » Haa, Thimphu, Punakha, Trashigang, Trongsa, Trashiyangtse

24 Lloydia longiscapa Hook. f.

Flowering stalk 10-30cm. Basal leaves to 6, apex blunt, sometimes darkened, almost equalling scape, somewhat flattened, 0.9-1.5mm wide. Leaf-like bracts to 5, lowest to 9cm. Flowers 1-2, drooping, white (sometimes flushed pinkish), with orange, brownish or reddish basal spot on lower half of tepals and veining of same colour in upper half. Tepals 1.5-2cm, deeply longitudinally ridged below, ridges clothed with short hairs; outer lanceolate to elletpic, slightly acuminate to subacute apex, sometimes laterally incised to trifid, 4.3-8mm wide; inner 4-8mm wide. Filaments with spreading hairs; anthers oblong, 1.4-2.5mm. Ovary 3-5mm, cylindric, gradually tapered into style; style 3.5-4.4mm; stigma capitates.

> » Among shrubs, grassy slopes
> » 3660-4270m
> » June-August
> » Trashiyangtse

388 Notholirion macrophyllum (D. Don) Boiss.

Stem 15-40 cm, 1.5-3.5 mm dia. Leaves 3-6 inserted evenly along stem, linear-lanceolate, tapering gradually from near base to blunt apex. Inflorescence 1-5 flowered raceme, flowers subtended by leaf-like bracts; lower pedicel to 2.5 cm, longer than upper. Flowers held horizontally or slightly upturned, weakly zygomorphic, purple or mauve, some times darker at base inside, smell offensive.

> » Found in open grassy hillsides, rocky banks, some times in Pinus forest
> » 1980-3960m
> » June-July
> » Haa, Thimphu, Punakha, Trongsa, Bumthang

25 *Streptopus simplex* D. Don
Eng: Simple Twisted Talk

An erect plant with zig zag, forked, leafy stem and with small white solitary, pendulous, long-stalked, bell shape flowers arising from the axil of most of the leaves. Flowers to 2.5 cm across; petals elliptic-acute; stamens much shorter tha petals. leaves ellpitic acute with heart-shaped clasping base, 5-12 cm, glaucous beneath; stems 60-120 cm. Fruit a berry, orange when ripe.

» 2500-3700 m
» June - August
» Punakha, Thimphu

....

Lythraceae
Loosestrife family

213 *Woodfordia fruticosa* (L.) Kurz.
Dzo: Zange Shing
Eng: Fire Flame Bush

Shrub 1-3m tall; stems pubescent, bark peeling. Leaves lanceolate, 7-11x1.2-3cm, acuminate, base round or shallowly cordate, sessile, minutely whitish or grayish puberilous and blackish gland-dots beneath, sparsely pubescent above. Cymes compact, 2-3.5cm long. Flowers bright brick-red. Calyx tube 10-13mm, lobes triangular, 2mm, alternating with small teeth c 0.6mm. Petals lanceolate, c 3mm. Filaments red, 12-17mm. Capsule ellipsoid, c 8x4mm.

» Stream side and scrub in dry valleys
» 610-1500m
» March-May.
» Mongar, Trongsa, Trashigang, Trashiyangtse
» An attractive ornamental shrub. Yellow dye made from dry flower is used for dying silk and. Also used for treating dysentery

Magnoliaceae
Magnolia family

16 Magnolia campbellii Hook. f.& Thomson
Dzo: Gong-Gong, Haley Meto
Eng: Campbell's Magnolia

Deciduous tree, 12-15m. Leaves appearing after flowers, elliptic to obovate, 22-33 x 10-14cm, acute tip, base rounded or heartshaped, pubescent at first, veins 10-15 pairs. Flowers erect c 15cm across, enclosed at first by spathe-like bract 4.5-6cm, densely sericeous; perianth parts c 12, outer ones yellowish, inner white, purple near base. Stamens several in series, purplish; carpels free, densely crowded on receptacle and purplish. Fruiting receptacle cylindrical, c 15-3cm; carpels obovoid, laterally compressed 1-1.5cm,

- » Moist Hemlock/Rhododendron forests.
- » 2000-3000m
- » March-May
- » Haa, Thimphu, Punakha, Trongsa, Trashigang, Gasa

17 Magnolia globosa Hook. f. & Thomson.
Eng: Globe Magnolia

Similar to *M. campbellii* but leaves unfolding before flowers, subcoriaceous, ovate-elliptic, 11-22x5-11cm, acute, base rounded, veins c 8 pairs, brownish hirsute beneath especially on veins; petioles 1.5-4cm, stipular scar +- as long; flower pendulous c 15cm across; perianth parts c 9, white or cream-coloured, stamens crimson; fruiting receptacle 3-5.5 x 2cm, carpels 12-20, elliptic-ovoid, 1-1.5 x 0.7cm, shortly (c 2mm) beaked at apex.

- » Moist Hemlock and Fir forest
- » 2440-3200m
- » May-July
- » Thimphu, Mongar, Gasa

18 Michelia doltsopa DC

Evergreen tree 8-25m, buds greyish-brown sericeous. Leaves elliptic or oblanceolate, 15-25 x 5-7cm, acute or gradually pointed tip, base wedge shaped, densely pubescent beneath at first, petioles 2-3cm. Flowers white, 10-15cm across, perianth parts 9-12, oblanceolate. Stamens yellowish in several series; carpels free densly crowding on receptacle. Fruiting receptacle 7-12cm, carpels ovoid, 1-1.5 x 0.7-1cm, acute, slightly compressed.

» Mixed evergreen forests.
» 1830-2500m
» February-March
» Chhukha, Thimphu, Sarpang, Punakha, Trongsa, Trashigang.
» Often cultivated, very valuable timber for building and furniture

....

Malvaceae
Mallow family

140 *Abelmoschus manihot* (L.) Medik.

A perennial herb or under shrub 1-2 m. Leaves deeply palmately lobed, broadly ovate to rhombic, lower ones obscurely 3-5 angled, upper more deeply lobed to hastate, 3-9x3-8 cm, acute, base cordate or sagittate, margins dentate; petiole 1-6cm; stipules linear. Epicalyx segments 4-6, ovate to lanceolate, c 2.5 cm. Flowers in terminal 2-7 flowered racemes with large flowers with purple centers. Fruits narrow, oblong-ovoid, 4.5-5.5x1.2–2 cm.

» Found in warm broad-leaved forest
» 600-1800 m
» August-December
» Punakha, Trashiyangtse, Mongar

....

Melanthiaceae
Bunchflower family

59 *Aletris pauciflora* (Klotzsch) Hand.-Mazz.

Rhizomatous perennial 5-16cm. Grass-like leaves in rosette of 4-10 with longest 4-18.5 x 0.3-0.5cm, and veins 8 or more. Scape earing flowers densely felted with short white hairs. Inflorescense with 10-20 flowers; each flower subtended by thin bracteoles longer than flower. Flowers pinkish or white and bell shaped with 6 lobes. Capsules ovoid.

» Alpine pastures and sometimes among alpine shrubs.

» 2290-4900m
» May-August
» Haa, Thimphu, Punakha, Trongsa, Bumthang, Gasa, Trashiyangtse

Melastomataceae
Meadow beauty family

377 *Melastoma normale* D. Don
Eng: Himalayan Melastome

Bushy shrub up to 4m. Stems with more or less spreading hairs. Leaves elliptic up tand acuminate with rounded base and 5 veins. Upper surface of leaves with leaves and soft to touch. Flowers with 5 petals mauve to rose purple. 10 unequal stamens (5 long with elongated connective and 5 short).

» Among scrubs and Forest Margins
» 305-1830m
» December - June
» Punakha, Wangdue, Tsirang

289 *Osbeckia nepalensis* Hook. f.

Shrub to 2m, stems appressed hairy, branched. Leaves narrowly ovate oblong to elliptic, 4-13.5x1.3-4cm, base rounded or heartshaped, with appressed hairs, sessile. Inflorescence mainly terminal with few to many flowers. Calyx 15-18mm with 5 lobes, oblong-ovate, 8-10mm, fringed with hair. Petals 5, pink, mauve or white, broadly obovate, 15-20mm, fringed at tip. Stamens 10, 13-15mm, anthers 7-10mm. Fruit 8-10mm capsule, hairy at apex.

» Steep hillsides or among scrub often near water.
» 610-1800m
» July-September
» Punakha, Wangduephodrang, Trongsa

311 *Osbeckia stellata* Wall. ex C.B. Clarke

Perennial herb or shrub 60-360cm. stems branched, sometimes winged, with dense or sparse hair. Leaves ovate-oblong or elliptic, 6.5-14.5x2.1-4.5cm, sparsely hairy on both surfaces, veins 5-7. Inflorescences terminal and in upper leaf axils, paniculate, few to many flowers. Calyx 13-25mm with 4 lobes, 8-13mm, subglabrous to densely hairy, some hairs tufted (star shape). Petals 4, pinkish to red-purple, obovate to broadly obovate, 16-27mm, usually fringed with hair. Stamens 8, 20-35mm, anthers 17mm. Fruit 10-20mm capsule, hairy.

Very variable species. Three varieties in Bhutan.

var. *stellata:* Stems with appressed hairs, not winged, calyx densely hairy, apendages on calyx tube with stellate hairs at apex.

» In grasslands and clearings in warm broadleaved forest.
» 305-1650m
» August-October.
» Chhukha, Sarpang, Samdrupjongkhar, Trongsa

var. *rostrata:* Stems with appressed hairs, sometimes winged; calyx without to sparsely haired, appendages on calyx tube sparse or absent, oten without hair at tip.

» Wet places in grassland or subtropical forests.
» 150-1220m
» December-January.
» Locality unknown in Bhutan.

var. *crinita:* Stems dense, spreading or sometimes reflexed hairs, not winged, calyx apendages oten dark purple, usually with stellate hairs at apex.

» Open hillside, rock crevices.
» 1550-2290m
» July-October.
» Punakha, Trongsa, Mongar, Gasa

....

Meliaceae
Mahogany family

276 *Toona ciliata* Roemer
Dzo: Chhuen Shing
Eng: Indian Mahogany

Large tree 20-27m. Leaves to c 40cm; leaflets 3-12 pairs, ovate-lanceolate, 11-12x3.5-6cm, acuminate, base obliquely rounded, glabrous or long-haired on veins beneath, veins about 18 pairs. Thyrses almost as long as leaves, sparsely pubescent. Sepals ovate, c. 0.8mm, pubescent. Petals ovate-oblong, 3.5-5.5x2-3mm, ciliate. Anthers shorter than filaments. Capsule oblong, 1.5-3.5cm; seeds c 15mm, equally winged at both ends.

» Subtropical forest
» 300–1760m
» November–March
» Chhukha, Sarpang

....

Myrsinaceae
Myrsine family

240 *Ardisia macrocarpa* Wall.
Dzo: Ressim
Eng: Himalayan Coralberry

Shrub 0.6-1.5m, glabrous, single-stemmed, branching near apex. Leaves coriaceous, elliptic or narrowly oblanceolate, 7-14x1-4cm, acute, base attenuate, margins undulate, with a line of raised gland-dots, glabrous and with scattered raised gland-dots beneath, lateral veins spreading, not prominent; petiole 3-8mm, winged. Flowers in umbels, each 2-5-flowered borne terminally and in upper axils on short peduncle 1-2cm at ends of leafy branches; pedicels 1-2cm; bracts ovate c 2mm, deciduous. Sepals oblong-spathulate 3-3.5mm, outside gland-dotted. Petals lanceolate 6-7mm, pinkish-white, gland-dotted. Style elongate c 5mm. Fruit globose c 1cm diameter, scarlet.

» Evergreen oak and cool broad-leaved forest.
» 1600-2400m
» May-July
» Chhukha, Samdrupjongkhar, Punakha, Trongsa and Mongar
» Flowers and fruit highly ornamental.

83 *Maesa chisa* D. Don

Shrub or more rarely a small tree 2-6m; branchlets glabrous. Leaves membranous, lanceolate or elliptic, 8-15x2.5-4.5cm, acuminate, base cuneate, margins subentire, sinuate or distantly and shallowly serrate, glabrous, minor veins reticulate, conspicuous and translucent; petioles 1-1.5cm.

Racemes simple or branched, 2.5-6cm; pedicels 2-2.5mm. Sepals ovate c 1mm. Corolla white, c 2mm. Fruit globose, c 4mm diameter.

» Margins of Evergreen oak and warm broad-leaved forests, often on rocky slopes and cliffs
» 250-2100m
» February-May
» Chhukha, Sarpang, Trongsa, Trashigang

Onagraceae
Evening primrose family

307 Epilobium angustifolium L.
Eng. Fireweed.

Robust herb forming large colonies, stems erect simple 30-250cm, almost smooth to covered in stiff hairs above. Leaves sublanceolate 2.5-20x0.4-2.5cm, smooth or with stiff hairs on midrib beneath, margin toothed and arranged spirally on stem. Inflorescence an elongated spike, with pedicels 0.7-1.2cm; flowers drooping when in bud. Flowers deep pink (rarely white) with 4 petals 12-15x7-8mm, ovaries hairy white, 1-2cm long, stigma 4 lobed and extending beyond anthers Stamens 8, capsules 4-7mm on pedicels 0.7-1.5cm

» Common in disturbed mountain areas
» 2800-4000m
» July-September
» Thimphu, Gasa

184 Oenothera biennis L.
Eng: Evening Primrose

Erect herb with a basal rosette, stems 30-200cm branching from base or above, with stiff hairs. Rosette leaves 10-30 x 2-5cm; stem leaves narrowly oblanceolate to oblanceolate or elliptic, 5-20 c 1-5cm, with stiff hairs. Inflorescence a simple spike, usually with secondary spike below main one, stiffly hair, flowers opening around sunset. Floral tube 2-4cm, yellowish, petals 4, yellow, 12-30x14-30mm. Capsules 2-4cm narrowly ellipsoid to ellipsoid, pubescent.

» Found in cultivation and in open grassy and disturbed areas.
» 1000-2400m

- » June - September
- » Thimphu
- » Native of North America, ornamental and now naturalised.

....

Oleaceae
Olive family

119 *Osmanthus suavis* Clarke
Dzo: Chhatshe Kam
Eng: Osmanthus

Evergreen shrub or small tree 2-10m. Leaves opposite, lanceolate to lanceolate ovate, 30-70m x 11-32mm, apex and base gradually tapering to point, margins toothed. Inflorescence of 3-9 flowers in axillary or terminal fascicle (bundle). Flowers very fragrant, white or cream with four rounded corolla lobes, tube 4-9mm long. Fruit blue black 5-12mm.

- » In a variety of sub-alpine habitats, Rhododendron forest, dry forest, open hillsides.
- » 2400-3700m
- » April- June
- » Haa, Paro, Thimphu, Chhukha, Punakha, Wangduephodrang, Trongsa, Bumthang, Mongar
- » Wood very hard.

38 *Jasminum grandiflorum* L.
Eng: Royal Jasmine

Robust almost self-supporting, scrambling shrub to 3m tall. Leaves opposite pinnate with 5-13 subsessile leaflets; petiole 7-25mm long. Leaflets very variable in shape; terminal leaflet 15-40x5-12mm, lateral leaflets 14-25x4-11mm. Inflorescence a widely branching 3-many-flowered cyme, rarely solitary; peduncles 15-40mm, pedicels 6-20mm. Calyx glabrous, teeth 5, setaceous, 4-7mm long. Flowers sweet scented, white, sometimes flushed purple-red, especially in bud. Corolla tube 14-22mm at anthesis; 5 lobes, 8-18x5-9mm. Fruit globose, glossy black, 5-9mm long, paired.

- » Dry, rocky areas in hot valleys, roadsides.
- » 1050-1450m

» June-October
» Punakha, Trashigang
» Widely grown throughout warm temperate and subtropical regions of the world. Used as source of "Oil of Jasmine" for perfume.

....

Orchidaceae
Orchid family

292 Aorchis spathulata (Lindl.) Verm.

Terrestial herb 7-18cm tall. Stem smooth, 6-13cm tall; basal sheaths 2, tubular, overlapping, 1-2.5cm long. Leaf ovate to ovate elliptic, 3-7x1.2-2.9cm. Inflorescence densely 1-4 flowered; Flowers 0.7-1.2cm across; sepals and petals purple-pink, lip purple pink, spotted with dark purple, base yellowish-green; pedicel an ovary slender, twisted, 0.9-1.5cm long.

» On turf on open hillsides, damp rocks, in the open, damp grazed meadow, among dwarf Rhododendron/ Abies.
» 3050-4500m
» June-July
» Haa, Paro, Thimphu, Punakha, Trongsa, Bumthang, Trashigang, Gasa, Trashiyangtse.

291 Anthogonium gracile Lindley
Eng: Slender Anthogonium

Terrestrial plant 14-40cm tall. Pseudobulbs ovoid, 0.5-1.9 x 0.8-1.6cm. Leafy stem sheathed at base, 2- to 5-leaved at apex, 3-6.5cm long. Leaves oblong-lanceolate to narrowly elliptic, many-veined, 7-30x0.4-3.2cm. Inflorescence laxly 5 to 10 flowered. Flowers 1-1.8cm long, dark pink to white, lip spotted dark purple, anther bright yellow; pedicel and ovary 1-1.8cm long. Fruit narrowly ellipsoid, 1-2.4 x 0.3-0.5cm.

» Shady banks, in warm broad-leaved forests, on dry exposed hilltops, on rock ledges.
» 1300-3000m
» June-October
» Chhuka, Samdrupjongkhar, Thimphu, Punakha, Trongsa, Zhemgang, Bumthang, Mongar, Lhuentse, Trashigang,

293 *Arundina graminifolia* (D. Don) Hochreutiner
Eng: Bamboo Orchid

Terrestrial plant to 3m tall. Stem erect, cane-like, leafy throughout, 0.7-1.3cm wide. Leaves distichous, linear lanceolate, acuminate, sessile, bases clasping, 8.5-24x0.7-2.5cm. Inflorescence erect, racemose or paniculate, few- to many-flowered; peduncle glabrous, intermittently sheathed. Flowers 4 x 4cm, magenta to pinkish-white, sometimes with a yellow throat; pedicel and ovary c.3cm long. Fruit long-ellipsoid, 3.5-7x0.8-1.5cm.

» In tropical valleys, dry roadside banks, among bamboo, in hot mixed forest and open spaces on hillsides, in tall grass, in scrub jungle on sandy soil.
» 200-2160m
» January-November
» Sarpang, Samdrupjongkhar, Punakha, Wangduephodrang, Trongsa Mongar, Lhuentse, Trashigang

379 *Bulbophyllum emarginatum* (Finet) J.J. Smith

Plant epiphytic to 10cm tall. Pseudobulbs conical-pyriform, 2-3 x 0.5-0.7cm. Leaf, linear-oblong to linear-ovate, 3.5-8.5 x 1.1-2.2cm. Inflorescence basal from pseudobulb, erect, umbellate, 2-3-flowers. Flowers 3.5-5cm long; sepals purple with darker stripes, petals white striped purple, lip purple; pedicel and ovary filiform, 1.8-2.2cm long.

» In rain forest on a narrow open ridge.
» 1460-2600m
» October-December
» Punakha

246 *Bulbophyllum leopardinum* (Wallich) Lindley

var. *leopardinum*

Epiphytic. Pseudobulbs clustered, cylindric-ovoid to cylindric-obpyriform. Leaf, apical, oblongelliptic, coriaceous, rigid, jointed, 7.5-20x2.5-6cm; petiole channelled, 2.5-7cm long. Inflorescence very short, 1-3 flowered. Flowers fasciculate, globose-campanulate, 2-3cm across; sepals and petals pale yellowish-brown to greenish, densely spotted with purple, lip deep crimson-purple, column pale yellow. Fruit stalked, cylindric, 3-3.6 x 1.1-1.5cm; stalk 4-5.7cm long.

» 1400-2300m
» (April-)June- October
» Punakha, Trashigang

var. *tuberculatum*

Differs from var. *leopardinum* as follows: Flowers 4.5 x 3.5cm; sepals and petals mottled with dark scarlet; pedicel and ovary 2cm long. Sepals and petals densely, minutely papillose internally. Lip ovate, acute, densely tuberculate-papillose on upper surface (lacking toothed auricles at base).

» 1800m
» March
» Trashigang
» Endemic

247 Bulbophyllum umbellatum Lindley
Eng: Umbrella Bulbophyllum

Epiphytic plant, 7-18cm tall. Psuedobulbs ovoid to broadly conical, 2.5-2x1-1.5cm. Leaf 1, coriaceous, narrowly oblong, 4-13 x 1-2cm; petiole 0.6-2cm long. Inflorescence shorter than leaves, umbellate to subracemose, 2-4 flowered. Flowers 1-1.5cm long; sepals and petals variable, yellow green, pale to yellow brown, unspotted or finely spotted with pink-purple, lip green yellow, green or green with purple, column foot green-white unspotted or spotted with purple; pedicels and ovary slender, 1.5-1.6cm long.

» On mossy cliff-face in evergreen forests.
» 1000-2000m
» March-May
» Punakha, Trashigang, Trashiyangtse

55 Cephalanthera damasonium (Miller) Druce

Terrestrial plant up to 60cm tall; rhizome short, creeping with thick roots. Leaves alternate up stem, oblong ovate becoming lanceolate above, 4-8x2-3.5cm; basal leaves reduced to sheaths 2.5-3.5cm long. Inflorescence laxly spicate, up to 15-flowered; rachis 6-7cm long. Flowers seldom fully opened, 1.5-2.5cm long; white with orange yellow markings on the lip; ovary ,sessile, spirally twisted, 1-1.5cm long. Fruit cylindric-fusiform, 2-3 x 0.3-0.5cm.

» In *Quercus griffithii*, *Lyonia ovalifolia* and *Pinus roxburghii* forest.
» 1990- 2550m
» May-June
» Punakha, Wangduephodrang, Trashigang, Trashiyangtse

384 *Chusua pauciflora* (Lindl.) P.F. Hunt

Terrestrial plant 5-40cm tall. Stem glabrous, 9-21cm tall. Leaves 1-5, distant along stem, narrowly oblong, sheathing at base, 3-15x0.5-1.8cm. Inflorescence secund, 3 to 6 flowered. Flowers 1.5-2cm across, uniformly purple-pink, pollinia white.

» On sandy flats by lake, alpine meadows, rocky areas and open ground among dwarf *Rhododendron* scrub, marshy streamside in open *Juniperus* and *Berberis* scrub, under and openings of fir/bamboo/ rhododendron forest.
» 2890-4880m
» June-September
» Haa, Paro, Thimphu, Punakha, Trongsa, Bumthang, Gasa, Trashiyangtse

249 *Cleisostoma racemiferum* (Lindl.) Garay

Epiphyte to 40 cm tall. Stem covered by leaf sheaths, 0.7-1.2cm wide; sheaths overlapping, 2-3cm long. Leaves oblong, spreading, coriaceous, keeled beneath, apex unequally 2-lobed, jointed, 14-36x1.8-3.5cm. Inflorescence lateral, paniculate, laxly many-flowered; peduncle sheathed, 15-25cm long. Flowers 6-8mm across; sepals and petals brownish-black, edged with yellow, lip yellowish, column white; pedicel and ovary 0.3-1cm long.

» In evergreen oak forest and on *Quercus griffithii*.
» 600-2150m
» May-June
» Chhukha, Punakha, Mongar, Trashigang, Trashiyangtse

385 Cleisostoma williamsonii (H.G. Reich.) Garay

Epiphytic plant sometimes lithophytic, clustered, pendent, 35-45cm long. Stem covered by leaf sheaths, 2-3mm wide. Leaves distichous, linear-terete, sessile, 9-13 x 0.1cm. Inflorescence lateral from half-way down leaf-sheath, racemose or paniculate, pendent, laxly many-flowered; peduncle sheathed at base, 1cm long; floral bracts triangular, 1 x 0.5mm. Flowers 3-5mm across; sepals and petals pink, lip pale purple; pedicel and ovary slender, 2-3mm long. Fruit ovoid, ridged, 5-7 x 3-4mm.

» On dry rock face in broad-leaved and *Pinus roxburghii* forest, in hot dry valleys.
» 1160-1910m
» May
» Punakha, Trongsa, Trashigang, Trashiyangtse

56 Coelogyne cristata Lindley
Eng: Crested Coelogyne

Plant epiphytic (occasionally lithophytic), 13-30cm tall; pseudobulbs spaced 5-6cm apart. Pseudobulbs cylindric-ovoid, smooth, 5-7.5x2-4cm. Leaves 2, linear-lanceolate, acute, margins slightly undulate, sessile, 15-30x2-2.7cm. Inflorescence heteranthous, pendent, 3 to 10 flowered opening together. Flowers 5-9cm across; sepals and petals white, lip white with yellow keels between the lateral lobes and crenulate plates on the mid-lobe . Fruit c.4 x 2cm.

» On large trees and rocks in shaded and upper montane forest, warm broad-leaved forest, on N-facing slope of valley.
» 1330-2600m
» February-July
» Punakha, Wangduephodrang

156 Coelogyne ovalis Lindley
Eng: Fringed Coelogyne

Plant epiphytic or lithophytic. Pseudobulbs ovoid-fusiform to fusiform, smooth. Leaves 2, narrowly elliptic, acute to acuminate, 9-17x2.5-4cm. Inflorescence few-flowered opening in succession. Flowers 3-4cm across, pale yellowish-green, lip marked brown, keels darker brown, column yellowish green; pedicel and ovary slender, 1-1.3cm long.

» On branches of trees, on humus covered rocks in hill forest, ravine in subtropical forest.
» 800-1800m
» March-July(-December)
» Samtse, Samdrupjongkhar, Punakha, Trongsa, Zhemgang

250 *Cymbidium erythraeum* Lindley

Plant epiphytic or lithophytic, 25-75cm tall. Pseudobulbs ovoid, 2.5-5 x 1.5-5cm. Leaves 5-9, distichous, linear-oblong, 35-90 x 0.8-1.6cm. Inflorescence erect to horizontal, arching, 5- to 14-flowered; peduncle sheathed, 9.5-20cm long; rachis slender, 13-25cm long. Flowers fragrant, c.4 x 5cm (across); sepals and petals greenish, spotted and striped red-brown, lip yellowish to white, spotted red-brown, callus cream-white, column yellow, lateral lobes red-veined; pedicel and ovary 1.1-1.7cm long. Fruit fusiform-ellipsoid, 5.5-6.5 x 2.5-3cm.

» In hot valleys, on trees, rocks, roadsides and steep banks, open mossy evergreen oak forest;
» 1660-2330m
» August-November
» Punakha, Trongsa, Zhemgang

251 *Cymbidium hookerianum* Rchb. f.
Dzo: Olachhoto

Plant epiphytic or lithophytic, 45-70cm tall. Pseudo bulbs narrowly ovoid, 3-6 x 1.5-3.5cm. Leaves 4-8, linear-elliptic, jointed, 40-80 x 1.4-2.1cm. Inflorescence arching to pendent, 6-15 flowers; rachis zigzag, slender, 20-30cm long. Flowers strongly fragrant, 5-7cm across; sepals and petals apple-green, red-spotted at base, lip cream to yellow with green margins, maroon-spotted or blotched, callus cream with red spots; pedicel and ovary 3.5-6cm long. Fruit fusiform-ellipsoid, stalked, beaked, c.13 x 4cm.

» On trees or steep banks in dense, damp forest, evergreen oak forest
» 1660-2330m
» February-May
» Chhukha, Samdrupjongkhar, Punakha, Wangduephodrang , Trongsa, Bumthang, Mongar

252 *Cymbidium iridioides* D. Don

Plant epiphytic or lithophytic, 45-85cm tall. Pseudobulbs 5-17 x 2-6cm. Leaves c.10, linear-elliptic, acute, mid-green, 35-90 x 1.5-4.2cm. Inflorescence 7- 20 flowers. Flowers 4-8cm across, fragrant; sepals and petals yellowish-green, veined red to ginger-brown, lip yellowish, red-spotted, lateral lobes red-veined. Fruit fusiform-ellipsiod, 6-8 x 3-4cm.

» On trees, in dense forest.
» 1160-2330m
» October-November
» Samtse, Chhukha, Mongar, Trashigang

207 *Cypripedium himalaicum* Rolfe.
Eng: Himalayan Garden Slipper Orchid

Plant 14-30 cm tall. Leaves 3-4, closely spaced on stems, elliptic-ovate, acute, slightly pubescent on upper surface, glabrous beneath, ciliate. Inflorescence one flowered and very fragrant 6 cm across; claret and green, crimson-purple or reddish chocolate, column yellow; pedicel and ovary long, pubescent, 1.6-2.9 cm long.

» Found in grass-clad limestone boulders, in crevices, among small shrub on steep hillsides, in alpine pastures with *Primula sikkimensis* and *Rhododendron anthopogon* and in *Cassiope* scrub, in partial shade in sub-alpine *Betula utilis* forest.
» 2800-4900m
» May-July
» Haa, Paro, Thimphu, Bumthang, Gasa

381 *Dendrobium aphyllum* (Roxb.) C.E.C. Fischer
Eng: Leafless Dendrobium

Plant epiphytic; 22-65cm long. Leaves lanceolate to ovate-lanceolate, 4.5-10 x 0.4-3cm. Inflorescence lateral, arising from nodes of old stems, 1-flowered; peduncle attenuate. Flower fragrant, 2-5cm across; sepals and petals pink to pale purple, lip pale yellow with purple lines basally. Fruit clavate, cylindric, 3-6 x 0.6-0.9cm.

» On trees on river banks in subtropical and open forest.
» 340-1660m
» March-June
» Samtse, Chhukha, Sarpang, Samdrupjongkhar, Punakha

165 Dendrobium chrysanthum Wall.
Eng: Golden Flowered Dendrobium

Plant epiphytic or lithophytic, pendent, 60-100cm long; 2-3mm thick. Stem pendent, straight to wavy, internodes covered by sheaths, yellowish beneath. Leaves distichous, elliptic-lanceolate, sessile, with 5-7 prominent veins, 5.5-21 x 1.5-4.5cm. Inflorescence on leafy or leafless stems, 2- to 4-flowered. Flowers fleshy, 1.5-2.5cm across, golden yellow, lip with two separate or confluent deep purple spots. Fruit ovoid-pyriform, long-stalked,2.5-4.5 x 1.5-2.2cm.

»   In warm broad-leaved forest, on north facing slopes.
»   900-2160m
»   February-October
»   Chhukha, Punakha, Trongsa, Zhemgang, Trashigang, Gasa

166 Dendrobium densiflorum Lindl.
Eng: Pineapple Orchid

Plant epiphytic or lithophytic, 30-45cm tall. Stems strongly club-shaped, yellow, sheathless. Leaves 3 or 4 on upper part of stem, oblong lanceolate to broadly elliptic-ovate, prominently veined, jointed, 12-16 x 2.6-6cm. Inflorescence pendent, axillary, densely many-flowered; rachis 6-16cm long. Flowers membranous, 3-4cm across; sepals and petals pale yellow, lip rich orange, paler towards margins; pedicel and ovary slender, 2.7-3.3cm long. Fruit clavate, 3.5-4.5 x 0.6-1cm.

»   In broadleaved riverine and wet forest, on *Rhododendron* and *Lithocarpus*, rarely on rocks.
»   330-2000m
»   April-July
»   Sarpang, Punakha, Trashigang

382 Dendrobium devonianum Paxton

Plant epiphytic or lithophytic, 30-50cm tall. Stem slender, erect or weakly zigzag, jointed. Leaves alternate, ovate-lanceolate to linear-lanceolate. Inflorescence lateral, arising from nodes, clustered, 1- to 3-flowered. Flowers 2-4cm long and wide; sepals cream to white, purple-tinged, petals cream to white with pink-purple towards apex, lip cream or white tinged with pink, yellow in centre. Lip simple, orbicular-cordate, shortly clawed at concave base, margins deeply fimbriate, 2-2.8 x 2-3.5cm.

» On *Quercus lamellosa* and *Citrus reticulata* trees,
   S-facing slopes and on rocks.
» 800-2050m
» (April-)May-August
» Chhukha, Punakha, Wangduephodrang, Trongsa,
   Mongar

383 *Dendrobium falconeri* Hook.

Plant epiphytic, pendent. Stem long, slender, branched,
pendent, jointed, bearing few leaves from bead-like nodes.
Leaves few, linear-oblong, jointed with internode sheath,
3-8 x 0.15-0.4cm. Inflorescence lateral, arising from
nodes, 1 flower from each peduncle (occasionally a second
peduncle creating a 2-flowered inflorescence). Flowers 3.4-
5cm long; sepals and petals pale pink tipped with purple,
lip white with a central dark purple spot surrounded by a
yellow-orange ring, apex purple; pedicel and ovary slender,
glabrous, 1.5-1.8cm long.

» On oak and other trees, hanging in clusters in full sun,
   in wet valleys, in *Quercus griffithii* and *Rhododendron
   arboreum* forest.
» 1660-2500m
» (March-)May-June
» Samdrupjongkhar, Punakha, Wangduephodrang ,
   Trongsa, Mongar, Trashigang, Trashiyangtse.

167 *Dendrobium hookerianum* Lindl.

Plant epiphytic or lithophytic, 30-70cm tall. Stems pendent,
curved, jointed, many alternate leaves. Leaves elliptic-
lanceolate to oblong-lanceolate, sessile, jointed, many
veined, 4-12 x 1.2-3cm. Inflorescences lateral, arising from
nodes on leafy-stem, 2- to 4-flowered; rachis weakly zigzag,
3-4cm long. Flowers 4-5cm across, pure rich golden-yellow,
lip usually with two oval purple-red blotches on the disc
with red striations extending to base, column with 2 red-
pink stripes. Fruit ovoid, 6-7 x 1.5-2cm.

» On oak and other trees and rocks.
» 330-2330m
» July-October
» Samdrupjongkhar, Trongsa, Zhemgang, Trashigang,
   Trashiyangtse

157 *Dendrobium jenkinsii* Wall.

Plant epiphytic or lithophytic, 6-7cm tall; roots fasciculate. Pseudobulbs aggregated, 1.5-2cm long. Leaf 1, apical from pseudobulb, oblong ovate, obtuse, shortly petiolate, 1.5-2.8 x 0.5-0.8cm. Inflorescence lateral from pseudo bulb, 1- or 2-flowered. Flower 4cm long, uniformly yellow-orange; pedicel and ovary slender, 4-5cm long.

» On *Quercus* sp., on North facing rockface.
» 1100-1400m
» April-May
» Samdrupjongkhar, Punakha, Wangduephodrang , Mongar

380 *Dendrobium nobile* Lindl.
Eng: Noble Dendrobium

Plant epiphytic or lithophytic, forming large clumps. Stems clustered, covered with sheaths, beaded, wavy to weakly zigzag, jointed, yellowish, 30-50cm long. Leaves oblong to spathulate, emarginate, many-veined, 7-13.5 x 1-3cm. Inflorescences lateral, arising from nodes, 2- to 4-flowered; peduncle 1-flowered from each node, 0.6-1.5cm long. Flowers variable, waxy, fragrant, 6-8cm across; sepals and petals white at base grading to pinkish-mauve above, lip rich maroon at base grading to yellow or white with mauve to purple margins; pedicel and ovary glabrous, 3-4.8cm long.

» On oak trees in warm dense broad-leaved forest, on rocks in river valleys, on citrus in plantation.
» 800-2000m
» March-May(-June)
» Chhukha, Sarpang, Punakha, Wangduephodrang, Mongar, Trashigang, Trashiyangtse

158 *Eria amica* H.G. Reichenbach

Plant epiphytic, 12-27cm tall. Pseudobulbs 4-17 x 0.7-1.5cm. Leaves 2, arising from pseudobulb apex, linear-lanceolate to oblonglanceolate, acute, tapered to petiolate base, 7-21 x 0.8-2cm. Inflorescence arising from axils of leaf-sheaths, 1-3 from each pseudobulb, erect to suberect, laxly 6- to 12-flowered; peduncle slender, 3-4cm long; rachis slender, pubescent, 5-6cm long. Flowers 7-9mm across; sepals and petals buff-yellow to greenish-yellow with red veins and yellow apices, lip pink with bright yellow apex and red lateral lobes and keels.

» 500-1660m
» March-May
» Punakha, Trongsa

57 *Eria coronaria* (Lindley) H.G. Reichenbach

Plant epiphytic, 12-38cm tall. Pseudobulbs cylindric, slender, 5-18 x 0.2-0.4cm. Leaves 2, elliptic to ovate-lanceolate, jointed, many-veined, subsessile, grooved, subopposite, thickly membranous, 8.5-18 x 2.3-4.8cm. Inflorescence, erect to arching, 4- to 6-flowered; rachis glabrous, 2-3cm long. Flowers 2-2.5cm long, white to pale purple, lip flushed with purple, lateral lobes striped with purple, mid-lobe yellow with purple dots; pedicel and ovary glabrous, 1.4-1.6cm long. Fruit ellipsoid, slightly dilated towards apex, 2-2.5 x 0.7-0.9cm.

» On trees and rocky banks
» 1160-2300m
» October-January
» Punakha, Trongsa, Zhemgang, Trashigang

233 *Gastrochilus acutifolius* (Lindley) Kuntse

Epiphytic plant 14-18cm tall. Stem slender, erect, weakly zigzag, 10-30x0.5cm; 1.4-1.6cm long. Leaves distichous, linear-lanceolate to oblonglanceolate, coriaceous, jointed, 8-15x1.7-4cm. Inflorescence corymbose, densely many-flowered. Flowers fleshy, 1.5-2cm across; sepals and petals orange-yellow, yellowish-red to yellowish-green, spotted or mottled with brown, lip white with a yellow centre, speckled with red, column stained with pale purple; pedicel and ovary slender, 1.5-1.7cm long. Fruit cylindric to ovoid, ridged, 4-6x0.7-0.9cm.

» 1000-2000m
» August-December
» Sarpang, Punakha

386 *Ione bicolor* (Lindl.) Lindl.

Plant epiphytic or occasionally lithophytic, 7-12cm tall. Pseudo bulbs obpyriform or flask-shaped, narrowed to apex, base broad, 1.2-2x0.6-1.8cm. Leaf linear-oblong, obliquely emarginated at apex, strongly keeled beneath, 4.8-

9.5 x 0.6-1cm. Inflorescences 1 or 2, laxly 6- to 8-flowered; peduncle filiform, glabrous, sheathed at base and above, 2.5-4.5cm long. Flowers 7-9mm long; sepals and petals white-transparent (or flushed purple), veined purple, lip deep purple, column green-yellow. Fruit ovoid, ridged, stalked, 4-5 x 2-3mm; stalk 3-4mm long.

» On small lichen-covered trees.
» 1700-2330m
» October-December
» Chhukha, Sarpang

253 *Ione cirrhata* Lindl.

Plant epiphytic, to 20cm tall. Pseudobulbs rugose, bright green, 2.5-3.5 x 1-1.5cm. Leaf erect, oblong to oblanceolate, obtuse, 9-16 x 2-3.1cm. Inflorescence laxly 4- to 8-flowered; peduncle slender, 15-22cm long; rachis slender, glabrous, 5.5cm long. Flowers pendent, smelling of honey, 2-2.5cm long; sepals and petals off-white with purple veins, lip rich purple; pedicel and ovary curved, 1-1.6cm long. Fruit pyriform, long-stalked, 1.5-1.9 x 0.6-0.7cm; stalk filiform, 1.5-2cm long.

» 1600-2000m
» October-November
» Punakha

254 *Oreorchis foliosa* var. *indica* (Lindl.) N. Pearce & P.J. Cribb
Eng: Indian Oreorchis

Terrestial herb 16-32 cm tall. Scape 11-28cm tall, lower part enclosed by tubular sheaths. Leaf 1 from psuedobulb apex, oblong-lanceolate, acuminate, 8-12 x 1-2.5cm; petiole 2-4cm long. Inflorescence laxly up to 7-flowered; Flowers c 1 cm long, purple to pink, blotched with reddish-purple, lip white with purple spots.

» On cliff faces, in *Picea/Tsuga* forest, dappled shade and open meadows.
» 2500-4500m
» June-August
» Haa, Paro, Thimphu, Punakha, Trongsa, Bumthang, Gasa

248 *Paphiopedilum fairrieanum* (Lindl.) Stein

Plant clump forming, to 27cm tall. Leaves 4-8, arranged in a fan on a straight stem, linear-oblong, acute, minutely toothed at apex, margins serrulate towards apex, mid-to dark green, 7.5-28 x 2-3cm. Inflorescence 1- (rarely 2-) flowered; peduncle 12-45cm long, slender, light green covered with purplish hairs. Flowers small to large, showy; sepals white, veined green and purple, dorsal sepal suffused with purple; lip yellow-green to olive with dark veining; staminode yellow, veined with green and purple in centre; pedicel and ovary purple pubescent, 3.5-6cm long.

» On outcrops of limestone, on dry, sheltered, grassy slopes.
» 1400-2200m
» October-December
» Sarpang, Mongar, Samdrupjongkhar

58 *Pholidota pallida* Lindl.

Plant epiphytic or lithophytic, 10-40cm tall. Pseudobulbs slender to swollen, sheathed, 2.5-6cm long. Leaf 1, oblong to linear-lanceolate, herbaceous, 6-30 x 1.5-6cm. Inflorescence densely many-flowered; peduncle wiry, 5-18 x 0.03-0.1cm; rachis 5-11cm long. Flowers membranous, fragrant, 5-6mm across, white or creamy-white, tinged with pink. Fruit ellipsoid, 1-1.5 x 0.5-0.8cm.

» On rock face and hanging over cliff edges in hot mixed forest.
» 1000-2330m
» May-August
» Sarpang, Punakha, Mongar, Gasa

53 *Pleione humilis* (J.E. Smith) D. Don

Plant epiphytic or lithophytic, 7-10cm tall. Pseudobulbs flask-shaped, 2-6 x 0.8-2cm. Leaf 1, oblanceolate to elliptic, acute, produced after the flowers, 18-25 x 2.8-3.5cm. Inflorescence 1-2 flowers. Flowers spreading to pendent; sepals and petals white, lip white spotted and streaked with crimson or yellow-brown, with a central pale yellow zone; pedicel and ovary 2-3cm long. Dorsal sepal linear-oblanceolate, 3.4-4.7 x 0.6-0.7cm; lateral sepals obliquely oblanceolate, 4-5.3 x 0.7-0.9cm. Petals obliquely oblanceolate, 3.1-4.2 x 0.5-0.7cm. Lip oblong-elliptic, obscurely 3-lobed in front, margin lacerate (in apical halo, 3.4-4.4 x 2.5-3.5cm; lateral lobes erect-incurved; callus of 5-7 bearded lamellae.

» On moss on trees, forming rings or collars around trunk, on moss-covered stones, in cloud forest.
» 1850-3200m
» January-March
» Thimphu, Punakha

290 *Pleione praecox* (J.E. Smith) D. Don

Plant epiphytic or lithophytic, 10-30cm tall. Pseudobulbs turbinate, contracted above into a beak, green mottled with reddish-brown or purplish, 1.5-3 x 1-1.5cm. Leaves 1 or 2, elliptic-lanceolate to elliptic, sheathed at base, 15-26 x 3-7cm; petiole 4-6cm long; sheath red-purple spotted. Inflorescence 1 (rarely 2)-flowered, produced after leaves have fallen. Flowers large and showy; white to pinkish-purple with yellow lamellae on the lip; pedicel and ovary c.1.5cm long.

» On moss-covered rock faces, in humus pockets, on Rhododendron and on ground in dense oak forest.
» 1200-3400m
» September-November(-December)
» Chhukha, Thimphu, Punakha, Wangduephodrang, Trongsa, Mongar, Trashigang, Trashiyangtse, Gasa

294 *Satyrium nepalense* D. Don

Terrestial plant to 30cm tall. Stem leafy below, densely covered with sheaths above. Leaves oblong-lanceolate, c 15x3cm long rather fleshy. Inflorescence densely flowered. Flowers small pink with spur shorter than ovary. Perianth segments recurved, subsimilar in length, up to 7 mm long; dorsal sepal linear-oblong; lateral sepals obliquely-oblong; petals linear. Labellum broadly oblong, erect, hooded, up to 9 mm long, 10 mm broad, with 2 slender spurs at base, tapering into a fine point, variable and sometimes unequal in length, 10-15 mm long.

» Forest openings, grassy patches.
» 1800-4350m
» July-November
» Haa, Paro, Thimphu, Punakha, Wangduephodrang, Gasa, Trongsa, Bumthang, Mongar, Lhuentse, Trashiyangtse.

387 *Schoenorchis gemmata* (Lindley) J.J. Smith

Small epiphytic plant, pendent. Stems curved, leafy, covered by leaf sheaths, 8-30cm long. Leaves distichous, linear-terete, fleshy, curved, apex unequally 2- to 3-lobed, base sheathing, jointed, 5-10 x 0.2-0.6cm. Inflorescence suberect to pendent, paniculate, laxly many-flowered; peduncle glabrous 2.5-4cm long; rachis glabrous, 4-5.5cm long. Flowers 3-4mm long; sepals white to bright purple with white apices, petals bright purple, lip white with purple on the spur and lateral lobes; pedicel and ovary stout, 1.5-2mm long. Fruit ovoid, ridged, shortly stalked, 3-4 x 2-2.3mm.

» In montane forests.
» 830-2000m
» May-June
» Samdrupjongkhar, Punakha

159 *Spathoglottis ixioides* (D. Don) Lindley

Terrestrial plant 5.5-22cm tall. Pseudobulbs globose-ovoid, fibrous-sheathed at base, 0.5-1.5 x 0.7-1.4cm. Leaves 2 or 3, linear to oblong, acuminate, sessile, sheathing at base, 3.5-17 x 0.1-0.7cm. Inflorescence slender, erect, laxly 1- to 3-flowered; peduncle slender, bearing few sheaths; rachis 1-4.5cm long. Flowers 2-3cm across, bright yellow with small purple spots at base oflip; pedicel and ovary pubescent, clavate, 1.8-2.6cm long.

» On moist moss covered rock in open *Pinus* and dense mixed forest, wet bank by roadside with scattered scrub, among matted roots of *Gaultheria* sp.
» 1950-3650m
» July-August
» Chhukha, Punakha, Bumthang, Mongar, Trashigang, Trashiyangtse

295 *Spiranthes sinensis* (Persoon) Ames
Dzo: Meto Yoenkom

Terrestrial plant to 45cm tall. Leaves 3-5, in a basal rosette, oblong-elliptic to linear lanceolate, acute, glossy dark green, 5-16 x 0.4-1cm. Inflorescence densely many-flowered, spirally arranged; peduncle glandular-hairy, bearing 2 or 3 distant sheaths. Flowers spreading, c.3mm long, pink with a white lip or white; pedicel and ovary glandular, 3-6mm long. Fruit ovoid, glandular-pubescent, 6 x 3.5mm.

» In damp, grassy clearings in juniper and rhododendron scrub, damp roadside banks, in subtropical forest, among boulders on open hillside.
» 300-3000m
» March-October
» Sarpang, Haa, Paro, Thimphu, Punakha, Wangduephodrang, Trongsa, Bumthang, Mongar, Trashigang, Trashiyangtse, Gasa

255 *Vanda bicolor* Griffith

Epiphytic plant. Stem leafy, 16-26cm long. Leaves oblong, curved, somewhat twisted in the middle, 7-21 x 1.1-2.3cm. Inflorescence piercing through the leaf sheath, laxly 3- to 6-flowered. Flowers 4-5cm across; sepals and petals tessellated, yellowish-brown inside, violet externally, lip violet and gold, spur white, column white, pedicel and ovary slender, 4.8 cm long. Fruit long stalked.

» On trees in open forest and on river banks.
» 700-2000m
» February – April
» Samdrupjongkhar, Trongsa, Mongar, Lhuentse, Trashigang
» Endemic

256 *Vanda cristata* Lindley
Eng: Comb Trudelia

Plant epiphytic, 12-30cm tall. Stem stout, covered by leaf sheaths, 7.5-15cm long. Leaves recurved, 7.5-12.5 x 0.6-1.8cm. Inflorescence 2- to 6-flowered; peduncle glabrous, sheathed, 2-3.5cm long; rachis glabrous, weakly zigzag, 2-5cm long. Flowers 3.7-5cm across; sepals and petals yellow to green, lip golden-yellow to white, striped with violet-purple to red-brown. Fruit long-stalked, cylindric-obovoid, 7-9 x 0.5-0.9cm (including the stalk).

» On tree trunks of *Rhododendron arboreum* and *Skimmia* spp.
» 1000-2100m
» April-June
» Chhukha, Punakha, Trongsa, Trashigang, Trashiyangtse

Oxalidaceae
Wood sorrel family

143 Oxalis corniculata L.
Eng: Creeping Wood Sorrel, Creeping Oxalis

Herb with creeping stems, up to 30cm, rooting at nodes with erect leafy branches. Leaves alternate and compound with three leaflets, each of which are heart shaped, 15-18mm long. Peduncles axilary, 3-8cm, 1-5 flowered. Sepals linear elliptic 3.5-5mm long. Petals yellow spathulate, notched at tip, mosty 5-7mm. Capsules 10-20 x 2.5mm, puberurlous.

» A cosmopolitan weed on disturbed soils roadsides and cultivation.
» 250-2450m
» February-August.
» Samtse, Chhukha, Sarpang, Samdrupjongkhar, Haa, Paro, Thimphu, Trongsa
» A widespread weed of unknown origin. Very variable species. Leaves eaten as vegetable and as cure for scurvy. Name oxalis comes from the Greek word "oxys" for sour referring to the acidic taste of the leaves.

....

Papaveraceae
Poppy family

135 Argemone mexicana L.
Eng: Mexican Poppy, Prickly Poppy

Annual branched herb, 0.3-1m. A prickly, glabrous, branching herb with yellow juice and showy yellow flowers,. Leaves elliptic-obovate, pinnatifid with 3-7 pairs of oblong, acute lobes, base cordate, margin coarsely spinous-dentate, glaucous-green with pale marking along veins, prickly on veins beneath. Capsules 2.5-3.5x1-1.5 cm

» Weed of waste ground in subtropical zone
» Upto 300m
» January – December
» Native to tropical America, widely naturalized. Seed produces oil used for burning in lamps and also used to treat skin diseases.

136 *Cathcartia villosa* Hooker
Eng: Himalyan Woodland-Poppy

Perennial herb with stout rootstock and persistent withered leaf bases, flowering stems erect, usually unbranched, 0.6-1.5m; brownish villous throughout. Basal leaves few, broadly ovate or suborbicular, 6-12 x 8-15cm, palmately 3-or 5-lobed, base cordate, 3-5 veined, lobes coarsely and bluntly toothed; petuioles 15-25cm; stem leaves smaller, upper ones sessile. Flowers solitary, terminal and axillary, 1-5 per stem, borne on slender pedicels 3-12cm. Petals always 4, suborbicular, yellow, 2.5-3cm. Ovary cylindric, glabrous. 1.5-2cm bearing sessile stigma with 4-7 radiating lobes. Capsules cylindric, 4-8x0.5-0.7cm, 4-7-valved, dehiscing almost to base leaving persistent placentae attached to stigma.

» Rocky streamsides in hemlock and fir forest
» 2700-4000m
» March-April
» Thimphu, Punakha, Trongsa, Trashigang, Trashiyangtse
» Endemic to Eastern Himalaya, valued horticulturally as an ornamental woodland garden plant.

336 *Meconopsis horridula* Hook. f. & Thomson
Med: Tsher Ngoen, Euit-Pel-Ngoinpo
Eng: Himalayan Poppy, Prickly Blue Poppy

Monocarpic herb with long slender tap root, stems 15-80cm, with dense pale, spreading prickles throughout. Leaves mostly basal, rosetted, oblanceolate, 5-12x1-3cm, obtuse or subacute, base long attenuate, margins entire or shallowly crenately lobed near apex; petioles 2-6cm; stem leaves absent or a few near stem base. Flowers 3-10 on pedicels 2-10cm borne in raceme on stout erect stem, often surrounded by 3-15 single-flowered leafless scapes present. Petals 4-8, usually blue, 2.5-3.5cm Ovary ellipsoid, densely prickly, 5-6 valved, splitting only near apex.

» Alpine cliffs and screes
» 3800-4700m
» July-August
» Haa to Trashigang, widespread.
» Plant used medicinally.

137 *Meconopsis paniculata* Prain.
Med: Euit-Pel-Sep
Eng: Golden Himalayan Poppy

Large monocarpic herb, 1-2.5m, softly yellowish rough hair throughout. Rosette leaves elliptic, 30-50 x 8-20cm, deeply divided; lobes ovate or oblong, coarsely toothed margins; petioles 15-25cm; stem leaves smaller, becoming sessile on upper part of stem. Flowering stem solitary, with short branches; flowers numerous, pendulous, borne singly in upper part and in 2 to 6 flowered lateral cymes in lower part; pedicels 2-6cm. petals 4 yellow, 3-5cm. Ovary subglobose, densely hairy, bearing style 7-10mm with capitate 6-10-lobed stigma. Capsules ellipsoid, 2.5-3 x 1.2-1.5cm, 6-10-valved, dehiscing only near apex, borne on elongated pedicels 5-15cm.

» Grassy and rocky alpine hillsides, amongst *Juniper/ Rhododendron* scrub and in *Fir* forest
» 3350-4260m
» June-August.
» Haa, Paro, Thimphu, Trongsa, Bumthang, Gasa, Lhuentse, Trashigang, Trashiyangtse
» Eaten to quench thirst by high altitude residents after removing the bark put into fire (Jigme, BWS, pers. comm.).

337 *Meconopsis simplicifolia* (D. Don) Walp.
Med: Tsher Ngoen, Euit-Pel-Ngoinpo
Eng: Common Blue Poppy

Herb 30-70cmm, covered in brownish bristles. Basal rosette with few withered leaf remains, leaves all basal, oblanceolate, 4-10x1-2cm, margins entire or with few teeth or shallow rounded lobes; petioles 4-15cm. Flowers solitary, nodding, on 1-5 scapes 30-70cm. Petals 5-8, purple or blue 2-4cm. Filaments same colour as petals. Ovary ellipsoid, without hair or bristly; style slender, with stout capitate stigma. Capsules oblong ellipsoid, 5-7x1-1.5cm, slightly constricted above base, thinly bristly, with 4-9 valves splitting in upper third.

» Juniper/rhododendeon scrub, rocky alpine screes.
» 3350-4600m
» May-July
» Haa, Paro, Thimphu, Punakha, Trongsa, Gasa, Trashiyangtse

Parnassiaceae
Grass of parnassus family

40 *Parnassia delavayi* Franchet

Herb 12-25cm with one white flower on a stem. Leaves broadly ovate 1.4-4cm long. Base of stem leaves surrounding the stem with a tuft of brown hairs in the axil. Flower with five white petals, obovate 7-9 x 3.5-5mm, and with short fringe of hair near base and sides. The connective between the anthers are elongated into a long thick point above the anther cells and sometimes longer than the anthers.

» Open alpine pastures and in fir forests.
» 3800-3950m
» June-July
» Thimphu, Trongsa, Gasa, Bumthang, Lhuentse, Trashiyangtse.

Philadelphaceae
Mock orange family

116 *Deutzia corymbosa* R. Br.

Shrub 1-3m. Leaves ovate, 3.5-7x1.5-2cm, tapering to tip, rounded base, margin finely toothed, sparsely hairy on both surfaces. Flowers in cymose corymbs; calyx 3-4mm including rounded lobes; 5 overlapping petals, white or pink tinged, broadly obovate, 4-6x3-5mm. Stamens 10 in two series, filaments broadened above and often ending in a tooth on either side of anther, 2-4mm long, inner ones shorter. Styles 3-3.5mm. Capsules broadly campanulate, 3-4mm.

» Blue Pine, Hemlock and Fir Forest margins.
» 2100-3350m
» June-July
» Chhukha, Paro, Thimphu, Trongsa, Bumthang, Mongar, Lhuentse, Trashigang

41 *Philadelphus tomentosus* Wall. ex G. Don
Eng: Mock Orange

Shrub 2-6m. Leaves ovate, 4-10x2-5cm, tapering to apex and rounded base, margin minutely toothed, pubescent below.

racemes 3-7 flowers, pedicels 5-10mm. Calyx tube 4-5mm, sparsely pubescent. Petals 4, white, obovate 10-15x7-12mm. Stamens numerous c8mm. Styles c 7mm, sometimes pubescent at base. Capsule c 10x5mm, slightly 4-angled.

» Margins or Blue Pine and Evergreen Oak forests and in dry scrub.
» 2250-3050m
» May-July
» Haa to Trashigang, Gasa and Trashiyangtse

Phytolaccaceae
Pokeweed family

268 Phytolacca acinosa Roxb.
Dzo: Kashakani, Baka, Kashakana
Eng: Indian Pokeweed

Fleshy perennial herb, with stems 0.5 -1.5m. Leaves, opposite, elliptic, 8-30 x 2.5-12cm, glabrous, petioles 1-4cm. Racemes dense, 8-20cm, pinkish, bracts and bracteoles linear. Perianth segments elliptic, c 5x3mm, green at first and becoming purplish. Fruit depressed-globose, 8-10mm across; carpels c 4mm, dark purple.

» Clearings and roadsides, around cultivated areas and settlements, warm broadleaved forests, coniferous forests.
» 900-3000m
» April - September
» Chhukha, Thimphu, Punakha, Trongsa, Wangduephodrang, Bumthang, Trashigang

Plumbaganaceae
Leadwort family

364 Ceratostigma griffithii C.B. Clarke
Eng: Burmese Plumbago

Bushy perennial subshrub 0.5-1.5m; young shoots covered in brownish stiff hair. Leaves obovate-spathulate, 1-8 x0.7-4cm, margins red, both surfaces ciliated. Flowers in rounded terminal and axillary heads, many-flowered. Bracts leaf-like tinged red ciliated. Calyx cilated, awl shaped 7-8mm. Corolla tube 1-1.5cm, pale pink; lobes deep blue, sometimes white, obovate c. 5mm, apex truncate with a small sharp point. Capsule ellipsoid, 3-5mm.

» Amongst scrub on dry hillsides.
» 2130-2400m
» June-October
» Thimphu, Paro, Punakha
» Valued as an ornamental shrub for its bright blue flowers and red foliage in autumn.

....

Poaceae
Grass family

271 *Thysanolaena latifolia* (Roxb. Ex Horneman) Honda.
Eng: Tiger Grass

Culms to 3m, c.0.5cm wide, often arching. Leaf blades 9-59 x1-6.5cm, glabrous, coriaceous, petiole-like base to 0.5cm, usually dark-coloured; sheaths glabrous, rigid, margins occasionally ciliate near apex; ligule c.1.3mm. Inflorescence purplish-brown, drying pale brown, 13-76cm, broadly cylindric, branches suberect, borne singly or fascicled, overlapping, shortly hairy at base on upper side, the lowest 19-56cm. Spikelets 1.4-1.9mm. Lower glume 0.6-0.9x0.4-0.6mm; upper glume 0.8-1.1x0.4-0.7 mm. Sterile floret: lemma 1.3-1.8mm x c. 0.7mm, margins occasionally minutely ciliate. Fertile floret: lemma 1.3-1.6mm, each half c.0.4mm wide, cilia to 1mm; palea 0.4-0.7x0.1-0.2 mm, oblong, apex truncate or slightly notched; anthers 0.4-0.9mm.

» Banks in subtropical forest, often disturbed places (e.g. roadsides); cliffs in disturbed scrub; sometimes cultivated in gardens.
» 200-1800m
» December-August
» Mongar, Trongsa, Thimphu, Chhukha, Trashigang, Trashiyangtse
» Used as brooms and roots used dry or fresh to make a paste to apply to boils and mouth wash

Podophyllaceae
May apple family

42 *Podophyllum hexandrum* Royle.
Eng: Himalayan May Apple, Indian May Apple

A herbaceous plant, with an erect unbranched stem bearing two large terminal lobed leaves encircling the single white pr pale pink flower. Flowers cup-shaped, 2-4 cm across; sepals 3, soon falling; petals 6; stamens 6. Fruit a large scarlet or reddish brown berry 2.5-5 cm, with many seeds imbedded in pulp.

» Open mountain slopes and shady coniferous forest
» 3100 - 4400m
» May - June
» Haa, Thimphu, Bumthang, Gasa
» Rhizome contains podophyllin, recently explored for its anti-cancerous property.

Polygalaceae
Milkwort family

185 *Polygala arillata* D.Don
Dzo: Baahu

Erect shrub or small straggly tree 1.5-5 m; leaves elliptic-ovate to oblong-lanceolate. Flowers yellow to deep orange, sometime tipped purple. Sepals fringed; outer paired one broadly ovate, 3–4mm; outer solitary sepal boat-shaped, 5-7mm; wing sepals obovate, 14–17mm. Keel petal 14–20mm, glabrous; crest laciniate. Filament free in upper 1/3. Style curve. Capsule winged, obong elliptic to suborbicular, 5-12x6-17mm, coriaceous, pubescent to subglabrous, dark reddish purple, conspicuously ribbed at maturity. Seeds subglobose, c 5x4mm, dull black, puberulent at apex; aril irregularly lobed, orange to yellow.

» Common in scrub, clearings and margins of mixed-broad leaved forest.
» 1065-3000m
» May-August
» Chhukha, Samdrupjongkhar, Thimphu, Punakha, Mongar, Trashigang, Lhuentse
» Roots used in the fermentation of beer.

Polygonaceae
Buckwheat family

296 Aconogonon campanulatum (Hook. F.) Hara

Herb, prostrate or erect, 0.3 -1m. Leaves elliptic-ovate, 5-12 x 2-5cm, acumimate, base rounded, appressed hair above, white or brownish tomentose below; petioles to 2cm; ocreae 7-12mm. Flowers in sparsely branched panicles. Perianth bell-shaped, about 5mm, 5 lobes, pink, pedicels c 3mm, scarcely exserted from acute bracts. Achenes strongly trigonous, c. 5.5mm, slightly exserted from perianth.

» Hemlock or fir forests in damp ground.
» 2900-4100m
» June-September(-October)
» Haa, Thimphu, Trongsa, Bumthang, Gasa, Trashiyangtse

77 Aconogonon molle (D. Don) Hara
Dzo: Chuchum, Shido

Subshrub 1-2.5m. Leaves elliptic, 10-18 x3-6cm, tapering to tip, pubescent on both sides, more densely below; petioles up to 2.5cm. Inflorescence of panicles with many branches. Flowers cream coloured, c3mm, white, segments oblong-elliptic; pedicels1-1.5mm, scarcely exserted from rounded bracts. Achenes c2.5mm enclosed in blackish fleshy perianth.

» Warm and cool broadleaved forests
» 900-4250m
» May-November
» Chhukha, Sarpang, Samdrupjongkhar, Haa, Paro, Thimphu, Punakha, Gasa, Wangduephodrang, Trongsa, Bumthang, Mongar.
» Tender young shoots edible as vegetable or in condiments.

297 Bistorta vaccinifolia (Meisner) Green
Eng: Rose Carpet Knotweed

Prostrate subshrub with trailing stolon-forming stems; flowering shoots suberect, up to 15cm. Leaves ovate-elliptic, 1-x 0.6-cm, veined, lacerate. Racemes terminal, sometimes branched, 3-8cm, sparsely flowered. Perianth c 6mm, pink. Stamens and styles shortly exserted. Achenes c 2mm, brown.

- » Edges of Fir and Rhododendron forests.
- » 3200-4400m
- » August- September
- » Haa, Paro, Thimphu, Trongsa, Bumthang, Mongar

298 *Bistorta vivipara* (L.) S.F. Gray
Med: Pangram
Eng: Alpine Bistort

Erect herb with thick fibrous rhizomes. Simple stems 8-30cm. Leaves on lower side ovate, 1.5-11x0.5-2cm, finely pubescent beneath; petioles 2.5-12cm; upper leaves linear and sessile. Racemes 2-7cm with bulbs on lower part. Flowers on upper part of raceme, white or deep pink, perianths 3mm, with stamens sticking out. Achenes c1.5mm, brown.

- » Hillsides, forest clearings
- » 3350-3950m
- » May-September
- » Haa, Paro, Thimphu, Bumthang, Mongar, Gasa, Lhuentsse, Trashiyangtse

103 *Fagopyrum dibotrys* (D. Don) Hara
Dzo: Thiu-Yoep
Eng: Wild Buckwheat

Erect annual herb. Stems up to 2-3m; Lower leaves broadly triangular, up to 13cm long and broad, petioles up to 9cm; ocrea sheathing stem at base 2-3.5cm, brown; upper leaves usually heart-shaped, sessile, semi-clasping stem at base. Flowers in slender branching, spike-like racemes; perianth segments c 3mm, white; achenes ovoid, c 7mm, sharply three-angular, surfaces flat or concave.

- » Roadside ditches and margins or cultivation.
- » 1400-3050m
- » June-October
- » Chhukha, Haa to Mongar
- » Young shoots sometimes eaten in spring.

315 *Persicaria capitata* (D. Don) H. Gross
Eng: Pink Knotweed

Decumbent annual with densly leafy and pubescent internodes. Leaves, ovate to elliptic 1.5-4 x 1-2.3cm, acute tip and rounded or wedge-shaped base, margins with hair, petioles 2-3mm with small rounded auricles at base. Flower heads pink and globose, 7-10mm diameter, usually solitary and on peduncles 1-4cm.

» Roadsides in warm and cool broadleved forests.
» 1200-2500m
» March-September
» Widespread. From Samtse to Sarpang, Thimphu to Trashigang.

104 *Persicaria chinense* (L.) H. Gross
Eng: Chinese Knotweed

Large scrambling subshrub. Leaves ovate, 2.5-12x1-7cm, tapering to tip, base rounded or cordate, margins entire or toothed, glabrous; petioles upto 1.5cm, sometimes with rounded ear-like lobe at base; ocrea sheathing stem at node for 1-2cm. Flowers in ovoid or rounded heads 0.5-1.5cm diameter, solitary or 3-5 or more at branch ends, peduncles glabrous or with bristles. Perianth white or pink, 4-5mm.

» Warm and Cool broad-leaved forests.
» 270-2600m
» From Chhukha to Samdrupjongkhar and Thimphu to Trashigang

316 *Persicaria nepalensis* (Meisner) H. Gross
Eng: Nepal Knotweed

Prostrate annual herb 10-45cm tall. Solitary globose flower heads up to 1cm in diameter arising from leaf axils. Pink or white flowers. Leaves ovate or elliptic with rounded base, upper leaves smaller and sub-sessile or clasping stem.

» Roadsides and damp places from warm to cool broad leaved forest to coniferous forests.
» 750-3050m
» April-October
» Common from Chhukha to Samdrupjongkhar and Haa to Trashigang

317 *Persicaria runcinata* (D. Don) H. Gross
Dzo: Lha-Lop

Prostate or ascending herb. Leaves runcinate-pinnatifid (sharply divided) with terminal lobe a rhombic ovate c 0.7cm long and broad and 1-4 pairs of lateral lobes, smooth or sparsely pubescent, sometimes with a dark V-shaped blotch on terminal lobe; petioles 0.5-3.5cm, rounded or auriculate at base. White or pink globular flowers, 1-3 flower heads, terminal or axillary, peduncles 1.5-7cm.

»   Roadsides and cliff faces
»   1000-3800m
»   May- October
»   Widespread. From Samtse to Sarpang, Haa to Trashigang including Gasa and Lhuentse.

370 *Polygonatum kansuense* Maximowicz ex Batalin
Med: Rangey

Small rhizome forming herb with a simple stem up to 19-53cm. Leaves in whorls of up to 4 leaves per node except lower ones which may have one leaf per node, lance shape narrowed to sessile base, 2.9-10mm wide, hooked when young. Flowers in pair emerging from leaf axils on lower nodes on peduncles 1.7-3.5cm. Berry red.

»   Clearings and margins of conifer forests, open grass slopes, Juniper and Rhododendron scrub.
»   2740-4270m
»   May-July
»   Haa, Thimphu, Punakha, Bumthang

222 *Rheum acuminatum* Hook. f. & Thomson
Eng: Himalayan Rhubarb

Herbaceous plant up to 1m tall and branched above. Large heart shaped leaves 15-30cm long, and sparsely pubescent below. Brown red stems. Deep red flowers in axillary or terminal panicales. Fruits orbicular, 7-8mm long and broad, notched at base and apex, achene 6-7 x c 3mm, wind c 3mm broad.

»   Fir/rhododendron forests
»   3400-4100m
»   June - September
»   Haa, Paro, Thimphu, Mongar, Gasa, Trashiyangtse
»   Distinguished from *R. australe* which are much larger up to 3m tall and leaves nearly hairless beneath.

186 *Rheum nobile* Hook. f. & Thomson
Med: Chukha Dongpo
Dzo: Chukha Meto
Eng: Noble Rhubarb

Perennial herb. Stems simple, 1-1.5m, densely covered in large pale reflexed bracts. Leaves broadly ovate or orbicular, up to 30cm long and broad, obtuse, base rounded or cordate, sparsely pubescent beneath, often tinged red below; petioles 15-20cm; ocreae almost as long. Bracts similar to leaves but smaller, yellow or white. Racemes or panicles 15-20cm, concealed by bracts. Perianth greenish, c 5x3mm, wings c1mm broad.

» Rocky hillsides
» 4250-4600m
» June-August.
» Thimphu, Paro, Gasa, Bumthang, Trashiyangtse

270 *Rumex nepalensis* Sprengel
Dzo: Shomda
Eng: Nepal Dock

Erect perennial herb. Stems 0.5-1.5m. Leaves oblong-ovate, lower ones 8-20x4-10cm, rounded tip, base heart-shaped, fine short hair on lower surface, petioles 6-15cm. Flowers in axillary clusters or in whorls, forming simple or branching racemes. Perianth segments 6, outer 3 oblanceolate and smaller at 2-2.5mm, inner 3 ovate and larger at 3x3mm when flowering, larger when flowering, one of the segments usually with an oblong median tubercle, prominently veined and surrounded with hook-tipped bristles. Achenes 3-4x2mm.

» Common in open waste grounds, areas grazed by cattle, around cultivation areas.
» 1500-2500m
» May-July
» Chhukha, Thimphu, Trongsa, Mongar, Trashigang, Gasa
» Leaves used in treatment of itchy skin.

Primulaceae
Primrose family

113 Androsace geraniifolia Watt
Eng: Geranium Leaved Rock Jasmine

Decumbent perennial with slender rhizome, somewhat stolon-forming. Leaves suborbicular, 0.7-3.5-6cm in diameter, divided in middle into 5-6 lobes, each with 3-5 teeth, white stiff hairs on both surface; petioles 1.5-14cm, densely white pubescent. Peduncles 1-several per rosette, 3-25cm, densely pubescent; umbels with 4-25 flowers, sometimes bearing a leafy rosette which develops into a new plant when peduncles becomes horizontal in fruit and rests on the ground. Calyx campanulate, 2-4mm, pubescent. Corolla pink or white with yellow eye; limb 4-8mm in diameter, lobes oblong or obovate 2-3x1.5-2.5mm, entire. Capsule globose 2.5mm.

» On shaded banks in coniferous forests and on open mountain grassy slopes.
» 2130-4270m
» April-July
» Haa, Paro, Thimphu, Gasa, Punakha, Trongsa, Bumthang, Mongar, Lhuentse

318 Androsace hookeriana Klatt
Eng: Hookers Rock Jasmine

Small herb in clumps and connected by stolons. Leaves ovate to elliptic 4-10 x 2-7mm with tips acute to rounded or notched and sparsely haired on both surfaces. Flowers in umbels of 2-10 on a penduncle 1.5-7cm tall which is sparsely hairy. Corolla pink with green, orange or dark red eye.

» Open grassland.
» 3350-4900m
» June- August
» Haa, Paro, Thimphu, Punakha, Trongsa, Bumthang, Trashigang

405 Primula calderiana Balfour f. & Cooper

Deciduous herb with winter resting bud. Leaves oblanceolate or like a spatula 5-30 x 1-6cm, obtuse to acute tip and base tapering to a winged petiole, margin toothed. Flower peduncle 7-28cm at flowering, with farinose near top, bearing an umbel of 5-25 flowers. Corolla purple (white in *forma alba*), with yellow eye. Capsule globose, included within calyx.

» Clearings and streamsides in fir forests, and damp alpine meadows
» 3000-4880m
» May-August
» Haa, Thimphu, Trongsa, Bumthang, Mongar, Trashigang, Gasa, Bumthang, Trashiyangtse

Two variants occur, *forma alba* has white flowers, and var. *aculescens* lacks a peduncle but has elongated pedicel 6-10cm.

406 *Primula denticulata* Sm.
Dzo: Doched Meto, Gurgur Meto
Eng: Drumstick Primrose

Deciduous herb. Leaves oblong-oblanceolate 5-30x1.4-5cm, blunt apex and tapering to base, toothed margin. Flower peduncle 7-25cm (-45cm in fruit), smooth or with fine hair, with or without mealy powder above. Flowers in compact globular head. Corolla purplish or white with yellow eye, tube 7-10mm, limb 10-25mm diameter, lobes are bilobed. Capsule oblong to subglobose within calyx.

» Open damp meadows and flushes, marshy clearings, in oak, pine and spruce forests.
» 1545-4110m
» February - June
» Chhukha, Haa, Thimphu, Punakha, Trongsa, Trashigang

362 *Primula glabra* Klatt

A rosetted herb forming small clumps. As the name suggests, this is a glabrous (smooth) plant. Leaves spoon shaped 1-3.5 x0.4-1cm , rounded tip and tapering to a winged petiole, with sharply toothed margins and glandular beneath. Slender peduncle 2-11cm with an umbel of 6-12 flowers. Corolla blue or purplish, rarely white, with yellow eye.

» Clearings among dwarf rhododendron and open alpine grass, mossy rocks, and grass slopes.
» 3650-4510m.
» April- August.
» Haa, Paro, Thimphu, Punakha, Bumthang, Trashigang, Gasa, Trongsa, Trashiyangtse

319 *Primula gracilipes* Craib
Eng: Slender Primrose

Evergreen herb; winter buds and persistent bud scales absent. Leaves rugose, at flowering oblanceolate, 3-6 x 1-2.5cm, obtuse, base attenuate, without petiole, margins finely irregularly spreading denticulate, efarinose or sparsely farinose when young; leaves after flowering ovate-oblong, 4-11 x 2.5-4cm, on long petiole 5-13cm. Flowers 5-20 borne amongst rosette leaves; peduncle absent; pedicels slender, 1-6cm; bracts linear-lanceolate, 5-15mm. Calyx campanulate, 5-9mm, farinose, divided to middle into oblong acute teeth. Corolla pinkish-purple with greenish-yellow eye, tube almost 2X length of calyx, limb 1 5-2.5cm across, with obovate irregularly dentate lobes. Capsule subglobose, included within calyx, ripening at ground level on recurved pedicels.

» 1980-4720m
» February-June
» Haa, Thimphu, Trongsa, Bumthang, Mongar, Trashigang
» The most frequent petiolarid Primula in Bhutan.

363 *Primula griffithii* (Watt) Pax

Deciduous herb with leaves oblanceolate to ovate with truncate or nearly heartshaped base, 4-9 cm x 1-6 cm (much larger when fruiting) and apex sharply pointed and margins coarsely toothed. Flower stalk 7-28 cm with an umbel of 5-25 flowers with blue petals and yellow eye, lobes notched at tip.

» Coniferous forests and rhododendron scrub, in marshes and by streams.
» 2600-3800m
» April-May
» Local endemic restricted to western Bhutan and Chumbi valley, but frequent in Paro and Thimphu.

190 *Primula sikkimensis* Hook.
Med: Shangshangdilbu
Eng: Himalayan Cowslip

Evergreen perennial herb. Leaves oblanceolate, 4-32x1-5 cm, rounded tip and base long and narrowing to a distinct petiole, margin finely toothed with smooth surface. Peduncle 10-50cm and covered in powder at apex with usually one umbel (rarely 2) of fragrant yellow flowers.

» Marshy grounds, damp meadows and among srcub in fir forests.
» 2475-4220m
» May – August
» Haa, Paro, Thimphu, Punakha, Trongsa, Bumthang, Mongar

191 *Primula smithiana* Craib

Evergreen perennial herb. Leaves oblanceolate, 7-20x 2-5cm, rounded tip with narrowing to base, smooth surface and sharply toothed. Peduncles 15-60cm with 2-5 distant umbels of yellow flowers and calyx covered in white powder. Corolla tube cylindric, 8-10mm; limb yellow, 10-15mm diameter, lobes oblong to obovate, slightly notched at apex. Capsule globose, about as long as calyx, splitting by 5 valves.

» Marshy areas besides streams.
» 2440-3350m
» April - June
» Haa, Paro, Thimphu, Punakha, Trongsa, Bumthang, Mongar

....

Punicaceae
Pomegranate family

204 *Punica granatum* L.
Dzo: Tsindu
Eng: Pomegranate

Shrub or small tree, 2-3m; branchlets often spiny. Leaves elliptic-oblanceolate, 3.5-7x1-2cm, without hair, petiole 2-10mm. Flowers axillary, 1-2 per axil, bright red, fleshy. Calyx red, 6-7 lobes. Petals 6-7, showy, crumpled, bright red, obovate, 1.5-2.2cm. Stamens numerous, yellow. Style bent near apex, 8mm; stigma capitate. Fruit globose, 4.5-6cm diameter, crowned by persistent calyx.

» Cultivated and among scrub on dry hillsides.
» 1200-2400m
» March-July
» Thimphu, Punakha, Trashigang

» Flowers yield red dye. Cultivated for flowers and fruit, but now naturalised in dry inner valleys.

Pyloraceae
Wintergreen family

84 *Pylora corbieri* Leveille

Erect glabrous herb 11-30cm tall. Scales at stem base 1-3mm broad, not or slightly sheathing; leaves ovate-elliptic, dark green with pale veins above, 3.5-7 x 1.5-3.5cm, subacute, base cuneate or attenuate, margins entire or shallowly crenate; petioles 1 - 3.5cm; racemes shorter, 1.5-4cm, 4-9 flowered; sepals c 4mm; petals white; anthers c 3mm; style distinctly curved.

» Streamsides in Blue pine forest
» 2100-2700m
» July-August
» Thimphu, Punakha

Ranunculaceae
Buttercup family

1 *Anemone rivularis* Buch.-Ham. ex DC
Med: Supka

Perennial herb. Leaves divided into three, leaflets broadly elliptic or rhombc, 4-7x3-5cm, toothed margin, stiffly pubescent, petioles 10-30cm; scapes 7-35cm. Umbellate cyme of long stalked flowers emerging from leafy involucres. Sepals obovate -elliptic 10-15x4-10mm, white within, purplish and silky outside. Petals absent. Achenes broadly elliptic, 1.5-2x0.7-1.2cm

» Streamsides and clearings in cool broadleaved, Evergreen oak, Blue Pine and Hemlock forests, more rarely in alpine meadows.
» 1980-3960m
» April-August
» Widespread. From Chhukha & Haa to Trashigang, including Gasa

2 *Anemone rupicola* Cambessedes

Small rhizome forming herb 3-10cm with solitary flowers. Leaves thrice divided with each leaflet further divided into 3-5 sharply toothed lobes, sparsely long hairy especially beneath. Petioles 4-20cm. Scapes 3-20cm, involucral bracts similar to leaves. Pedicels 4-15cm. Flower petals absent, sepals broadly elliptic, white inside and purplish outside.

» Alpine meadows in juniper/rhododendron scrub, cliff edges, screes and moraines
» 2830 - 4800m
» May- July
» Thimphu, Trongsa, Gasa, Trashiyangtse, widespread.

3 *Anemone vitifolia* Buch.-Ham. ex DC.
Eng: Grape Leaf Anemone

Perennial herb, up to 100cm tall. Leaves simple broadly ovate, 7-20cm long and broad, 3-7 lobes, base heart shaped, marging toothed, white hair below, petioles 15-50cm. Scapes 20-50cm. Umbellate cymes usually branched. Sepals obovate-elliptic, 1.5-2x0.7-1.2cm, white within, purplish and pubescent outside. Petals absent. Achenes ellipsoid, c 1mm surounded in wooly hair.

» Clearings in cool broadleaved forests, Evergreen oak and Fir forests.
» 1525-2745m
» July-September
» Widespread. Chhukha, Samdrupjongkhar, and from Thimphu to Trashigang including Gasa

368 *Clematis acutangula* Hook. f. & Thomson
Med: Emong

Stems herbaceous to woody, erect or weakly scandent, 0.3-3m. Climbing by twining petioles. Leaves compound with three leaflets arising on opposite sides of stem., leaflets ovate, 2-5x1-3cm, toothed margins and often 3-lobed, sparsely or densely pubescent with straight hairs. Solitary (or few) purple flowers in axils, pedicels 2-20cm; sepals, oblong-elliptic, purple 1-1.5 x 0.4-0.6cm, with 3 narrow wings on back. Stamens densely covered in long white hair. Achenes pubescent.

» On scrub under pine and cool broadleaved forests.
» 1500m-2740m

» August - October
» Widespread. From Haa to Trashigang

243 *Clematis buchananiana* DC

A strong woody climber. Leaves ternate or rarely pinnate, leaflets 3-5, broadly ovate, 6.5-12 x 4-10 cm, acute or shortly acuminate, base rounded or cordate, margins coarsely serrate or 3-lobed, sparsely pubescent above, denser beneath; petioles sometimes broadened and thickened at base and narrowly connate; panicles bearing a pair of coarsely toothed leafy bracts at each node. Flowers cream or yellow in long leafy branched clusters, sweet scented, with narrow-oblong pointed petals recurved only at the tips.

» Warm broad-leaved, Hemlock and Fir forest, on shrubs.
» 1000-3650m
» July - October
» Chhukha, Sarpang, Haa, Trashigang, Trashiyangtse.

4 *Clematis montana* DC.

Woody climber. Leaves with three leaflets and margins coarsely toothed or lobed, rounded base, sparse hair below, petioles 4-7cm. Flowers 2-3 in axillary fascicles, pedicels 3-8cm. Petals absent; Sepals 4, white or pinkish, elliptic, 1.5-2x0.7-1.25cm, obtuse or acute, pubescent outside, hairless within. Numerous stamens with yellowish anthers. Achenes ovate, c5x4mm compressed, glabrous.

» On shrubs in dry valleys, blue pine and spruce forests and Juniper and Rhododendron scrub
» 2100-4100m
» April-July
» Common from Haa to Bumthang

5 *Clematis tongluensis* (Bruehl) Tamura

Similar to *C. montana*. Woody climber. Leaves ternate, with leaflets acute and coarsely toothed or lobed, with sparse flat hair, especially below. Flowers usually 1 per axil, with pedicels 12-30cm. Sepals 4, white or pinkish. anthers purple.

» Cool broad-leaved, spruce, hemlock and fir forests on shrubs and bamboo
» 2300-3500m

- » June-July
- » Haa to Mongar

375 *Delphinium cooperi* Munz.

Med: Jakang

Erect perennial herb with slender stems 10-45cm. Leaves palmately kidney shaped, 3-5cm long, divided into 3-5 broadly ovate segments, margins broadly toothed. Pedicels -8cm, hairy/glandular. Sepals 5 (look like petals), purplish violet with yellowish hairs; uppermost sepal elongated into a spur spreading or decurved, 15-17mm and 3m broad. Petals 4 (inside the hood), dark blue-black, much darker than sepals; lamina of upper pair oblong and curved at tip, entire, lower lamina borader with a notch at tip and covered in hair.

- » Dry banks and evergreen oak forest
- » 2400-3000m
- » August - October
- » Paro, Thimphu, Punakha, Trongsa

264 *Delphinium viscosum* Hook. f. & Thomson

Perennial herb. Stems 15-80cm, pubescent. Leaves suborbicular, 3-10cm diameter, divided to middle with 5-7 broad lobes, toothed at apex; petioles to 20cm. Flowers few, greenish to blue or purple, in lax racemes; bracts oblong, 3-5cm, bracteoles near flower, 1-2cm. spur c15-5-8mm, upper sepal 18-23mm long and broad.

- » Alpine cliff ledges, screes, gravel.
- » 3660-4730m
- » July-October
- » Paro, Thimphu, Trongsa, Gasa, Bumthang, Lhuentse

126 *Oxygraphis endlicheri* (Walpers) Bennet & Chandra

Dwarf perennial stemless herb. Leaves all basal, leathery and ovate or suborbicular, 5-25mm long and broad, margins with few teeth. Scape 1-flowered 1.5-10cm. Flowers with 10-15 yellow or bronze petals 4-10mm x1.5-2mm. Stamens many. Achenes obovate, 1.5-2mm.

- » Damp clearings in fir forests and in alpine meadows, mossy rocks and grassy slopes

- » 3350-4900m
- » May
- » Paro, Thimphu, Trongsa, Bumthang, Trashigang, Gasa

127 Ranunculus brotherusii Freyn
Med: Chetsha

Suberect herb, stems 2-25cm. Basal leaves reniform in outline, 1.5-3cm long and broad, stem leaves deeply cut into long thin segments 1-2mm broad, sparsely hairy below, glabrous above; petioles 2-6cm. Flowers usually solitary, pedicels sparsely pubescent. Sepals broadly ovate, 2.5-3.5mm, sparsely pubescent, spreading. Petals 5, obovate, 4-6mm long and broad, yellow with nectar pit at base. Stamens many. Carpels many, style short. Achenes glabrous or pubescent.

- » Damp clearings in Spruce, Hemlock and Fir forests, in alpine meadows and scrub
- » 2560-4570m
- » April-August
- » Haa, Paro, Thimphu, Mongar, Gasa, Bumthang, Trashiyangtse.

128 Ranunculus chinensis DC

Annual or biennial herb 20-40cm. Leaves ternately divided into 3 leaflets, each leaflet deeply cut into oblanceolate lobes, with short pressed hair. Sepals elliptic 5x3mm and bent backwards. Petals 5, obovate 7-8 x 3-5mm, yellow, numerous stamens, Achenes broadly elliptic c2.5-2mm, pale and thickened at margins, depressed and darker in middle, style minute, more or less straight, receptacle elongated up to 1.5cm, hairy.

- » Paddy fields and cultivated grounds, ditches.
- » 1400-2500m
- » April-May
- » Thimphu, Paro, Punakha
- » *R. cantoniensis* is very similar but has achenes broadly elliptic c 2mm long and broad, compressed, surrounded by a narrow marginal rim, style persistent more or less straight, receptacle subglobose. Weed of irrigated fields.

398 *Thalictrum chelidonii* DC.

Eng: Meadow Rue

Erect perennial herb 40-200cm. Leaves 8-30cm, dissected into 15 or more leaflets, leaflets broadly ovate or sub orbicular, margins coarsely toothed or lobed, minutely pubescent. Flowers in racemes or panicles. Sepals 4-5, ovate, 8-15 x 5-10mm, mauve or purplish. Petals absent. Stamens many.

» Fir forests and Juniper/Rhododendron scrub.
» 2130-4570m
» June-September
» Common. From Haa to Mongar, Gasa, Bumthang, and Lhuentse.
» *T. reniforme* is similar but has smaller greenish-white flowers.

Rosaceae
Rose family

6 *Cotoneaster microphyllus* Lindley

Low growing much branched shrub. Leaves elliptic or obovate and leathery with margins more or less inrolled, smooth above and pubescent beneath. Flowers solitary. Petals (c 3mm) white or tinged pink and almost orbicular in shape. Fruits almost globular 7-10 mm diameter and scarlet.

» Rock faces and gravel banks
» 2100 - 4570m
» April- July
» Haa, Thimphu, Mongar, Trashigang, Gasa, Trashiyangtse
» Fruit used medicinally. Valued as ornamental shrub in Europe

7 *Cotoneaster sherriffii* Klotz

A shrub 1-2 m. Leaves elliptic or obovate, 7-20x4-10mm, glabrous above, sparsely hairy beneath. Cymes or 2-10 flowers. Petals 5, white, almost circular in shape and spread open, 3-4mm. Fruit ellipsoid or globular 5-7mm, red.

» On dry open hillsides
» 2100-2400m

» April-May
» Paro, Thimphu
» Very similar to *C. racemiflorus* which has leaves broadly elliptic or ovate and 1.5-2.5cm.

129, 235 Duchesnea indica (Andrews) Focke
Eng: False Strawberry, Indian Strawberry

Herb with slender stolons. Similar to *Fragaria* but leaves always palmately 3-foliate, leaflets elliptic or obovate, 0.75-3x0.75-2cm, obtuse, margins toothed, with hair, petioles up to 10cm. Peduncles 2.5-5cm. Flowers solitary, Petals 5, yellow, obovate 4-6x2-4mm. Red fruit like strawberry with minute achenes on surface.

» Warm broadleaved forests to above treeline.
» 1060-4420m
» February-June.
» Chhukha, Sarpang, Haa, Thimphu, Bumthang, Mongar, Trashiyangtse

8, 236 Fragaria nubicola (Hook. f.) Lacaita
Dzo: Batshi Tsheloo, Thseloo Meto
Eng: Himalayan Strawberry

Prostrate herb. Leaves palmately compound with three leaflets, each of which are elliptic with 7-14 sharp teeth on each side and silky white beneath. 1-3 flowers on a scape 2-8cm. Petals 5 white, broadly obovate and 7-10mm long, Stamens numerous. Achenes on fleshy red and round receptacle 10-15mm in diameter, with sweet sharp flavour.

» Open grass on margins of cool broadleaved and coniferous forests.
» 2000-3600m
» April-June
» Chhukha, Thimphu, Punakha, Trongsa, Gasa

9 Malus baccata (L.) Borkh.
Dzo: Khomang Shing
Eng: Siberian Crab Apple

Deciduous shrub or tree 3-5m. Leaves simple, elliptic lanceolate, rarely ovate, 3.5-8x1.5-5cm, margin finely toothed, sparsely pubescent along veins and sometimes along lateral veins mostly beneath; petioles 2-3.5cm, slender. Calyx tube 3-4mm, constricted above ovary, 5 lobes lanceolate. Petals 5, obovate 10-15x7-10mm white, often tinged pink. Styles 4-5, stamens numerous. Pomes fleshy, ellipsoid 7-8x4-5mm, thinly fleshy, red.

» In scrub among blue pine forest.
» 1800-3050m
» April-May
» Haa, Paro, Thimphu, Punakha, Trongsa, Gasa, Bumthang

239 *Neillia rubiflora* D. Don
Dzo: Totuma

Shrubs to 2 m tall. Branchlets red-purple, angled, hairy when young, glabrescent; buds purple-red, ovoid, with 2 or 3 scales glabrous or slightly pubescent at margin, apex acute. Stipules ovate-lanceolate or linear-lanceolate, membranous, slightly pubescent, margin entire, apex acuminate; petiole 1–2 cm, pubescent; leaf blade broadly ovate to triangular-ovate, 4–6 × 3–4.5 cm, glabrous on both surfaces or abaxially slightly pubescent, base cordate, rarely rounded, margin sharply doubly serrate, apex acuminate. Raceme 2–4 cm, 5–12-flowered; peduncle and pedicels glabrous. Flowers 5–6 mm in diameter; pedicel 2–3 mm. Hypanthium urceolate-campanulate, 2–3 mm, abaxially pubescent. Sepals triangular-lanceolate, shorter than or nearly equaling hypanthium, densely pubescent, margin entire, apex acuminate. Petals pinkish white, obovate, ca. 3 mm. Stamens 25–30. Ovary subglobose, slightly hairy at apex; ovules 8–10. Follicles ellipsoid, glabrous. Seeds ovoid.

» Found in cool wet broad-leaved forest.
» 2100 - 3300 m
» May – July
» Samdrupjongkhar, Thimphu, Punakha, Trongsa, Bumthang, Mongar, Trashigang

130 *Potentilla arbuscula* D. Don
Med: Penma
Eng: Bush Cinquefoil, Shrubby Cinquefoil

Shrub from 0.6-1.5m Compound leaves with 3 or 5 leaflets with silky hairs on both surfaces, leaflets 6-15x3.5-6mm. Flowers solitary at ends of branches with peduncles up to 5cm. Petals 5, obovate, 10-16x8-13mm, rounded yellow.

Achenes 1.5-2mm, ovoid, sparsely white long-haired, concealed by long straight white hairs on receptacle.

» Rocky hillsides, and among juniper and rhododendron scrub
» 3050-4100m
» May-August
» Leaves burned as incense
» Haa, Paro, Thimphu, Gasa, Bumthang, Trashiyangtse

10 *Potentilla coriandrifolia* D. Don
Eng: Coriander Leaved Cinquefoil

Rosette herb with thick woody rootstock and persistent leaf remains. Leaves pinnate, 3-10cm, lateral leaflets 4-5(-9) pairs, 3-12mm, deeply divided cut pinnately, with linear segments, sparsely pubescent. Flowers 2-5 in corymbs on peduncless 7-15cm. Calyx lobes 2-3mm. Petals 5, obovate 6-7mm, notched in middle of rounded tip, white with deep crimson at base. Achenes oblong ellipsoid 1.5-2mm.

» Open grassy hillsides
» 2900-4570m
» July - September
» Haa, Paro, Bumthang, Trongsa, Gasa

131 *Potentilla cuneata* Lehmann
Eng: Five Finger Cinquefoil

Rosette or mat forming perennial herb, stems woody at base; rhizomes slender, naked. Leaves 3-foliate, leaflets obovate, 6-12 x 4-10mm, apex shallowly 3-toothed, base cuneate, pubescent or glabrous above, appressed hirsute beneath; petioles 0.5-3cm; stipules lanceolate 8-10mm, leaf. Flowers solitary, c 2cm diameter, on peduncles 2-6cm. Calyx lobes ovate, 4-7mm, appressed pubescent; epicalyx segments elliptic, slightly shorter. Petals yellow, broadly obovate, c 10 x 7-8mm, slightly emarginated. Achenes ovoid, c 1mm, covered with straight pale brown hairs, and hidden by hairs of receptacle.

» On rocky streamside, cliffs and boulders
» 2500-3650m
» May-July
» Haa, Thimphu, Trongsa, Trashigang, Gasa, Bumthang, Trashiyangtse

132 *Potentilla griffithii* Hook. f.
Dzo: Choga Sey Sey

Perennial herb, prostate or decumbent with shoots 15-55cm, covered in white silky hair. Basal leaves pinnate, 5-20cm, with 2-4 pairs of lateral leaflets, margins coarsely toothed, green above, white hairy below. Stem leaves similar but smaller with 1-2 pairs of leaflets. Flowers in loose terminal cymes. Calyx lobes 5, ovate, 5-6mm, covered in white hair. Petals 5, broadly obovate 7-10mm, notched at rounded tip, usually yellow. Achenes ellipsoid, c 0.75mm.

» Roadsides, margins of cultivation, distrubed areas in blue pine forests.
» 2300-3350m
» June-September
» Chhukha, Haa, Thimphu, Punakha, Wangduephodrang, Trongsa, Bumthang, Gasa

133 *Potentilla microphylla* D. Don

Dense cushion plant or mat- or rosette-forming herb, with stout tape-root or long slender roots. Leaves pinnate, leaflets 3-15 pairs, shallowly to deeply toothed or pinnatifid, often silky hairy beneath. Flowers usually solitary (-2), subsessile or on peduncles 1-5cm. Calyx lobes 4-5mm. Petals yellow, obovate, 7-8mm. Achenes obovoid, c 2.5mm, densely hairy.

» Rocky riverbanks and screes
» 3650-4400m
» June-July
» Thimphu, Gasa, Trongsa, Bumthang, Trashiyangtse

134 *Potentilla peduncularis* D. Don
Dzo: Saley Dem

Perennial rosette herb with thick woody rootstock covered with leaf remains. Leaves mostly regularly pinnate oblong or oblanceolate in outline, 5-20cm; lateral leaflets 9-12 pairs, oblong-elliptic 0.5-3x0.25- 0.75cm, +- obtuse, base rounded or cuneate, margin serrate, sparsely pubescent above, usually white sericeous beneath; stipules ovate-lanceolate 1-3cm, brown. Flowers 2-5 +- corymbose, borne on almost leafless peduncles 6-25cm. Calyx lobes ovate 5-6mm. Petals obovate, 8-13x8-10mm, rounded, yellow. Achenes obovoid 1.5-2mm, glabrous.

» Open hillsides and in Fir forests.

- » 3650-4400m.
- » June-July
- » Thimphu, Punakha, Trongsa, Bumthang, Gasa, Trashiyangtse

11 *Prinsepia utilis* Royle
Dzo: Dushi Tsang

Shrub 1-4m, branches bearing ascending spines (modified lateral shoots) 0.7-3.5cm. Leaves elliptic-lanceolate 2.5-7x0.5-2.5cm, acuminate, base attentuate or rounded, minutely serrate, subsessile or on petioles upto 10mm, glabrous. Racemes 3.5-7cm, 2-5 flowered. Calyx lobes suborbicular, 4-6mm. Petals elliptic or obovate 6-7x5 mm, white. Stamens 2-3mm, filaments crimson at base. Drupes 10-15mm, borne on persistent calyx cup, purplish, styles near base due to unequal growth.

- » River banks, edges of blue pine and *Quercus* forests
- » 2200-2750m
- » March-April
- » Haa, Thimphu, Trongsa, Bumthang, Trashiyangtse, Chhukha, Sarpang
- » Used as a hedge plant and seeds contain an oil used in lamps

320 *Prunus cerasoides* D. Don
Eng: Wild Himalayan Cherry

Tree 5-15m, flowering in autumn and winter. Leaves ovate or oblong-elliptic, 5-12x3.5-4cm, margin finely toothed, glabrous; petioles 1-2cm. Flowers 1-3 in fascicles unfolding with young leaves, pedicels 1-2cm. Calyx cup tubular-campanulate c 1cm, glabrous, green flushed pink, lobes c5mm ovate, acute. Petals 5, alternating with calyx, lobes, obovate, 1.5-1.8x0.8cm, pink, spreading. Stamens 10-35, filaments of outer stamens as long as petals. Drupes ellipsoid 1-1.3x0.8cm.

- » Warm broad-leaved forests
- » 1050-2000m
- » October-November
- » Chhukha, Samdrupjongkhar, Haa, Trongsa, Punakha, Wangduephodrang, Lhuentse
- » Wood used in furniture making, often cultivated for ornamental flowers, fruit edible.

109 *Rosa brunonii* Lindley
Dzo: Taktsher Karp

Scrambling shrub 3-10m, with recurved prickles on stem. Compound leaves 8-15cm with 5-9 leaflets, pointed or tapering to point, rounded base and finely toothed on margins. Flowers in large fragrant terminal corymbs. Petals creamy white, rarely pink. Styles united and club shaped 8-10mm.

- » Scrambling climber on shrubs and small trees in moist forests
- » 1370-2550m
- » May - July
- » Chhukha, Sarpang, Samdrupjongkhar, Thimphu, Punakha, Mongar, Gasa

283 *Rosa macrophylla* Lindley
Dzo: Taktsher Marp
Eng: Himalayan Rose, Large Leaf Rose

Erect shrub. Stems 1-5m, sometimes bearing paired straight prickles below leaves. Leaves 7-20cm, pinnately compound with 7-11 leaflets, ovate elliptic, margins finely toothed, smooth above, sparsely pubescent below. Flowers 1-2 on short lateral shoots. Calyx tube ellipsoid c.1cm, purplish, densely covered in glandular bristles. Petals 5, obovate 2.5-3x2-2.5cm, deep pink. styles 5-7 free, almost concealed by white hairs. Stamens numerous.

- » Hillsides and forest margins.
- » 2100-2800m
- » June-July
- » Haa, Thimphu, Punakha, Bumthang, Mongar, Gasa

12 *Rosa sericea* Lindley
Dzo: Sew Shing
Med: Sewai Meto
Eng: Silky Rose

Erect shrub 1-4m, stems naked or with scattered slender or broad prickles. Leaves 3-9cm with 7-11 leaflets which are oblong shaped and toothed margins, and sericeous (silky) beneath. Flowers solitary with usually 4 yellow or creamy white petals 1.5-2cm long. Hips more or less globular up to 1cm, orange red.

- » Open dry hill slopes

- » 1220-3800m
- » April – June
- » Chhukha, Haa, Paro, Thimphu, Bumthang, Trashigang
- » Flowers used medicinally and fruits edible.

13 *Rubus biflorus* Buch.-Ham. ex Sm.
Med: Kentakare, Taktse Meto
Eng: Silver-Stemmed Bramble

Shrub 1-2m, stems smooth, with white bloom and stout recurved prickles 5-9mm. Leaves compound with 3 leaflets (occasionaly 5), ovate, doubly serrate or shallowly lobed, pubescent above and white soft hair below, with few prickles along midrib. Flowers axillary and terminal, solitary or in fascicles of 2-3 pedicels, 1.5-2cm. Calyx cup without prickles, 5 ovate lobes, 6-9mm, smooth, short pointed. Petals 5, white, obovate, 7-10mm. Fruit glabrous, orange.

- » Blue pine forests, in clearings and amongst shrubs
- » 2300-3500m
- » May-July
- » Haa, Thimphu, Trongsa, Bumthang, Gasa, Trashiyangtse
- » Fruits edible

14 *Rubus ellipticus* Smith.
Dzo: Tshema Tshelu ·
Eng: Yellow Himalayan Raspberry

A robust scrambling shrub 2-3m tall. Stems pubescent, with scattered prickles and dense spreading bristles 3-6mm. Leaves pinnately trifoliate, leaflets elliptic-obovate to suborbicular, terminal 4-10x3-7cm, margins shallowly serrate, pale puberulous beneath, midrib prickly; lateral leaflets slightly smaller; petioles 3-8cm; stipules linear, 6-8 mm, caducous. Panicles axillary and terminal, few to many flowered. Calyx cup bristly, lobes ovate, 5-6mm, acute, entire, softly pale pudescent. Petals white, obovate, c6mm. Fruit yellow, druplets many.

- » Along roadside scrub and abandoned cultivation in Warm broadleaved and evergreen oak forest
- » 1200- 1900 m
- » Feb-April
- » Samtse, Chhukha, Sarpang, Trashigang, Trashiyangtse, Thimphu
- » Fruit edible

284 Rubus hypargyrus Edgeworth

Arching or scrambling shrub 2-3m, leafy shoots with scattered to dense weak prickles. Leaves with 3 leaflets which are ovate and tapering tips and rounded to cuneate base, and toothed margins, thinly haired above and white short hair below or rarely green and smooth beneath. Flowers solitary or 2-5 in short axillary racemes, calyx lobes lanceolate 8-12mm with long awl-like apex and covered in fine hair. Petals pink or red 5-6mm. Fruit red or orange about 1cm.

- »   On banks and in scrub in fir/rhododendron forests
- »   2750-3660m
- »   June- August
- »   Paro, Thimphu, Bumthang, Mongar, Trashigang, Gasa, Lhuentse, Trashigang

15, 237 Rubus indotibetanus Koidzumi

Scrambling shrub 1-2m with long slender branches and numerous straight or curved prickles, leafy branchlets short with slender hooked prickles. Leaves pinnately compound with mostly 5 leaflets, leaflets ovate tapering to point and rounded base, sharply toothed. Stems and petiotles covered in short straight gland tipped hairs. Flowers 1-2 in terminal on leafy shoots, calyx covered in glandular bristles, lobes 13-17mm with triangular base and stringy tips; petals 5, white 10-13mm; stamens numerous. Fruit red, large oblong-globose 2cm diameter, not very tasty.

- »   Warm and cool broadleaved forests, evergreen oak forests
- »   1400-3000m
- »   March-May
- »   Chhukha, Sarpang, Samdrupjongkhar, Thimphu, Punakha, Trashiyangtse

110 Sorbus microphylla (Wenzig) Hook. f.
Dzo: Tsema Shing
Eng: Small Leaf Rowan

Shrubs or small trees, 2–5 m tall. Branchlets reddish brown when young, grayish brown when old, puberulous when young. Leaves imparipinnate, together with rachis 11–14 cm; petiole 1–1.5 cm; leaflets 10–17 pairs, linear-oblong, 0.7–2 cm × 4–8 mm, both surfaces glabrous, margin sparsely sharply serrate. Compound corymbs terminal, 2–6 cm, laxly flowered. Flowers 7–10 mm diam. Hypanthium dark purplish black, broadly campanulate, 2–3 mm, glabrous. Sepals triangular, 1.5–2 mm. Petals pink, suborbicular, 3–4 mm. Stamens ca. 20, slightly shorter than petals; filaments rose; anthers nearly purplish black. Styles 5, ca. as long as stamens. Fruit white or flushed pink or crimson, globose or ovoid, 8–12 mm in diam.

» Common in Fir, Hemlock and Spruce forest
» 3050 - 4100 m
» June – July
» Samdrupjongkhar, Mongar, Trashigang, Trongsa

321 *Spiraea bella* Sims
Eng: Pretty Spiraea

Rhizomatous shrub, stems 1-2.5m, branched. Leaves narrowly ovate 3-6x0.7-1.5cm, acuminate, base rounded, margins serrate or doubly serrate. Corymbs 2-7cm broad, terminal on lateral shoots. Calyx cup concave, 5 triangular lobes. Petals 5, white or pink, obovate 2.5-3x3mm. Stamens 20-25, reduced to staminodes in female flowers.

» Among scrub and by streamsides, openings of forests, roadside.
» 2300-3950m
» May-August
» Samdrupjongkhar, Haa, Paro, Thimphu, Mongar, Trashigang, Bumthang, Lhuentse

Rubiaceae
Madder family

82 *Leptodermis stapfiana* Winkler

Shrub up to 2.4m with hair in two rows or more. Opposite leaves, pubescent surfaces and cilliate margins elliptic shape up to 2cm long. Stipules to 4mm at leaf pedicel. Inflorescence of compact clusters of up to 20 flowers at end of new growth. Bracteoles subtending flowers longer than calyx. Corolla white or deep maroon or violet or bicoloured and pubescent outside.

» Scrub on dry banks and hillsides

» 1300-3350m
» May- September
» Chhukha, Thimphu, Punakha, Trashigang

324 *Luculia gratissima* (Wall.) Sweet.

Dzo: Tongden Meto
Eng: Sweet Luculia

Shrub 1-3m. Leaves elliptic to oblanceolate, 5-19x1,5-6.5cm, abruptly or gradually acuminate, base acute to attenuate, glabrous and shiny above, pale green beneath, matt and long-haired, especially on veins; petioles c 1cm, tomentose. Stipules ovate, c 1cm, cuspidate. Peduncles tomentose. Flowers very fragrant. Hypanthium tomentose; calyx lobes +- elliptic, 8-25mm, usually acuminate. Corolla white or pink, tube 2-4cm; lobes ovate, spreading, 1-1.5cm, without appendages. Capsule obovoid, 1-1.5cm, sparsely long-haired.

» Riversides, hillsides in scrub or open forests.
» 1000-2200m
» August-October
» Samdrupjongkhar, Punakha, Trongsa, Mongar, Trashigang
» Leaves used in dyeing.

232 *Mussaenda roxburghii* Hook. F.

Much branched shrub 1–4.5m. Stems glabrous or with spreading hairs. Leaves petiolate, usually elliptic, rarely ovate or oblong, 5–25x4–9cm, subglabrous or thinly long-haired above, more densely haired below, veins with hairs on both sides; petioles 2–15mm; stipules broadly triangular, 6–14mm. Inflorescence a dense terminal head, usually 3-branched from base, but undifferentiated, many-flowered, Calyx lobes filiform, tapering from base, 6–9mm x 1mm, densely covered in long silky hairs, Corolla tube 2.4–2.8cm, densely covered in long silky hairs; lobes narrowly ovate, 4–8x2–2.5mm, terminating in long fine hairpoint. Berry globose, 6–10mm, glabrous calyx persistent until fruit is ripe.

» Locally common in secondary scrub and margins of sub-tropical forest
» 100–1850m
» May–August
» Chhukha, Punakha, Wangduephodrang

120 *Pavetta indica* L.
Eng: Indian Pavetta

A shrub to 3m or a small tree with smooth brownish-grey bark, leaves opposite leathery elliptic acute leaves, flowers terminal domed clusters of many fragrant white flowers with long slender corolla-tubes and long projecting slender styles.

» Moist sub-tropical forest especially in clearings
» 270-1070m
» April to June
» Mongar, Chhukha, Sarpang, Trashigang
» Roots and leaves used medicinally

223 *Rubia manjith* Roxb.
Dzo: Tsoy
Eng: Indian Madder

Climbing herb to 3m, reddish-tinged throughout especially when dry; stems quadrangular, weakly strigose-hooked to almost smooth. Leaves in whorls of 4, occasionally opposite, often strongly reddish tinged beneath, ovate-lanceolate to ovate, 3.5-8 x 1-4cm, 3-5-veined; petioles 2.5-10cm. Flowers in axillary and terminal panicles to 20x8cm. Flowers red or orange, 3.5-4.5mm diameter, 5-merous. Corolla tube c 0.6mm; lobes ovate, c 1.4mm with very short point. Styles 2, short, free. Fruit black when ripe, bilobed-globose, 3.4-5mm broad.

» Along footpath, hedgerows in sub-tropical and warm broad-leaved forest
» 1150-2300(-1850) m.
» June-October.
» Chhukha, Sarpang, Samdrupjongkhar, Punakha, Mongar, Thimphu, Trashigang, Trashiyangtse.
» Stems used to produce red dye.

74 *Wendlandia coriaceae* DC.

Shrub or small tree 2- 6m. Branchlets red-brown, glabrous. Leaves in opposite pairs, oblong, 5-18x2-5cm, acuminate at both ends, coriaceous, glabrous on both surfaces, with prominent brown midrib; petioles 0.4-2cm. Pannicles ovoid, disctinctly longer than broad, usually compact, c 7-15x5-10cm; branches glabrous to indistinctly scruffy. Corolla white, tube 4-4.5mm; lobes ovate-oblong, rounded or shallowly emarginate, 1.25-1.5mm. Anthers oblong, 1-1.75mm shortly exserted. Style glabrous, exserted 2 – 2.5mm; stigma bilobed. Capsule glabrous, reddish brown.

» On well drained rocky slopes in low land valleys
» 450 – 900 (-1500) m
» February-April

....

Rutaceae
Rue or Citrus family

32 Citrus limon (L.) Burman f.
Eng: Lemon

Small tree to 4m, twigs with spines up to 1.5cm. Leaves ovate, 5-9.5x3-5cm, rounded or pointed tip and rounded base, margin toothed, petiole 2cm with narrow wings. Flowers solitary or few, axillary, with 4-5 petals, white inside and purplish outside and in bud. Calyx 4-5mm. Petals oblong 17 x 5mm. Stamens numerous c 15mm. Ovary oblong, 5mm, tapering gradually into style. Fruit oblong or obovoid, 8-12 x 6-8cm, distinctly mamillate at apex Peel yellow, closely attached, 7-15mm thick.

» Warm, broadleaved forest. Occasionally cultivated for edible fruit.
» 1800m
» May
» Punakha
» Lemon is cultivated worldwide but thought to originate in India, Burma, Himalayan region.

118 Murraya paniculata (L.) Jack
Eng: Orange Jasmine

Evergreen shrub to tree to 6m. Leaves 12-15cm, 3-7-foliolate; leaflets ovate, 5-10x2-5cm, bluntly acuminate, base asymmetrically cuneate, margin entire, glabrous. Inflorescence up to 20 flowered. Calyx c 1mm. Petals greenish white, oblanceolate, c 1.8 x 0.5cm. Stamens 8-10mm. Style c 12mm. Berry ovate, c 8 x 5mm.

» Sub-tropical forest slopes
» 200-1250m.
» March-April
» Samtse, Chhukha, Sarpang, Trongsa, Mongar

Salicaceae
Willow family

210 Salix calyculata Andersson

Decumbent shrub, branchlets ascending, up to 40cm, dark brown, glabrous. Leaves obovate, 1- 4 x 0.5-1.5cm, obtuse or subacute, base cuneate, margins serrulate near apex, or entire, sometimes blackish when dry, long silky villous beneath at first, later glabrous; petioles 5-7mm; stipules minute. Catkins terminal on leafy shoots, 2-6cm. Male catkins 1-1.5cm; bracts oblong, c 4 x 1mm, reddish brown, glabrous or ciliate, c 3 x 2 mm, glabrous, otherwise similar to male; gland oblong c 1.5mm. Capsules narrowly ovoid, c 4mm, glabrous, shortly pedicelled; style c 1mm, deeply divided, branches entire or shortly bifid.

» Edges of stream on open hillside
» 3800-4750m
» June-July
» Haa, Gasa, Bumthang, Trashiyangtse

211 Salix serpyllum Andersson

Low prostrate shrub with creeping and rooting branches and stems. Leaves obovate or elliptic-lanceolate, 0.8-1.5x 0.3-1.0cm, with toothed margins near apex, dark green above, pubescent at first, later without hair beneath. Catkins many-flowered on leafy shoots. Male catkins 0.8-1.2cm; bracts rounded, cuneate, blackish-crimson, crisped hairy at first, later glabrous except for ciliated margins; stamens 2, filaments free, brownish wooly. Female catkins 1-3 (-6) cm; bracts similar to male. Capsules ovoid-conical, glabrous, c4mm; styles 1.5-2mm, divided to middle, branches capitate or bilobed.

» On mountain slopes and peat
» 3200-3950m
» May-June
» Haa, Paro, Thimphu, Gasa, Bumthang, Trashiyangtse.

Saururaceae
Lizard tail family

37 *Houttuynia cordata* Thunberg.
Eng: Lizard Tail, Chameleon Plant

Stems 15-45 cm. Leaves broadly ovate, 3.5-9x3-8cm, acute or shortly acuminate, base cordate; petioles 2-4 cm; stipules oblong, 1.5-2.5 cm, adnate to petiole in lower half. Flower spikes 1-2.5cm; basal bracts white, oblong or obovate, 1-1.5x0.7-1 cm, obtuse.

» Weeds of cultivation and on roadsides in cool broad-leaved forest.
» 1000-2400 m
» June – August
» Chhukha, Punakha, Trongsa, Mongar, Trashigang, Trashiyangtse.

....

Saxifragaceae
Saxifrage family

114 *Bergenia ciliata* (Haworth) Sternberg
Eng: Frilly Bergenia

Flowering stems 7-30cm, reddish brown, with glands and hair. Leaves broadly ovate 4-15x 4-14cm, rounded apex and base with smooth surface, margins finely toothed and ciliated. Flowers 1-20, with petals obovate, 11-15x7-13mm, white tinged pink; stames 6-12mm

» Rocks and cliff faces
» 1500-3050m
» February-April
» Chhukha, Samdrupjongkhar, Haa, Mongar

304 *Bergenia purpurascens* (Hook. F & Thomson) Engler
Eng: Purple Bergenia

Perennial herb. Flowering stem 7-30 cm, reddish brown, glandular-pubescent. Leaves elliptic or ovate-elliptic, rounded, base cuneate or rounded, margins entire or shallow sinuate, glabrous or cilate near base, flowers 1-8, bright pink

» On rock ledges, cliffs, under rhododendron forests and scrub.
» 3800-4550m
» May-July
» Haa, Paro, Bumthang, Gasa, Bumthang and Trashiyangtse

200 Saxifraga parnassifolia D. Don
Eng: Himalayan Saxifrage

Perennial herb. Slender stems 10-30cm, usually without hair at base, glandular hairs above. Basal leaves broadly ovate, 1-3.5x1-3.5cm, base heart shaped, usually fringed margins. Flowers 1-6 in more or less flat topped cluster. Calyx 4-5mm, lobes ovate, c 3x3mm, erect at first and later spreading or bent back, glandular hairs. Petals 5, obovate 7-8x3mm, yellow.

» Cliff ledges and open, grassy banks.
» 3050-3800m
» August-October
» Thimphu, Trongsa, Bumthang, Mongar

....

Schisandraceae
Magnolia vine family

286 Schisandra grandiflora (Wall) Hook. f. & Thomson
Eng: Bay Star Vine

A woody climber with toothed leaves. Leaves lanceolate, elliptic or oblanceolate. Flowers with stamens or carpel borne on a conical or cylindric column. Perianth parts fleshy, white or plate pink, 7-8 in 3 series. Climbing on trees or shrubs in cool broad leaved and moist coniferous forests.

» Climbing on trees or shrubs in cool broad leaved and moist coniferous forests.
» 2440-4100m
» May- June
» Paro, Thimphu, Mongar, Gasa
» Fruit edible

145 *Schisandra neglecta* A.C. Sm.

Climber. Similar to *S. grandiflora*, but smaller, leaves 5-15x2-7cm, toothed margins, sometimes sinuous; male flowers on pedicels 1-5cm, perianth parts yellowish, 5-10x5-10mm, anthers 1-2mm, outerones on filaments, c.0.5mm; female flowers like males but carpels ellipsoid, 1-2x1mm, on column 1.5-1.8mm; fruiting column 4-12cm, bearing 10-30 oblong-ellipsoid carpels 5-7x3-4mm

- »   Climber on shrubs in moist broad-leaved forests.
- »   1500-2100m
- »   April-June
- »   Sarpang, Punakha, Trongsa

....

Scrophulariaceae
Figwort family

80 *Digitalis purpurea* L.
Eng: Foxglove

Tall herb, biennial or rarely perennial. Stems 25-180cm, with dense short hair above and hairless towards base. Basal leaves with long winged petiole, lamina ovate to lanceolate, 4-30x2-13cm, margins toothed, hairy above and beneath. Raceme simple or slightly branched, with many flowers. Pedicels with hair, longer than calyx. Corolla purple, mauve, pink or white outside, usually whitish with darker purple spots inside, 40-50mm, glabrous or pubescent to villous outside, shortly ciliate and with few long hairs inside. Capsule ovoid, at least as long as calyx.

- »   Cultivated and occurring as escape in forest clearings
- »   May-August
- »   2100-3000m
- »   Paro, Thimphu, Wangduephodrang
- »   Native of Europe.

343 *Mazus delavayi* Bonati

Annual herb, with numerous stems trailing on the ground or slightly erect, 6-26cm, densely covered in glandular hair. Basal leaves 15-40x9-16mm oblong obovate tapering to base and an indistinct petiole and margin with rounded teeth. Stem leaves subsessile. Main inflorescence with 8-15 flowers more or less secund (on one side of stalk), later inflorescence not secund, shorter and fewer flowers. Corolla 5.5-7.5mm longer than calyx. Corolla white or pale mauve. lower lobe with palate (raised appendage) yellow to brown markings. Capsule obovoid to almost globular with pointed appendage.

» Streamsides, roadsides and as a weed in wheat and rice fields.
» 250-2800m
» March-June
» Chhukha, Haa, Thimphu, Punakha, Trongsa

344 *Mazus surculosus* D. Don

Perennial herb with arching aerial stolons. Flowering stems decumbent to suberect, 4-14cm, glandular pubescent. Leaves mortly all basal; petioles 5-20mm; lamina mostly obovate, 4-40x4-25mm, with 5-7 teeth per side. Inflorescence up to 14 flowered, subsecund. Bracts 2-4mm, linear. Pedicels 2.5-8mm in flower, c.8mm in fruit. Corolla 7-13mm; upper lip mauve, lower lip white with 2 yellow or orange ridges, throat with red or brownish-yellow spots. Capsule ovoid or subglobose, 4-4.5x3mm.

» Warm broadleaved forests, steep grassy hillslopes, field margins, short grassland, roadside, ditches.
» 1260-3050m
» April-August
» Chhukha, Thimphu, Punakha, Gasa, Trongsa, Lhuentse, Trashiyangtse

301 *Pedicularis elwesii* Hook. f.

Herbaceous with several stems, 5-20cm. Leaves mostly from root and clustered. Stems leaves broadly linear or oblong, 40-100 x 5-20mm, pinnatiesct or pinnapartite. Inflorescence a short raceme on a long scape. Bracts leaf-like with broad petioles expanded at base, pinnatifid, densely puberulent. Corolla deep pink, crimson or magenta; tube c 10mm, galea with erect basal part 3-5mm, anther-bearing part hooked and decurved near middle, c 8mm, enclosed by lower lip, suddenly narrowed into downwards-directed, straight, twisted beak c 4mm with deeply 2-lobed apex; lower lip large, enclosing galea, 3-lobed, with densely ciliate margin; lateral lobes reniform, 9-14mm wide, middle lobe orbicular with shallowly emarginated apex.

- » Moist alpine grassland (often by streams)
- » 3050 – 4877m
- » June – September
- » Haa, Gasa, Bumthang, Trashiyangtse

180 *Pedicularis longiflora* Rudolph

Herbaceous, stems 1-50cm, usually several,. Leaves linear to oblong, 10-40 x 3-10mm, pinnatifid with 6-10 pairs of segments, margins toothed. Inflorescence several-flowered terminal raceme. Bracts leaf-like with petioles broadened at base. Flowers erect at anthesis, strongly recurved to touch ground after pollination. Corolla bright golden yellow, with 3 reddish-brown, chocolate or purple comma-like marks in throat and pale yellow tube, slightly scented; tube 25-50 x 1.5mm, pubescent; galea abruptly bent at top, anther-bearing part directed forwards but becoming strongly twisted, narrowed into slender beak with 2-lobed apex, turning orange-red after pollination; Capsule lanceolate-ellipsoid, 13-17 x 4-5mm, acuminate.

- » Swamps and marshy meadows, often in water.
- » 3050-5560m
- » June-October
- » Haa, Thimphu, Gasa, Bumthang, Trashiyangtse

302 *Pedicularis megalanthe* D. Don

Perennial herb. Stems 1- several, 10-80cm. Leaves linear-lanceolate to ovate-lanceolate, 40-120x10-40mm, pinnatifid to pinnatipartite with 7-14 pairs of segments; both surfaces sparsely long-haired. Inflorescence elongated or almost condensed raceme of 5-20 flowers. Bracts leaf-like but usually more ovate. Corolla deep reddish-purple or cerose with white galea and throat, or rarely entirely white, 45-75mm; tube 28-60mm, very slender, straight; galea erect in the centre of the lower lip which forms a deep cup around it, strongly twisted and forming a nearly complete ring, anther-bearing part almost sessile on top of corolla tube, gradually tapering to a long coiled beak 10-14mm with, deeply emerginate apex. Capsule oblong-ovoid, c 12 x 4mm,.

- » Clearings in Fir and bamboo forest and scrub, grassy alpine hillside (often by streams)
- » 3960 – 4270m
- » June – August
- » Thimphu, Punakha, Gasa, Trongsa, Bumthang

181 *Pedicularis scullyana* Maximowicz

Robust perennial herb, stems erect, 15-100cm, with wooly hairs, sometimes nearly glabrous. Leaves alternate, clustered near base with several on the stem; lamina linear to linear-lanceolate, 50-210 x 12-50mm, with winged rachis and pinnatipartite with 10-25 pairs of segments, coarsely and deeply lobed. Inflorescence very conspicuous, long and dense terminal raceme of many flowers. Corolla pale lemon- or primrose-yellow with galea tipped purple with faint lemon scent, 30-35mm; tube straight, 15-20mm, equallling cayyx, glabrous; galea strongly falcate, erect part 6-8mm, anther-bearing part c10mm, tapering to an abruptly incurved beak 4-5mm with 2-lobed apex; lower lip 12-18 x 25-30mm, middle lobe orbicular to obovate-orbicular, entire, c 8 x 10mm, lateral ones c 10 x 15mm, enclosing galea. Capsule obliquely lanceolate, 20-25 x 6mm.

» Open grassland hillside and screes.
» 3,350-4,725m
» June–August (-early September)
» Trongsa

303 *Pedicularis siphonantha* D. Don
Med: Lukro Marpo

Perennial herb. Stems erect, decumbent or sometimes prostate 5-35cm, glabrous or pubescent. Leaves alternate, mostly radical except on plants with well-developed stems, linear oblong, 10-40 x 2-15mm, with narrowly winged rachis, pinnately divided with 5-8 pairs or segments; segments variable size and shape, margins doubly toothed; Inflorescence of several axillary flowers in upper part of stem. Calyx tube with two lobes at tip. Corolla bright rose-purple or pink with white throat, Corolla tube 3x longer than calyx tube. Lower petal with three lobes, and upper petal strongly curved galea with white base, u-shaped and poining upwards.

» Fir forests, Rhododendron scrub, damp alpine meadows and sedge moorland.
» 3200-4270m
» May-September
» Haa, Paro, Thimphu, Punakha, Trongsa, Bumthang, Mongar, Gasa, Trashiyangtse

187 *Verbascum thapsus* L.

Dzo: Kachum

Eng: Common Mullein

Stout, erect biennial, 30-50cm, densely tomentose. Basal leaves ovate to oblong, 8-50 x 2.5-14cm, crenate to subentire, tomentose. Cauline leaves decurrent, oblanceolate to obovate. Inflorescence dense, simple or very rarely branched, spike-like, 15-90cm, tomentose; axis scarcely visible. Flowers in clusters of 2-7, sweet scented. Calyx 7-12mm. Corolla yellow, 12-20mm diameter, punctuate with pellucid glands, stellate-pubscent outside, ciliate to base of upper lobes within. Capsule broadly ovate-elliptic, 7-10 x 4-6mm, stellate-tomentose.

- » Dry often abandoned fields, clearings in Blue pine forest, often on sandy soil
- » 1220-3048m
- » June-October
- » Chhukha, Thimphu, Bumthang
- » The seeds are used for stupefying fish; plant used for pulmonary disease, asthma, diarrhoea and bleeding of the lungs and bowel.

Solanaceae
Nightshade family

19 *Brugmansia suaveolens* (Willd.) Berch. & Presl

Eng: Angels Trumpet

Shrub or small tree 1-6m, with brittle branches and young branches pubescent. Leaves ovate-elliptic, 9-25cm x 5-12cm tapering to a point at tip and base wedge-shaped, and more or less smooth except for veins with fine hair and petiole with dense fine hair. Flowers hanging from horizontal branches sometimes fragrant. Large corolla (20-30cm) funnel-shaped with a narrowly cylindrical shape emerging from calyx tube 6-11cm, cream at first then turning white.

- » Ravines in subtropical forests and by streams, near villages.
- » 500-1800m
- » February-September
- » Samtse, Sarpang, Mongar
- » A narcotic species, used as ornamental hedge plant in the Himalayan region. Native to Southeast Brazil.

20 *Datura stramonium* L.
Eng: Thorn Apple

Erect annual herb 10-100cm. Leaves with coarsely toothed margins and smooth surface. Solitary flowers emerging from axils of leaves. Corolla white and cylindrical to funnel shaped with five edges. Fruits are spiny egg-shaped capsules.

» Commonly found in fields, stony roadside, camps and villages.
» 1200-2440m
» March-October
» Sarpang, Thimphu, Trongsa, Trashigang
» All parts of plant are narcotic, especially the seeds which have a stupefying effect and can be fatal. Plants with purple flowers are called. *D. tatula* L.

338 *Nicandra physalodes* (L.) Scopoli
Eng: Apple of Peru

Stems 20-200cm, minutely but densely white-glandular at petiole bases, otherwise glabrous. Petioles 20 - 80mm; lamina elliptic to broadly ovate, 25-220 x 15-210mm, sinuate-dentate or -crenate, rather bluntly acuminate, base obtuse to truncate, upper surface densely but minutely sessile-glandular, lower surface glabrous, margins minutely scabrid. Pedicels 15-25mm. Calyx segments sepal-like, 15-20x10-12mm in flower, to 30mm in fruit, cordate at base, green becoming whitish and membranous in fruit, prominently 25-35mm across. Anthers pale yellow, c 3.5mm. Berry yellow or brownish-yellow, pendulous. Seeds red brown, 1.5-1.8 x 1.3-1.6mm, reticulately pitted.

» Roadside, field margin and secondary scrub
» 1070-1950m
» May-October.
» Chhukha, Thimphu
» Native of Peru, now found in warmer parts of the world

21 *Solanum pseudocapsicum* L.
Eng: Jerusalem Cherry

Unarmed shrub 90-120cm with minute hairs on stems. Leaves lanceolate or elliptic ovate, narrow, 40-80 x 10-20mm, without hair. Inflorescence a 1-3 flowered pedunculate axillary or extra axillary cyme, peduncle short. Calyx lobes 3-5mm in flower, narrow triangular shape. Corolla white, rotate, 5 petals in star shape and orange yellow anthers 2.5mm long and style extending beyond. Round berry 8-15mm diameter and scarlet in colour.

» Cultivated as ornamental.
» 2400m
» Flowering fruiting almost year round.
» Thimphu
» Native to Brazil, Poisonous

22, 275 *Solanum viarum* Dunal
Eng: Tropical Soda Apple

Spiny herb or undershrub 50-150cm. Stems densely covered in glandular hairs. Pale yellow prickles on stems, petioles, both leaf surfaces, pedicels and calyces (few). 6-25mm. Leaves broadly ovate to sub-orbiucular 45-140 x 45-125mm, shallowly or deeply lobed, lobes and apex obtuse or acute, base almost equal, truncate to heartshaped, veins densely covered in simple hairs, upper surface less har, and lower surface with much fewer hairs. Flowers outside of axils, solitary or in groups up to 3. Calyx lobes triangular about 3mm with hair and few small prickles. Corolla of 5, white petals, hairy outside and smooth inside. Stamens forming a cone in center with pale yellow anthers 5.5-6.5mm. Berry round and covered in fine short hair, green with white blotches when young and yellow when mature.

» Evergreen oak forests, warm broad-leaved forests, fields and field margins, shingle and roadsides.
» 200-2100m
» May - October
» Samtse, Sarpang, Samdrupjongkhar, Thimphu, Paro, Punakha, Trongsa.
» Native of South America, invasive in many places. Introduced in India, Nepal, Myanmar etc for medicinal purposes (solasodine).
» Frequently misidentified as *S. khasianum, S. myriacanthum or S. melongena.*

371 *Solanum virginianum* L.
Eng: Thorny Nightshade

Very spiny diffuse prostate herb 30-120cm across. Stems sparsely stellate-pubescent. Prickles very numerous and on all parts except corolla, to 18mm. Leaves ovate or elliptic oblong, 30-80x25-50mm, margins shallowly or deeply lobed. Inflorescence 1-4 flowered racemose pedunculate cyme; peduncles 10-20mm; pedicels 5-8mm inflower, 10-15mm in fruit. Calyx c5mm, 5 lobes acute. Corolla mauve or violet, 20-28mm across; lobes 10-12mm, ovate-triangular, with hair in a band outside and a narrow line inside along mid-vein, with simple hairs on inner surface and margins. Anthers linear 7-8mm, yelllow. Berry globose, 15-20mm, green turning yellow.

» Weed of open disturbed areas, like roadsides, edges of cultivated areas.
» Upto 1300m
» April
» Wangduephodrang. Other localities not recorded.
» Roots and fruits used for asthma and other chest related complaints and for toohache.

122 *Solanum verbascifolium* sensu F.B.I. non L.
Dzo: Namphai

Unarmed shrub or small tree 1-6 m. Young branches terete, densely stellate-tomentose, older ones with greyish bark. Leaves lanceolate-elliptic 10-30x5-13 cm, dull dark green or brownish-green and sparsely stellate above, greyish-tomentose beneath; petiole 10-55mm. Inflorescence a dense axillary, long-pedunculate corymbose cyme near tip of branch. Calyx 6-8mm, stellate-tomentose outside and less densely inside; tube 3.5-5mm. Corolla white (often creamy), 8-12 mm; lobes 4-5 mm, densely stellate outside and much more sparsely (but not glabrous) within. Berry globose, c 10mm dia, yellow; seeds ovate-discoid, c 1.5-1.2 mm, reddish-brown, reticulate.

» 250-1450 m
» Flowering and fruiting most of the year
» Samdrupjongkhar, Thimphu, Punakha, Trongsa, Trashigang
» The fruit is used as an edible vegetable in Sikkim.

Symplocaceae
Sweet leaf family

123 Symplocus paniculata (Thunberg) Miquel
Dzo: Pangtse Shing

Tree or shrub 3-10m. Leaves membraneous or leathery, broadly elliptic or ovate and sharply toothed and veins impressed above. White flowers in terminal panicles 3-9cm long with 30-40 stamens.

» Blue pine forests and among shrubs on river banks
» 1600-2850m
» April-June
» Chhukha, Haa, Paro, Thimphu, Punakha, Bumthang, Gasa
» Leaves and bark used to make yellow dye, seeds for edible oil.

....

Tamaricaceae
Tamarisk family

310 Myricaria rosea W.W. Smith

Prostrate, much-branched shrub with densely leafy branches 10-30cm. Leaves on main vegetative shoots lanceolate, 4-6x1-1.5mm, subacute, base narrowed, sessile, margins entire; leaves on lateral shoots linear, 2.5 x 0.5mm. Flowers fragrant, in dense bracteate racemes 3-7cm; bracts lanceolate 10x3mm; pedicels 2-3mm. Sepals linear-lanceolate, 6x2mm, white margined. Petals oblanceolate, 7 x 3mm, pink or purplish, Capsule narrowly ovoid, 3-angular, 10-12mm; seeds oblong 1.5mm.

» Stream side
» 3350-4250m
» May-August
» Haa, Thimphu, Trongsa

Theaceae
Tea family

43 Schima wallichii (DC.) Korthals.

Dzo: Puyam

Eng: Chinese Guger Tree

Tree upto 30m. Leaves ovate-elliptic, 9-16x4-6cm, acute or acuminate, base rounded or cuneate, margins entire, glabrous above, usually pubescent beneath; petioles 1.5-2cm. Flowers fragrant, 3.5-5cm across, pedicels 2-3cm, bracteoles oblong, c 5x2mm. Sepals suborbicular, c 4mm, ciliate on margins, otherwise glabrous. Petals white, obovate, up to 3x1.5cm, minutely pubescent externally at base, otherwise glabrous. Stamens yellow. Capsule subglobose, 2-2.5cm diameter, woody, dehiscing in upper two-thirds into 5 valves. Seeds c 7x4mm, surrounded by wing 2-3mm.

- » Sub-tropical and warm broad-leaved forest
- » 300-2000m
- » May-July
- » Samtse, Sarpang, Punakha
- » Contact with bark causes intense itching.

....

Thymelaceae
Paper bush family

115 Daphne bholua D. Don

Dzo: Dey Shing, Deyna

Eng: Daphne

Evergreen shrub 1-3.5m with tough fibrous inner bark. Branchlets with small fine hair becoming hairless. Leaves clustered at branch ends, leathery but thin, elliptic-oblanceolate 3.5-13 x 1-2.5cm, with tapering ends, smooth and without stalk. Inflorescence at ends of branches with 5-15 flower clusters. Flowers very fragrant, sessile. Perianth tube pink or purplish, 7-12mm, silky. Lobes white, rounded or pointed tips and spreading. Drupes ovoid, black 8x5mm

- » Evergreen oak, blue pine, spruce, hemlock and fir forests
- » 1980-3400m
- » February-May
- » Bark is used for paper making. The species is also a

prized ornamental due to strong fragrant flowers.
» Chhukha, Samdrupjongkhar, Haa, Thimphu, Punakha, Trongsa

198 *Edgeworthia gardneri* (Wall.) Meisner.
Dzo: Dey Shing, Deykarp
Eng: Paper Bush

Shrub 2-4 m. Leaves elliptic-oblanceolate, 5-20 x 1.5-4.5cm, acute, base cuneate or attenuate, glabrous above, sparsely appressed silky beneath; petioles 0.5-1cm. Flowers numerous in pendulous heads 3-4.5cm diameter, sweet-scented; peduncle 1-6cm, silky; bracts linear, 1-1.5cm, silky. Perianth tube 10-15mm, densely creamy-white silky; lobes yellow, broadly ovate, 2-4 mm, recurved-spreading. Fruit ovoid, c 5 x 3mm, covered with long, stiff, pale hairs.

» Commonly found in cool laurel-dominated and evergreen oak forest.
» 1670-2400m
» February-May
» Chhukha, Trongsa
» Bark used for papermaking

....

Trilliaceae
Trillium family

244 *Paris polyphylla* Smith
Eng: Himalayan Paris

A creeping rhizomatous forest plant with erect stem growing to 40 cm. It has 4-9 elliptic leaves occuring in a whorl. Flowers occur single at the end of branches. The flower has a ring of 4-6 green leaf-like perianth segments (which play the role of sepals/petals), which are 5-10 cm long. There is an inner ring of long purple or yellow perianth segments which look like spider legs. Ten short stamens are arranged again in a ring. Flowers are followed by a globular fruit with scarlet seeds. The botanical name Paris means equal, and polyphylla means many-leaved.

» Broad-leaved forest including Hemlock and oak forest
» 1300-3960m

» April-June
» Haa, Thimphu, Punakha, Gasa, Trongsa, Bumthang, Mongar

....

Umbelliferae
Carrot family

85 *Heracleum obtusifolium* Wall. ex DC.
Med: Trucha, Tukar

Finely hairy plant 30-150cm tall. Large compound leaves, 3-45cm x 5-25cm including petiole, with 3-5 leaflets, each leaflet 3-lobed and rounded. Leaves with dense white hair below. Flowers in umbels with white to pinkish petals with outerones larger to 6x7mm.

» Pastures in dry areas
» 1500-4600m
» April-September
» Haa, Paro, Thimphu, Punakha, Gasa, Bumthang

86 *Oenanthe javanica* (Blume) DC.
Eng: Water Dropwort, Water Celery, Water Parsley

A robust stolon-forming herb of marshland. Stems erect 60-120cm, often rooting at lower nodes. Leaves up to 30cm long, divided twice or thrice into groups of three leaflets, margins toothed. Umbels large 5-8cm across, 16-20 rayed; rays 2-3cm long, bracteoles c. 4mm, Calyx teeth 0.5-1.5mm. Petals white or greenish-yellow, c. 1.5mm. Fruits ellipsoid, c 2.5x1.5mm

» Marshy ground, roadside ditches.
» 150-2600m
» April-October
» Samdrupjongkhar, Thimphu, Trongsa, Trashigang
» Plant is edible in salads or cooked in many oriental dishes.

87 *Selinum wallichianum* (DC.) Raizadae & Saxena

Dzo: Rabe

Med: Tsed

Eng: Milk Parsley

Smelly herb 50–120 cm high, surrounded by fibrous leaf remains at base; stem 3–6mm thick, ridged, upper parts sparingly leafy. Leaves 3-pinnate, ultimate segments ovate-oblong, deeply pinnatifid; basal leaves to 40 x 20cm (including petiole), usually finely pubescent on the rachis and veins beneath; petioles to 25cm long, with narrow sheathing base c 1.5cm broad (c 8mm broad in upper leaves). Main umbels 6–8cm across, 15–30 rays; rays 2–3.5cm in flower, elongating to 5cm when fruiting; umbellules c 1cm across. Petals white, c 1.5–2 x 1mm, somewhat unequal. Fruit elliptic to circular in outline, 3–5 x 2.2-3.5mm; dorsal ribs prominent, scarcely winged.

»   Open well drained rough grassland, yak pastures, trackside, in coniferous forest clearings, scrubland.
»   2300-4000m
»   July – September
»   Paro, Thimphu, Gasa, Common in Eastern Bhutan
»   Roots used to treat cough and cold

88 *Tongoloa loloensis* (Franchet) H.Wolff

Erect herb to 30cm or more. Leaves 3-18x1.5-4cm, 2-3 times pinnately divided into small long segments; ultimate segments 2-8x0.3-0.5mm and tipped with a sharp point. Petiole sheathing to 8mm broad. Umbels 3-8cm across with 8-15 rays. Umbels 3-8cm across, 8-15 rayed; rays 1-5, subequal; bracts 0-3, linear-sububulate, to 5mm, falling early; umbellules 6-12mm across, 14-25 flowered, bracteoles numerous, to 6mm long, about equalling the flowers. Petals white or flushed pink, 1.5x1mm. Stylopodium (base of style) flattened, dark purple, domed. Fruits ovoid with ribs moderately prominent

»   Alpine turf and amongst rocks
»   3150-4100m
»   September-October
»   Chhukha, Dagana, Paro, Thimphu

89 Torilis japonica (Houttuyn) DC
Eng: Japanese Hedge-Parsley, Upright Hedge-Parsley

Stem 20-100cm, much branched, with downward pointing hairs. Leaves pinnately divided but overall shape is triangular in outline, with fine hair on both surfaces. Peduncles 2-17.5cm; umbels 6-12-rayed. Petals white or pale pink, c 2mm. Fruits often blackish-purple when mature, 2-5 x 1-2.5mm, covered with upwardly hooked bristles.

»   A common weed around houses, field margins, meadows, roadsides and waste ground, etc.
»   1200-3050m.
»   July-September
»   Haa, Thimphu, Bumthang, Mongar

....

Urticaceae
Nettle family

266 Girardiana diversifolia (Link) Friis
Dzo: Zocha

Herb up to 2m tall with stinging hairs. Leaves alternate on stem and margins are saw-toothed and strongly three veined at base; shape is highly variable as the name suggests - from broadly ovate to shallowly lobed or deeply lobed. Greenish flowers in axillary and terminally branched spikes.

»   Sub-tropical and warm broadleaved forest and rarely to cool broad leaved forests.
»   850-2750m
»   July- September
»   Chhukha, Sarpang to Samdrupjongkhar, Thimphu, Punakha, Gasa
»   Fibres used to make ropes, bow-strings and coarse cloth.

Uvulariaceae
Bellwort family

33 *Disporum cantoniense* (Loureiro) Merrill
Eng: Chinese Fairybell

Stems 50-150cm, 2.2-5mm diameter, dichotomously branched above, branches ascending, sometimes branched again. Scale leaves to 7 or more, loosely shething, brownish, membraneous. Leaves lanceolate, finely tapering, base cuneate, to a short petiole, 5-14x 1.8-3.7cm, main veins 5-9, raised and papillose beneath. Inflorescence of 4-9-flowered, apparently lateral fascicles inserted opposite leaves on upper part of stems; pedicels papillose, 1.1-2.1cm, becoming rigid and deflexed in fruit. Flowers greenish cream of dull purple, tepals oblong to oblanceolate, tapered to apex, narrowed below, variable in size on same plant, largest 11.5-20x2-5.5mm, papillose; basal sacs rounded. Berry black, 3 seeded, 0.6-0.8cm diameter.

» Among shrubs and on banks in forest (mixed, *Quercus, Castanopsis, Pinus*); marshy ground at edge of paddy fields
» 1370-3350m
» April-June
» Thimphu, Punakha, Trongsa, Mongar, Trashigang, Gasa, Lhuentse
» *D. calcaratum* is similar but has basal tepal spurs which are 4.2-5mm long.

....

Valerianaceae
Valerian family

125 *Valeriana jatamansi* Jones
Eng: Indian Valerian

Perennial herb with thick rhizome upto 4.5 cm with fibrous roots. Basal leaves simple, cordate, persistent, 2.5-11.8 X 1.6-7.8 cm, appressed hairy above, pubscent below, margins usually obscurely dentate, some times sinuate; petioles 1.5-17.5 cm. Cauline leaves few, opposite, upper usually ovate with a pair of small lobes at base, upto 3-5cm, acuminate, margin obscurely dentate. Flowers unisexual flowers white tinged pink or purple. Fruits elliptic 2.4x1mm

» Moist shady areas near streams or in oak forest
» 1200-2000
» February-June
» Samdrupjongkhar, Haa, Thimphu, Punakha, Bumthang, Trashigang, Trashiyangtse
» Rhizome and roots have medicinal properties.

Verbenaceae
Verbena family

410 Callicarpa arborea Roxb.
Dzo: Khalema

Tree 5-20m, branchlets closely yellowish stellate tomentose. leaves coriaceous, ovate-elliptic, 11-28 x 5-13cm acuminate, base cuneate, margins entire, almost glabrous above, closely yellowish stellate tomentose beneath, with hidden small yellow gland dots; petiole 3-7 cm. Flowers in rounded axillary cyme 7-14 cm, penduncle 3-6 cm; bracts minute, linear, 1-1.5mm; pedicels 0.5mm. Calyx funnel shaped, tube c 0.5 mm, stellate pubescent, lobes shallow, Corolla pinkish or mauve, tube 2-2.5mm; lobes 1mm. Drupes black or purple when ripe, lobose, c 3mm

» 250-1520m
» April-June
» Chhukha, Sarpang, Mongar, Trashigang, Trashiyangtse
» Wood is used for fuel and charcoal

356 Caryopteris bicolor (Hardwicke) Mabberley
Eng: Bluebeard, Blue Mist Shrub

Scrambling or spreading shrub 2-3m; branches finely grayish-tomentose when young, becoming glabrous. Leaves elliptic-lanceolate, 6-13 x 1.5-5cm, acuminate, base cuneate, margins distantly sharply to bluntly serrate, pubescent on veins beneath, densely minutely reddish gland-dotted beneath; petiole 5-15mm. Flowers fragrant, in dense many-flowered panicles 5-14 x 2-3cm, finely tomentose; bracts narrowly lanceolate, 1.5-4mm; pedicels 2-4mm. calyx tomentose with glands obscured, tube c 3mm; lobes triangular, 1.8-2mm. Corolla tube c 5mm; lobes pale blue, upper 4 oblong, rounded, 5-7mm, lip 7-9mm, bilobed. Stamens 2-2.5cm. Style 2.5-3cm. Capsule subglobose, with

4 rounded angles, 3.5-5mm, hairy.

»   Amongst shrubs in hot dry valleys.
»   200-1500m
»   December-February
»   Chhukha, Samdrupjongkhar, Punakha,
    Wangduephodrang.

219 Holmskioldia sanguinea Retzius.
Eng: Chinese Hat Plant, Cup and Saucer Plant

Shrub, often scrambling, 2-5m; stem short gland-tipped
hairs and longer eglandular hairs. Leaves ovate, 4-11x
2.5-7cm, acuminate, base truncate or rounded, margins
shallowly serrate, thinly pubescent with eglandular hairs
and with sessile glandular scales; petioles 1-3cm. Racemes
3-6 flowered. 2.5-6cm; peduncle glandular-hairy; pedicel
5-13mm. Calyx cup 2-2.5cm diameter, bright crimson,
glandular-pubescent. Corolla orange or crimson, tube
curved, 17-22mm, glandular pubscent; lip 4-5mm, other
lobes c 1.5mm. Drupe 4-lobed, obovoid, 6-8 mm diamters,
scaly, subtended by enlarged calyx.

»   October-March
»   Scrubby hillside and forest margin
»   230-1220 m
»   Samtse, Chhukha, Sarpang, Trashigang, Trashiyangtse

197 Lantana camara L.
Eng: Spanish Flag, West Indian Lantana, Ham 'n Eggs

Sprawling or scrambling shrub 1-3m, often forming thickets;
stems quadrangular, with recurved prickles. Leaves foetid
when crushed, ovate, 4-9 3-5cm, margins serrate-crenate,
upper surface scabrous, lower surface stiffly hairy and with
sparse minute gland dots; petiole 1-3cm, hairy. Flowers
showy, in round flat-topped heads 2-3cm diameter, in axils
of upper leaves; peduncle stout, 2-7.5cm; bracts lanceolate,
3-5mm, hairy. Corolla white, creamy, yellow, orange, pink
or red, with buds at centre of head darker; tube cylindric
9-10mm, pubescent outside; lobes 4-5, unequal, rounded.

»   River shingle and roadside
»   250-600m
»   May-August
»   Chhukha, Sarpang, Samdrupjongkhar
»   Native of tropical America; some showy forms

cultivated as ornamentals but generally an invasive weed; foliage poisonous to livestock. Those with glabrous unarmed stems belong to var. *camara* and those with prickly stems (the commonest form) belong to var. *aculeata*.

399 *Verbena officinalis* L.
Eng: Vervain

Perennial herb woody at base. Stem erect or reclining on ground 20-70cm with stiff hairs. Leaves oppposite on stem, deeply lobed and toothed, ovate in outline, deeply pinnatifid or coarsely double toothed, 2-8 x 1.5-5cm, base attenuate, sessile, margins bluntly toothed. Flowers on slender spikes, 5-25cm, subtended by lanceolate bracteoles 2.5mm. Calyx 2.5-3mm, including short lobes, pubescent. Corolla pale mauve or purple; tube 3.5-4mm, hairy within throat, five lobes weakly bilabiate, 2-2.5mm.Fruit c 2mm.

» Field Margins, roadsides, grassy banks and waste grounds.
» 1220-2470m
» March - November
» Chhukha, Sarpang, Thimphu, Punakha, Trongsa, Trashigang, Gasa
» Sometimes an agricultural weed

357 *Vitex negundo* L.
Eng: Five-Leaved Chaste Tree

Shrub or small tree 2-10m; branchlets minutely white tomentose. Leaves palmately compound, leaflets 3-5, narrowly lanceolate, acuminate, base cuneate, glabrous above, densely matted white tomentose, petiole winged. Flowers in long slender panicles 10 – 26 x 2 – 4cm, terminal and in upper leaf axils; branches cymose; peduncle minutely white tomentose; pedicels 0 – 1.5mm. Fruit c 5mm, black when ripe, enclosed by persistent cup-shaped calyx.

» Cultivated and possibly naturalized on scrubby hillside
» 300-1700m
» May-November
» Chhukha, Sarpang, Trashigang

Violaceae
Violet family

349 Viola betonicifolia Sm.

Estoliniferous perennial herb. Leaves narrowly oblong-ovate, more than twice as long as broad, 2.5-5.5cm long, rounded tip, base truncate or shallowly heart-spahed, margins shallow round teeth, sometimes hair on lower surface. Peduncles 5-15cm, with our without hair; bracts linear-lanceolate c 6mm. Sepals ovate 5-6mm, acute. Petals bluish or white with purple lines, 8-10mm; lateral petals pubescent inside; spur thick, 5-6mm, obtuse. Capsule ovoid c 7mm.

» River banks and damp ground.
» 2370-2500m
» May-June
» Thimphu, Punakha

54 Viola bhutanica Hara

Perennial herb without stolons. Leaves, basal, ovate and heart-shaped base, obtuse or acute tips, toothed margin, pubescent or glabrous; stipules lanceolate, c 10mm, sparsely glandular toothed, adnate to petiole in lower half. Peduncles 2-12cm, glabrous or pubescent; bracts linear, c 4mm. Sepals ovagte, 4-5mm, acute; appendages c 1mm, rounded, glabrous or pubescent. Petals 10-14mm, white or purplish with dark purple streaks. Lateral petals pubescent within. A small spur 2-3mm shaped like a sac. Capsule ovoid c 7mm.

» Damp wooded banks
» 2450-3500m
» April - June
» Thimphu, Punakha, Trongsa, Bumthang, Mongar

164 Viola biflora L.
Eng: Yellow Wood Violet

Perennial herb up to 15cm. Leaves broadly ovate, 6-20x10-30mm, base heartshaped, margins shallowly toothed, pubescent; petioles up to 4cm, without hair. Peduncles with weak linear bracts 1-3mm. Sepals lanceolate, c 4mm, with short fringe. Petals 8-11mm, yellow, upper 4 sharply pulled back, without hair inside, lower most petal strongly streaked with reddish-purple, all petals purplish-reticulate outside, spur bag-like c. 2mm. Capsule ovoid c. 6mm, without hair.

» In damp, shaded margins of Fir forests.
» 2285-3350m
» May-June
» Haa, Paro, Thimphu, Trongsa, Bumthang, Mongar.
» var. *hirsuta* has much shorter stems and petioles which are densely short spreading stiff hairs (hirsute).

....

Zingiberaceae
Ginger family

173 *Cautleya gracilis* (Sm.) Dandy

Leafy shoot to 40cm. Leaves 4-6, lanceolate, long caudate, sessile, 6-20x2.5-3cm, usualy dark purple beneath; ligule entire, 3-5mm. Inflorescence 4-10cm (elongating with age); bracts usually red, 1-2.5cm. Inflorescence terminal with bracts below each flower. Calyx red, splitting on one side, 1-1.5cm. Corolla tube1.5-2cm, petals oblong, rounded, 2cm. Lateral staminodes almost spathulate, 2cm. Lip bilobed to halfway, 2x1.25cm. Filaments very short; anther 2cm. Capsule red, globose, to 1cm diameter.

» Moist banks and rocks (sometimes epiphytic) in mixed and Evergreen Oak forest.
» 1500-3000m
» May-August
» Chhukha, Thimphu, Punakha, Trongsa, Gasa, Trashiyangtse

174 *Cautleya spicata* (Sm.) Baker

Leafy shoots to 1m. Similar to *C. gracilis*, but has a more robust habit with more densely flowered inflorescence, with larger flowers.

» Shady gullies and cliffs in mixed broad-leaved (including oak) and *Rhododendron grande* forest.
» 1500-2400m
» June-September
» Chhukha, Samdrupjongkhar, Wangduephodrang

306 *Cucurma aromatica* Salisbury
Dzo: Dum

Rhizome yellow within, aromatic. Leaf tufts to over 1m, 5-7 leaved; lamina broadly lanceolate, acuminate, 40-70 x 10-14cm, shortly pubescent beneath; petiole sometimes equaling lamina. Inflorescence 9-20 x 6-10cm, commonly appearing before, and produced laterally to, leaves. Coma bracts pink. Fertile bracts recurved at tips, to 6cm, minutely pubescent at least in upper half; bracteoles c. 2cm, lightly pubescent. Flowers whitish, pink tinged, not exserted, lip yellow, obscurely 3-lobed.

» Open slopes in hot, dry valleys; secondary scrub at margins of sub-tropical forest; shady forest floor
» 150-1830m
» March-July
» Samtse, Sarpang, Punakha, Wangduephodrang, Trongsa.

117 *Hedychium ellipticum* Buch.-Ham. ex Sm.

Leafy shot with many leaves 1-1.5m. Leaves elliptic, 7-15x25-30cm, petioles 1cm; ligules bright red. Inflorescence terminal with many flowers, ellipsoid in outline, flat-topped. Bracts overlapping, ovate acute, to 2-2.5x1-1.5cm, below a single white flower. Calyx equal to bract. Corolla tube 6-7cm, petals linear, 5-6cm. Lateral staminodes spathulate, 4-5cm; lip clawed, narrowly oblong, entire or notched at tip of rounded apex, 2.5-4cm. Stamens orange red, sticking out, 8-9cm.

» Dry rocky hillside, rocky banks at margins of subtropical forest; sometimes epiphytic.
» 305-2440m
» June-August
» Chhukha to Samdrupjongkhar, Mongar, Trongsa, Gasa

62 *Hedychium gardnerianum* Roscoe
Eng: Kahili Ginger

Leafy shoots 1-2m, robust. Leaves lanceolate, 20-40cm; bracts narrowly cylindric, 2-3cm, each below 1-3 very fragrant, lemon yellow flowers. Calyx almost equal to bract. Corolla tube 6-7cm; petals linear, 2.5-3cm; lip obovate, shortly bilobed or entire, 3x2cm. Stamens red, longer than petals, 6-7cm.

» Broad-leaved forests (including oak).
» 910-2130m
» July-September
» Chhukha, Thimphu, Wangduephodrang, Punakha, Gasa

63 *Hedychium spicatum* Buch.-Ham. ex Sm.

Leafy shoots 0.5-2m. Leaves lanceolate, 10-45x3-10cm, pubescent beneath; ligule entire, 1-2cm. Inflorescence narrowly cylindric, 15-30cm; bracts oblong, obtuse, convlute, 2-3cm x1cm, each below a single flower. Flowers white tinged yellow or reddish at base; corolla tube 5-6cm; petals linear, 2-3cm. Lateral staminodes narrowly lanceolate, almost equal to lips; lip 3.5-4cm, shortly clawed with almost orbicular limb, or with a cuneate with limb more deeply divided into 2 almost acute lobes. Stamen shorter than lip, usually orange. Fruit yellow, orange inside, seeds red.

» Broad-leaved forest, sometimes epiphytic.
» 610-2630m
» July-October
» Chhukha, Sarpang, Samdrupjongkhar, Paro, Thimphu, Wangduephodrang, Trongsa
» Two varieties in Bhutan; var. *acuminatum* has shorter inflorescence with fewer flowers and consistently orange stigma; var. *trilobum* has a small tooth between the lobes of the lip.

378 *Roscoea alpina* Royle

Small leafy shoot 10-20cm. Leaves 2-3 not developed during flowering. Inflorescence up to 5 flowers but appearing only one at a time. Corolla purple with tube much longer than calyx, and lower lip with two lobes.

» Meadows, dry peaty soil.
» 3500-3960m
» June-August
» Paro, Gasa

IV: Appendices

Glossary

Achene: A small, dry, indehiscent fruit with a single locule and a single seed.

Alternate leaves: Borne singly at each node, as leaves on a stem. (compare opposite)

Annual: A plant which germinates from seed, flowers, sets seed, and dies in the same year.

Anther: The expanded, apical, pollen bearing portion of the stamen.

Axil: The upper angle between the stem and any part (usually a leaf) arising from it.

Banner: The upper and usually largest petal of a "butterfly-like" flower, as in peas and beans.

Basal leaf: Leaves arising from the base of the stem.

Biennial: A plant which lives two years, usually forming a basal rosette of leaves the first year and flowers and fruits the second year.

Blade: The broad part of a leaf or petal.

Bloom: A whitish, waxy, powdery coating on a surface, eg. on primulas.

Bract: A reduced leave or leaf-like structure at the base of a flower or inflorescence.

Bractlet: A small bract borne on a petiole.

Bud: An undeveloped shoot or flower.

Bulb: An underground bud with thickened fleshy scales, as in the onion.

Calyx (pl. **calyces**, **calyxe**s): The outer perianth whorl; collective term for all of the sepals of a flower.

Campanulate: Bell-shaped.

Capsule: A dry, dehiscent fruit with more than one carpel.

Capitula: Small flower heads.

Compound leaf: A leaf with two or more distinct leaflets.

Corolla: The collective name for all of the petals of a flower; the inner perianth whorl.

Cyme: A flat-topped or round-topped determinate inflorescence, paniculate, in which the terminal flower blooms first.

Deciduous: Falling off, as leaves from a tree; not evergreen.

Dentate: Toothed along the margin.

Dioecious: The staminate (male) and pistillate (female) flowers borne on different plants. (Compare **monoecious**)

Disk: An enlargement or outgrowth of the receptacle around the base of the ovary; in the Compositae (Asteraceae) the central portion of the involucrate head bearing tubular or disk flowers.

Disk Flower: A regular flower of the Compositae (Asteraceae).

Epiphyte: A plant which grows on another plant but does not draw food or water from it.

Filament: A thread-like structure; the stalk of the stamen which supports the anther.

Glabrous: Smooth, hairless.

Glandular: Bearing glands.

Head: A dense cluster of sessile or subsessile flowers; the involucrate inflorescence of the Compositae (Asteraceae).

Herb: A plant without a persistent above-ground woody stem, the stems dying at the end of the growing season.

Hypanthium: A cup-shaped extension of the floral axis usually formed from the union of the basal parts of the calyx, corolla, and androecium, commonly surrounding or enclosing the pistils.

Inflorescence: The flowering part of a plant; a flower cluster; the arrangement of the flowers on the flowering axis.

Involucre: A whorl or bracts subtending a flower or flower cluster.

Keel: A prominent longitudinal ridge, like the keel of a boat; the two lower united petals of a "butterfly-like" flower.

Leaflet: A division of a compound leaf.

Ligule: A tongue-shaped or strap-shaped organ; the flattened part of the ray corolla in the Compositae (Asteraceae).

Linear: Resembling a line; long and narrow with almost parallel sides.

Lip: One of the two projections or segments of an irregular, two-lipped corolla or calyx; the exceptional petal of an orchid blossom.

Lobed: Bearing lobes which are cut less than half way to the base or midvein.

Monoecious: The staminate (male) and pistillate (female) flowers borne on the same plant. (Compare **dioecious**)

Naturalised: Plants introduced from elsewhere, but now established.

Node: The position on the stem where leaves or branches arise.

Opposite leaves: Borne across from one another at the same node, as in a stem with two leaves per node. (compare **alternate**)

Panicle: A branched, racemose inflorescence with flowers maturing from the bottom upwards.

Pappus: The modified calyx of the Compositae, consisting of awns, scales, or bristles at the apex of the achene.

Peduncle: The stalk of a solitary flower or of an inflorescence.

Perennial: A plant that lives three or more years.

Perianth: Collective term for calyx and corolla of a flower, especially when they are similar in appearance.

Petal: An individual part of the corolla, usually colored or white.

Petiole: A leaf stalk.

Pistil: The female reproductive organ of a flower, typically consisting of a stigma, style, and ovary

Pith: The spongy, central tissue in some stems and roots.

Pod: Any dry, dehiscent fruit, especially a legume or follicle.

Pubescent: Covered with short, soft hairs.

Raceme: An unbranched, elongated inflorescence with pedicellate flowers maturing from the bottom upwards.

Ray Flower: A ligulate flower of the Compositae (Asteraceae).

Recurved: Curved backward.

Reflexed: Bent backward or downward.

Rhizome: A horizontal underground stem; rootstock.

Rosette: A dense radiating cluster of leaves (or other organs), usually at or near ground level.

Rotate: Disc-shaped; flat and circular, corolla with widely spreading lobes and little or no tube.

Runner: A slender stolon or prostrate stem rooting at the nodes or at the tip.

Scale: Any thin, flat, scarious structure.

Sepal: A segment of the calyx.

Sessile: Attached directly, without a supporting stalk, as a leaf without a petiole.

Setulose: Covered with minute bristles.

Shrub: A woody plant, with several stems, that is shorter than a typical tree.

Spadix: A spike with small flowers crowded on a thickened axis

Spathe: A large bract or pair of bracts subtending and often enclosing an inflorescence.

Spike: An unbranched, elongated inflorescence with sessile or subsessile flowers or spikelets maturing from the bottom upwards. (compare **raceme**)

Spur: A hollow, slender, saclike appendage of a petal or sepal, or of the calyx or corolla.

Stamen (pl. **stamens**, **stamina**): The male reproductive organ of a flower, consisting of an anther and filament.

Standard: The upper and usually largest petal of a "butterfly-like" flower, as in peas and beans.

Stigma: The top part of the pistil which receives the pollen.

Stipule: One of a pair of leaf-like appendages found at the base of the petiole in some leaves.

Stolon: An elongate, horizontal stem creeping along the ground and rooting at the nodes or at the tip and giving rise to a new plant.

Style: The usually narrowed portion of the pistil connecting the stigma to the ovary.

Tendril: A slender, twining organ used to grasp support for climbing.

Tomentose: With a covering of short, matted or tangled, soft, wooly hairs.

Toothed: Dentate.

Umbel: A flat-topped or convex inflorescence with the pedicels arising more or less from a common point, like the struts of an umbrella.

Verticillasters: A pair of axillary cymes arising from opposite leaves or bracts and forming a false whorl.

Whorl: A ringlike arrangement of similar parts (eg. leaves or flowers) arising from a common point or node.

Wing: A thin, flat margin bordering a structure. One of the two lateral petals of a "butterfly-like" flower.

Photo & illustration credits

Photographs

All numbers are the serial number of the photographs in Section II.

Thinley Namgyel: 1, 2, 3, 4, 5, 6, 7, 8, 9, 10, 12, 13, 15, 16, 18, 19, 20, 21, 22, 26, 27, 29, 32, 33, 34, 35, 36, 38, 39, 40, 41, 44, 45, 46, 47, 48, 49, 50, 51, 52, 54, 55, 59, 61, 62, 63, 64, 65, 66, 67, 68, 70, 71, 72, 76, 77, 79, 80, 82, 85, 86, 88, 89, 90, 91, 92, 93, 94, 97, 98, 99, 100, 102, 103, 104, 105, 106, 107, 108, 109, 111, 113, 114, 115, 116, 117, 119, 121, 123, 124, 126, 127, 128, 129, 130, 132, 137, 141, 142, 143, 144, 145, 147, 148, 149, 150, 151, 152, 153, 154, 160, 161, 162, 163, 164, 169, 170, 171, 173, 174, 175, 176, 178, 179, 184, 186, 188, 189, 190, 191, 192, 194, 195, 196, 198, 199, 200, 204, 205, 206, 209, 211, 214, 216, 218, 221, 222, 225, 226, 227, 229, 230, 231, 232, 235, 236, 237, 242, 244 (inset), 245, 248, 254, 258, 259, 260, 261, 262, 263, 264, 266, 268, 269, 270, 272, 275, 278, 279, 281, 282, 283, 284, 285, 287, 288, 289, 291, 292, 294, 295, 296, 297, 298, 299, 300, 303, 304, 305, 307, 308, 309, 311, 312, 313, 314, 315, 316, 317, 318, 319, 320, 321, 322, 323, 324, 325, 326, 328, 329, 331, 333, 334, 335, 336, 337, 339, 340, 341, 342, 343, 344, 345, 346, 347, 348, 349, 350, 351, 352, 353, 355, 358, 359, 360, 362, 363, 364, 365, 366, 368, 370, 371, 372, 373, 374, 375, 376, 377, 378, 380, 384, 389, 391, 392, 393, 394, 395, 396, 397, 398, 399, 400, 401, 402, 403, 404, 405, 406, 407, 408, 409

Karma Tenzin: 11, 14, 17, 23, 24, 25, 30, 31, 37, 43, 53, 56, 57, 58, 60, 69, 74, 75, 78, 81, 83, 84, 87, 96, 101, 110, 118, 120, 122, 125, 131, 133, 134, 135, 136, 138, 139, 140, 146, 156, 157, 158, 159, 165, 166, 167, 168, 172, 182, 183, 185, 187, 193, 197, 203, 207, 208, 210, 212, 213, 215, 217, 219, 220, 223, 224, 228, 233, 234, 238, 239, 240, 241, 243, 244 (main) 246, 247, 249, 250, 251, 252, 253, 255, 256, 257, 265, 267, 271, 273, 274, 276, 277, 280, 286, 290, 293, 306, 327, 338, 354, 356, 357, 367, 369, 379, 381, 382, 383, 385, 386, 387, 388, 390, 410

Phurba Lhendup: 28, 73, 95, 112, 155, 177, 180, 181, 202 (main), 301, 302, 310, 330, 332, 361

Rebecca Pradhan: 201, 202 (inset)

Kinley Tshering: 42

Illustrations

All illustrations by Thinley Namgyel.

Bhutan Administrative Map by Thinley Namgyel, based on Population and Housing Census of Bhutan 2005 GIS data layers.

Bhutan Land Cover map, courtesy WWF-Bhutan.

Species index

The first number after the species name (in italics) refers to
photograph number in Section II and the second number refers to
the page with its description in Section III.

W

Y

Z

Family index